SOCIAL
GROUP
WORK: A Helping Process

PRENTICE-HALL SOCIOLOGY SERIES
Herbert Blumer, Editor

PRENTICE-HALL INTERNATIONAL, INC., *London*
PRENTICE-HALL OF AUSTRALIA, PTY., LTD., *Sydney*
PRENTICE-HALL OF CANADA, LTD., *Toronto*
PRENTICE-HALL FRANCE, S.A.R.L., *Paris*
PRENTICE-HALL OF JAPAN, INC., *Tokyo*
PRENTICE-HALL DE MEXICO, S.A., *Mexico City*

SOCIAL
GROUP
WORK: A Helping Process

GISELA KONOPKA

Prentice-Hall, Inc., Englewood Cliffs, N.J., 1963

*"Group Work is a mental hygiene experience –
a venture in sanity. Small groups, conscious
discipline in human relations, nuclear democracy, leadership laboratory . . . "*

Edward C. Lindeman

Introduction

The foolishness of my writing in comparison with what I wanted to write
infuriated me for years. Greatness, greatness, greatness is what I wanted
and insisted upon, only to notice that everything I wrote was small and
miserable. I couldn't understand it. My soul was great, it *was* astonish-
ingly great, and yet, it was captured in a little, feeble body and could not
get itself free. I had in my soul the greatest truths to tell but when I came
to the work of telling them I couldn't do it, I couldn't find a starting
place . . . Where could I begin?

I was long years discovering the secret that it does not matter at all
where one begins, and that it is not necessary for anything one writes to
be instantly great, the important thing is for a man to resign himself to
the truth that he is only a man, and to work . . .[1]

To start a book which is some kind of a text book with such a quote must
seem strange. These words had been written in the anguish of the creative
writer, not by the scientist or instructor. Yet in writing this book, the same

[1] William Saroyan, *The Bicycle Rider in Beverly Hills*, New York: Charles
Scribner's Sons, 1952, p. 99.

anguish is present, partially because of the always creative process of writing, but mostly because of the vastness and importance of the subject of social group work. Any endeavor directed toward helping people in whatever area is an audacious undertaking, since human beings are powerful and weak creatures at the same time, regardless of whether they are the helper or the one to be helped. Helping people in a group and through a group is especially demanding and difficult. Groups are the basic expressions of human relationships; in them lies the greatest power of man. To try to work with them in a disciplined way is like trying to harness the power of the elements and includes the same kind of scientific thinking, as well as serious consideration of ethics. Like atomic power, groups can be harmful and helpful. To work with such power is a humbling and difficult task.

The group work process—as developed in the last thirty years—has great promise. To write about it so that both actual practice and theory become alive presents more than one problem. The writing must be logical and scientific; at the same time it must paint the picture of a work of art. Every writer, every practitioner, in this helping endeavor called social group work, has written parts of this book. The thinking of other writers from different disciplines is also incorporated. Insight has come from those being served as well as from lay people in the communities. All the contributions by others are gratefully acknowledged. This book is an attempt to present this intricate subject as a whole piece of cloth; the threads from which it is made are not always recognizable, but they are there. Without them, without the untiring work of others, it could not be written.

Recent years have seen a great increase in interest in the group approach to treatment of a variety of problems. It is time to pull together our existing knowledge. Several years ago Gertrude Wilson and Gladys Ryland wrote the first comprehensive book on social group work[2] In the meantime, the method has been developed and has entered many additional fields of practice. New knowledge has arisen. This does not detract from the importance of this first pioneering work, and the contribution of its authors is gratefully acknowledged.

The reader must be prepared for the fact that he will miss not only extensive quoting, but also a complicated scientific language. The avoidance of such language does not mean that the subject is simple or that the

---

[2] Gertrude Wilson and Gladys Ryland, *Social Group Work Practice*, Boston: Houghton Mifflin Co., 1949.

approach to it will be simplified. It is the author's conviction that thoughts —especially in the field of human relations—must and can be expressed in the clear language of good literature. This is no easy task and, without question, this writer will not always achieve the necessary simplicity. Yet the clearer the thought the less involved and obscure the language will be.

A professional effort means translation of thought into action, and the conversion of highly complicated knowledge into seemingly effortless doing. Knowledge and skill are constantly in the state of development.

> The best of us, however vigorous our search for truth, will always leave at the outer reaches, frayed edges of knowledge or uncertainly grasped truths, and will at the last recognize how true it is that our greatest contribution to and through education is in the excitement and development of students, who, becoming equally interested in the search for truth, can complete what we imperfectly begin."[3]

It is hoped that the student, the practitioner, and the teacher who read this, will read the book in this spirit.

[3]   O. Meredith Wilson, "A Message from the President," *The Minnesotan*, Vol. XIV, No. 1, Oct. 1960, p. 2.

Acknowledgment

Thanks for help should go to so many: to teachers, colleagues, students, group members, and clients. Yet they cannot all be named. I want to mention those who gave special help and encouragement:

Thanks go to:

my teachers, Gertrude Wilson; Ruth Garland, who died too early, and Grace Coyle who had wanted to see this writing, but who, unfortunately, passed away before the manuscript was finished;

my colleagues, Ruby Pernell, Miriam Cohn, and Frances Guzie, who were willing to discuss the many problems of social group work and who offered case material;

many of my former students, among them Sarah Churchill, Perry Roth, and Vernon Bloom who also helped with a supply of pertinent case material.

No manuscript can be written without painstaking attention to detail. Very special thanks for help with this and editorial comments go to Vernie Mae Czaky who read and reread the manuscript and the footnotes.

And few books can be written without some encouragement and the support of people close to the writer. For both I thank Dr. Theodore H. Blegen who, through the many years he was the dean of the graduate school at the University of Minnesota and after his retirement, has given me help and warm, constructive criticism, especially supporting me in the use of a simple language.

And finally, the deepest thanks—as always—to my patient and thoughtful husband who lives with the endless hours, nights, weekends, that must be taken to write a book.

TABLE
OF
CONTENTS

xi

CHAPTER ONE

History of
Social Group Work

*✓ Social work's secret tool is the infinite
untapped, unused, unsuspected capacity
for growth in the sovereign individual
personality. . . . Of all types and breeds
of social worker, the social group worker
most consciously accepts this democratic
premise in his work.*[1]

Sigmund Freud began his famous lectures on Introduction
to Psychoanalysis with a deceptively simple definition of the new
method:

> . . . psychoanalysis is a method of medical treatment for those suffering
> from nervous disorders. . . .[2]

He then proceeded to discuss not only the "method," but also the
assumptions on which it was based, the kind of "nervous disorders" he
was treating and his own concept of "medical practice." The same pro-

---

[1] Louis Towley in Frank J. Bruno, *Trends in Social Work, 1874-1956*, New
York: Columbia University Press, 1957, pp. 421-422.
[2] Sigmund Freud, *A General Introduction to Psychoanalysis*, English translation by Joan Riviere, New York: Liveright Publishing Corp., 1935, p. 17.

1

cedure will be necessary to discuss social group work. Since its conscious beginning the practitioners using the social group work method have searched for a simple definition. This definition has changed somewhat in the course of history, and there is not yet a generally accepted one. The most abstract and encompassing concept recently expressed can be found in the *Curriculum Study* where Marjorie Murphy defined *social group work as a method of social work* and as *"enhancement of persons' social functioning through purposeful group experience."*[3] This definition parallels closely the one given by Helen Harris Perlman when she describes casework, the oldest method in social work:

> Social casework is a process used by certain human welfare agencies to help individuals to cope more effectively with their problems in social functioning.[4]

Neither definition—as is always the case with definitions—gives a total and complete picture; both need interpretation and amplification.

Let us consider the first part of the group work definition. This part places social group work within the context of social work as one of the methods through which this profession renders its service. Group work as a *method of social work* is only a recent concept. Originally it was conceived of as a movement, a way of democratic action, and a part of several fields of social services. Foremost among these were informal education, youth services, recreation, camping, the labor movement, settlement houses and community centers. We must understand the historical development of what is today called the group work method to appreciate its underlying philosophy, to understand the particular form of working with people and the way in which it has contributed to widen the concept of social work—a fact still disturbing to those who want to limit severely the functions of this profession. We will return to this after we have tried to trace the historical evolvement of the present concept of social group work.

---

[3] Marjorie Murphy, "The Social Group Work Method in Social Work Education," *A Project Report of the Curriculum Study*, **XI**, Werner W. Boehm, Director and Coordinator, New York: Council on Social Work Education, 1959, pp. 39-40.

[4] Helen Harris Perlman, *Social Casework*, Chicago: University of Chicago Press (copyright 1957 by the University of Chicago), p. 4.

Group work did not spring up suddenly as Athena from the head of Zeus. It was not discovered like a new drug, which can be dated, at least according to the day of its publication. It cannot even be traced to a certain person, as the original formulation of the other method of social work, casework, which usually is credited to Mary Richmond. This method too has changed in the course of history, but it owes its first development to one person in the service of one particular organization, the Charity Organization Societies.

The history of the development of modern group work is part of the history of social agencies evolving within a changing society. Industrialization brought with it slums, movement of the farm population into the cities, and large-scale immigration to the United States. The older social services distinguished sharply between the giver and the receiver. Yet among newer services there were the beginnings of an idea turned into action: self-help, self-help of a group nature. "Whereas philanthropy was generally of middle class origin, mutual self-help, as the name implies, developed from the need for mutual aid and support."[5] There were the beginnings of the labor movement —not only related to improvement of wages, but having a strong cultural aspect, with beginnings of adult education, and with camp vacations for their children financed by the workers' own efforts. There were the brotherhoods which developed their own centers, such as the Jewish centers. The Jewish centers were developed partially by the older, more privileged immigration for the new poor Eastern Jewish immigration, and they partially presented the effort of the new immigrants to help themselves. These were nationality groups, helped by the "outsider" in the settlement houses, but increasingly taking on their own responsibilities. And there were youth agencies with strong and significant participation by the adult volunteer. In all these groups burned a fire of "citizen action," either to improve their own lot or to help improve that of others, by involving those others, not by acting for or in behalf of them. The proud preamble of the *Girl Scout Constitution* expresses the approach to many social problems, found in all these different movements:

> We maintain that the strength of the Girl Scout movement rests in the voluntary leadership of its adult members, in the cooperation and support

---

[5] Peter Kunstler, *Social Group Work in Great Britain*, London: Faber and Faber, Ltd., 1955, p. 40.

of the community, and in the affiliation with Girl Guide and Girl Scout movements of other countries through the World Association of Girl Guides and Girl Scouts.

We declare that the democratic way of life and the democratic process shall guide all our activities.

We hold that ultimate responsibility for the Girl Scout movement rests with volunteers.[6]

The recreation movement too, was a vital root of group work. At the turn of the century it was a social movement. It was closely related to the unions' fight for the eight-hour-day, for the right to a creative life after long hours of deadening mechanical work. It opened new outlets for the "culturally and educationally disadvantaged." The recreation movement fought for playgrounds for children in the slums, for summer camps and swimming pools. It was not a movement for "entertainment," but for vital necessities of body and soul, especially for children. Most of the activities were conducted in groups. Eventually, group interaction itself became the dominant concern. For many years group work and recreation/informal education were erroneously considered synonymous. In fact, even in the present day, this confusion often persists despite the change in the concept of group work and the changes in the field of recreation.

The organizations which built the foundations of group work were the self-help and informal-recreational ones: settlement houses, neighborhood centers, Y's, the Scouts, Camp Fire Girls, Jewish centers, and camps. Later they were designated as "group work agencies," but at their inception they worked separately.

Participation in small groups, the democratic way of life, community responsibility, and membership in a worldwide effort were new concepts which united these services and movements without their being aware of it.

In the period after World War I, social casework, used predominantly in the Charity Organization Societies, gained additional insight from psychoanalytic theory. This was necessary and valuable to its practice, but it was sometimes over-used.

At that time, the social group work method was hardly consciously

[6]   From the Preamble to the Constitution of the Girl Scouts of the United States of America and used by permission. This was formulated only recently, but represents the philosophy which has prevailed since the beginning of the movement.

developed, yet the services from which it grew increased, not only in number, but in significance as well. This was the period when most European monarchies tumbled, when countries in central Europe without any experience in self-government tried hard to develop a democratic society, and when the emancipation of women radically changed family relationships. In the USA there was disappointment that the war had not made the world "safe for democracy," but the picture of the roaring twenties is very incomplete if it omits the enormous growth of voluntary associations and their impact on a rapidly changing society. It was during this time that an investigation into the unexplored area of group association started, not as a dispassionate research into small group behavior (this occurred later, after World War II), but as a way of achieving a better society and to develop a true "democratic way of life." This is the reason why social group work was not conceived of as a method but as a goal, a philosophy, a movement, a psychology, and a profession all rolled into one.

The settlement's goal was described by Robert Woods,

> The social worker thus serves to unite the new scattered industrial, racial and religious elements that are thrown together to make up the population of our great city communities.[7]

And the function of Workers Education was seen as:

> Workers Education will stimulate the student to serve the labor movement in particular and society in general, it is not education to be used for selfish personal advancement.[8]

This was the period that saw the beginning of research into the phenomenon of group behavior. Mary Richmond wrote in 1920:

> . . . a tendency in modern casework which I seem to have noted and noted with great pleasure. It is one which is full of promise, I believe, for the future of social treatment. I refer to the new tendency to view our clients from the angle of what might be termed small group psychology.[9]

[7] Robert A. Woods, *The Neighborhood in Nation Building*, Boston: Houghton Mifflin Co., 1923, p. 94.
[8] President's Report, 5th Convention Workers Education Bureau, 1927; quoted by Mark Starr in, *Workers Education Today*, New York: League for Industrial Democracy, 1941, p. 3.
[9] Mary Richmond, "Some Next Steps in Social Treatment," *Proceedings of the National Conference of Social Work*, 1920, New York: Columbia University Press, 1939, p. 258.

And Mary Parker Follett, the political scientist and active settlement worker, who saw the possibility of a new and just society on the horizon, wrote:

> The great cosmic force in the womb of humanity is latent in the group as its creative energy; that it may appear the individual must do his duty every moment. We do not get the whole power of the group unless every individual is given full value, is giving full value.[10]

The goal again was the democratic society as a means to provide for the highest fulfillment of the individual and allow him to take his place as a responsible member of the human race.

These movements and thinkers increasingly realized that *a way of working with groups* could hinder or help this goal. The insights and concepts did not come mainly from the social work profession. They came more from education, especially the ideas of John Dewey, and from sociologists who were active in these self-help movements and entered schools of social work as teachers.

Mark Starr described Workers Education in 1937:

> This training is often a learning-by-doing process. It engages in a great number of educational activities which are not "courses" at all, but projects created spontaneously out of problematic situations "here and now" . . . The aim is to preserve the balance of "ideas and fun," to remember "ultimates" as well as "immediates."[11]

Here were concepts of the group work method, as the "learning-by-doing," the "starting where the group is" and the use of informality. They clearly showed the influence of John Dewey.

Eduard C. Lindeman developed in his early book, *The Community*,[12] the important technique of allowing conflict to come into the open in groups, and Grace Coyle started in 1923 the first course in group work at the School of Social Work at Western Reserve University; this course was taught partially as a method and partially as a field of practice.

Despite group work being taught early in a school of social work,

10 Mary Parker Follett, *The New State*, 4th edit., New York: Longmans, Green and Co., Inc., 1934, p. 342.
11 Mark Starr in Theodore Brameld, ed., *Workers Education in the United States*, Fifth Yearbook of the John Dewey Society, New York: Harper & Row, Publishers, 1941, p. 91.
12 Eduard C. Lindeman, *The Community*, New York: Association Press, 1921.

its integration into the social work profession was not an easy one. Group work seemed like a foreign body in social work. Social work, after all, had grown out of the Charity Organization Societies, which were geared to the relationship of helper to the one being helped. They put pride in their highly formalized approach and in their new-found focus on the individual and the inner forces influencing him.

Group work, by contrast, grew out of neighborhood approaches and self-help movements. It considered informal relations one of its basic approaches. It focused strongly on group interaction and group strength. It hardly seemed concerned with individual dynamics, but was vitally concerned with environmental and social impact. It was also highly action-oriented, but was not well-developed as a conceptual system, and it was only partially identified with the profession of social work whose field of interest seemed, to group workers, too limited.

Group work in the years after the 1920's was developed mainly through increasingly conscious group efforts of people from different professions, especially education, psychology, and social work. In 1936 the American Association for the Study of Group Work was founded. Its aim was to "clarify and refine both the philosophy and the practice of group work."[13] Yet, as late as 1939, group work was treated as a separate subject at the National Conference of Social Work. Its relationship to the field and the profession of social work was still tenuous. Group workers still saw themselves as a separate profession, and social work could not yet envision the group approach as an integral part of its function. Mary Richmond's insight seemed to be forgotten. Lindeman's words sounded more like a plea:

> A group is a specific form of human interrelation, namely a collection of individuals who are experimenting for the purpose of determining whether their needs are more likely to be satisfied by means of collaboration than through individual effort. I cannot see why, then, groups and group experiences do not stand at the very center of social work's concern.[14]

The period immediately preceding World War II and the war years themselves had a strong impact on the development of group work, and hastened its identification with the social work profession.

13 Harleigh B. Trecker, Ed., *Group Work Foundations and Frontiers*, New York: Whiteside, Inc., 1955, p 3.
14 Eduard C. Lindeman, "Group Work and Education for Democracy," *Proceedings of the National Conference of Social Work*, 1939, New York: Columbia University Press, 1939, p. 344.

The advent of the Nazis in Germany emphasized the importance of a constant and conscious work for democracy, not only as a political form of government, but as a way of life. Eduard C. Lindeman wrote in 1939:

> . . . the roots of democratic culture do not lie in theories and conceptions, but rather in conduct, in experience and its satisfactions. If these roots do not strike deep into the "soil" of human personality, they will be easily destroyed by their external enemies, or they will wither away and die for want of nutriment and exercise. Whenever in history the people have thought and felt and lived democracy there has been cast upon human experience a sharp luminosity. Fears were dispelled and hopes renewed and, whenever in history, tyranny and despotism have succeeded to power, human experience has been shadowed by suspicion, anger and bitterness.[15]

The shadows of fascist Germany heightened the light that those interested in group work had tried to shed on the importance of qualitative group life, which meant increased participation by citizens in community life, of strength that grows in the individual and in the group from the feeling of "self-help," and of the need to work with intelligent leadership in all strata of the population and in all groups. On the other hand they also told the story of the disastrous power of group associations and of the skilled misuse that could be made of them. It taught group workers, who at times had considered group activities a value in themselves, that these activities, too, could be used to enslave youth as well as to help them freely participate in a human society. It forced them to look deeper into human movement to learn about the unique forces within each individual and not to rely alone on programs and group process. The insanity which was gripping whole societies at this time seemed to bring about, among caseworkers, a greater appreciation of the group and, among group workers, a greater appreciation of individual dynamics.

There were other reasons for this rapprochement. War services, on the home front and in the armed forces, brought caseworkers and group workers together as practitioners on a larger scale than ever before. The psychiatric professions, which had strongly influenced social casework and which were accorded high status in the eyes of

---

[15]   Eduard C. Lindeman, "The Roots of Democratic Culture," in Trecker, Ed., *op. cit.*, pp. 24-25.

social caseworkers, began to experiment with groups as therapeutic devices. This in itself did not yet bring more appreciation of social group work, but the idea of using the group as a helping element did impress many.

Perhaps one must also mention (although I do this with hesitation, since it may be viewed subjectively) the influence of refugees from central European countries on the use of group work for the purpose of therapy.[16]

These refugees came with a combined tradition of psychoanalytic thinking and group experiences that had been of deep significance to them; they had practiced in a milieu in which groups played an important part in education and therapy. Having grown up in an authoritarian family culture—and resented it—they realized the significance of voluntary group participation to individual development. Psychoanalysis had neither the dramatic nor the exclusive impact on them that it frequently had on the person reared in a highly individualistic and puritan culture such as that of the USA. Analytic therapy was seen by many middle European refugees as only one form of treatment among others; it was to be used with discrimination. They had grown up with the beginnings of the psychoanalytic movement; they accepted the theory as valuable, but not as dogma. Added to this were their own painful experiences in Nazi Germany and Austria, which intensified their motivation to work on human relations.

For myself, if I represent at all—at least in some ways—this group of immigrants, I must say that my first encounter with social group work in 1941 was a revelation. Having just come from a society that seemed to present an inescapable gulf between the individual and the group —which insisted that the individual be sacrificed to the interests of the group—I found the concept of individualization in and through the group exhilarating. Sallie Bright, in 1948, called this "individual de-

---

16 See the works of such social workers as Morris F. Mayer, director of Bellefaire, an institution for disturbed children, who has written extensively on casework and institutions with much appreciation of the importance of group work; Henry Maier, who writes in the same field; Susanne Schulze who emphasized group work and casework in the total child welfare field; Fritz Redl, who has strongly influenced development of group therapy; Bettelheim and his work with disturbed children; Walter A. Friedlander's sympathetic treatment of group work in his basic texts, and myself. This should not detract from the great or greater influence of American-born social workers in this same field (e.g., Samuel R. Slavson, Gertrude Wilson, Grace Coyle, Margaret Svendsen, or Raymond Fischer).

velopment within the group" the answer to a "national dilemma." She also saw in it the potential of a method to combine two purposes: the therapeutic goal of mental hygiene related to the individual, and the society-directed goal of keeping a democracy alive. In her own words:

> True, the settlement house group may not be able to affect the Turkey and Greece situation directly; but a democratic nation is the sum total of democratic neighborhoods and communities, and what you are doing in group work is to give people a chance to practice the methods of democracy in their own backyards. And, from a mental hygiene point of view in a frustrated nation, you are relieving the frustration of the citizen who can't make himself heard on a global scale by giving him a chance to make himself heard in the neighborhood. It is a thrilling thing to realize, then, that if the citizen can be heard in all the neighborhoods, his collective voice will, in the end, have global carrying power.[17]

This dual focus on democracy in action and mental health is very significant in the development of the group work method itself. It has led to controversy within the ranks of group work practitioners. Practitioners from the traditional field of informal education and recreation feared that the concern with mental hygiene and the focus on therapy would detract from the valuable use of the group work method to help with citizen action and services to normal youth. Actually, both foci were kept, even during the period when the healing power of the group was first recognized and used by social group workers. This occurred with sufficient emphasis in the late years of the 1930's. Papers on the use of the group work method for therapeutic purposes appeared in the *Proceedings of the National Conference of Social Welfare*.[18] The dual goal direction is symbolized by a paper presented by the author at the Annual Meeting of the American Orthopsychiatric Association and entitled, "Group Therapy in Overcoming Racial and Cultural Tensions."[19]

[17] Sallie E. Bright, "Letting the Public in on Group Work Objectives," in Harleigh B. Trecker, Editor, *op. cit.*, p. 48.

[18] See Gisela Konopka, "Therapy through Social Group Work," *Proceedings of the National Conference of Social Welfare*, New York: Columbia University Press, 1946, pp. 228-236; see also Samuel R. Slavson, "Group in Development and in Therapy," *Proceedings of the National Conference of Social Work*, 1938, New York: Columbia University Press, 1938, pp. 339-349.

[19] Gisela Konopka, "Group Therapy in Overcoming Racial and Cultural Tensions," *The American Journal of Orthopsychiatry*, XVII, No. 4, Oct. 1947, pp. 694-699; also in Arnold M. Rose, ed., *Race Prejudice and Discrimination*, New York: Borzoi Book, Alfred A. Knopf, 1951, pp. 565-572.

During the war years the members of the rapidly developing American Association for the Study of Group Work still hesitated to identify themselves with any specific profession. In 1940, William Heard Kilpatrick, the great educator and friend of John Dewey, wrote in a book published under the auspices of the AASGW:

> This group work is, however, not to be thought of as a separate field of work, but rather as a method to be used in all kinds of educational effort. "Group Work" in this sense is now more or less of a movement, and as such deserves support and success. But its success will be achieved when, and to the degree that, effective working in groups has established itself as an essential part of any adequate education of youth, however and wherever conducted.[20]

Kilpatrick thought that group work should be identified with the profession of education. Yet the agencies from which it had grown, the developments described on the preceding pages, the change in social work itself, which had moved away from its strong emphasis on psychiatry, and the fact that group work was taught in a few schools of social work identified it more closely with social work. Although it is almost impossible in the development of the method itself to name an individual who alone "invented" group work or to cite a certain point in history when it was first employed, the turning point in the identification of group work with social work can be dated and credited to a person. The date that is recognized is 1946; the person, Grace Longwell Coyle.

At the meeting of the National Conference of Social Work in Buffalo, New York in 1946, the members of the American Association for the Study of Group Work met in the auditorium of the Kleinhaus Music Hall. It was only a year after the end of World War II. Hopes were high for a "new society" and civic responsibility was strongly felt. The audience listened to the "dean" of social group work, Grace Coyle, who had helped develop objectives and methods and who had established the first course in group work at Western Reserve University in Cleveland. Her subject was "On Becoming Professional."

[20] William Heard Kilpatrick, *Group Education for a Democracy*, New York: Association Press, 1940, p. vii. The author became aware of this statement through an especially perceptive article dealing with the development of group work written by William Schwartz and entitled, "Group Work and the Social Scene," in Alfred J. Kahn, Ed. *Issues in American Social Work*, New York: Columbia University Press, 1959, pp. 110-137.

Her presentation was not concerned with the privileges or the status of a profession, rather, it was concerned with the responsibilities and the prerequisites of a professional endeavor. Her first sentences established the seriousness of such a claim:

> Within the ten years since the American Association for the Study of Group Work was born, there has been increasing evidence that group workers were coming to regard themselves as professional and that other groups were demanding of us the assumption of such responsibilities. As the founders of the organization will, I am sure, all agree, this was not our intention in the beginning. . . .[21]

She proceeded to discuss the attributes of a profession, each time evaluating with strict honesty whether group work came up to the required standard. She then entered the controversial discussion of group work's alignment:

> One baffling problem has plagued the development of professional consciousness among group workers over this decade. It is usually phrased in terms of alignment, and a dilemma is presented. We must, it seems, be either educators or social workers. . . .[22]

She discussed the great variety of agencies grouped under health and welfare services. They were more or less bound to social work through tradition. She continued:

> A large part of our difficulty in knowing what we are has come out of the words "social work." To many people they connote relief, or dealing with the poor, or uplift, or some other unpleasant facet of life. We need to realize that not only we but other people are changing. . . . My own hope is that the emerging definition of social work may define it as involving the conscious use of social relations in performing certain community functions, such as child welfare, family welfare or health services, recreation and informal education. Casework, group work, and community organization have this common factor, that they are all based on understanding human relations. While the specific relations used in each are different, the underlying philosophy and approach are the same: a respect for personality and a belief in democracy. This we share with caseworkers and expert community organization people. It is for this

[21] Grace L. Coyle, "On Becoming Professional," in Trecker, ed., *op. cit.*, p. 328.
[22] *Ibid.*, p. 338.

reason that I believe group work as a method falls within the larger scope of social work *as a method* and as defined above.[23]

When the assembly accepted this reasoning and decided to become a professional membership organization, group work entered the family of social work. This process was finalized in 1955 when the AAGW joined the newly formed National Association of Social Workers.

One of the insights gained from work with groups is that any person entering a group constellation changes through his interaction with others; conversely, the given group changes in turn by the entrance of a new member. The same happens in the realm of ideas and organizations. Social group work changed through its close association with the profession of social work and also with the older method, social casework. In turn, it changed the profession and widened the concept of the social welfare field. It took insight and certain concepts from the earlier method and added concepts and approaches, not only to the total profession of social work but to the practice of casework. The recent trend of a more aggressive and more outgoing approach in casework is related, for example, to the original more informal and neighborhood-related practice of group work while the more conscious purposefulness seen in modern group work practice is influenced by the clear and more formalized approach of social casework. (Caseworkers and group workers do not always credit each other for the help they gain from each other. Sibling rivalry also exists in the realm of ideas.)

With the new concept of group work as a *method of social work,* the integrative process had only begun. The years after World War II placed demands on the development of the method through actual practice and through better conceptualization and formulation of theory. The process is in no way finished. The years after the war saw an immense rise in group work literature.[24] Gertrude Wilson's *Social Group Work Practice* (1949), Harleigh B. Trecker's *Social Group Work* (1949), Grace Coyle's *Group Work with American Youth* (1948), and Gisela Konopka's *Therapeutic Group Work With Children* (1949) appeared in a timespan of only two years. These books

---

23 *Ibid.,* pp. 339-340.
24 This writer studied social work with a specialization in social group work during the war years, 1941-1943. At that time no textbook in group work was available; in fact, most of the literature consisted of articles.

all made the attempt to clarify the orderly process of social group work as part of the helping function of social work on the wide scale from healthy to sick individuals and groups. Definitions were sought for, but not easily formulated. In 1949 a committee of the American Association of Group Workers published a report entitled "Definition of the Function of the Group Worker." To define the method alone, seemed to be too difficult. The report showed the interrelation of goal, function, method and required underlying knowledge. It was for years the official definition of group work. Though loosely conceived it did show many concepts that are worked out more thoroughly today. It is therefore reproduced here:

The Group Worker enables various types of groups to function in such a way that both group interaction and program activities contribute to the growth of the individual, and the achievement of desirable social goals.

The objectives of the group worker include provision for personal growth according to individual capacity and need, the adjustment of the individual to other persons, to groups and to society, and the motivation of the individual toward the improvement of society; the recognition by the individual of his own rights, abilities, and differences of others.

Through his participation the group worker aims to effect the group process so that decisions come about as a result of knowledge and a sharing and integration of ideas, experiences and knowledge, rather than as a result of domination from within or without the group.

Through experience he aims to produce those relations with other groups and the wider community which contribute to responsible citizenship, mutual understanding between cultural, religious, economic or special groupings in the community, and a participation in the constant improvement of our society toward democratic goals.

The guiding purpose behind such leadership rests upon the common assumptions of a democratic society; namely, the opportunity for each individual to fulfill his capacities in freedom, to respect and appreciate others and to assume his social responsibility in maintaining and constantly improving our democratic society.

Underlying the practice of group work is a knowledge of individual and group behavior and of social conditions and community relations which is based on the modern social sciences.

On the basis of this knowledge the group worker contributes to the group with which he works a skill in leadership which enables the members to use their capacities to the full and to create socially constructive group activities.

He is aware of both program activities and of the interplay of personalities within the group and between the group and its surrounding community.

According to the interests and needs of each, he assists them to get from the group experience the satisfactions provided by the program activities, the enjoyment and personal growth available through the social relations, and the opportunity to participate as a responsible citizen.

The group worker makes conscious use of his relation to the group, his knowledge of program as a tool, and his understanding of the individual and of the group process, and recognizes his responsibility both to individuals and groups with whom he works and the larger social values he represents."[25]

Another committee of the American Association of Group Workers worked on the new relationship to therapeutic services. Its work deepened the concept of group work as a method to be used in many different agencies if it was used purposefully and with increased skill in diagnostic thinking about individuals and their situations. Its final report strengthened the bond with the entire profession of social work and prevented the danger of creating a hierarchy in the use of the method according to the function it had to fulfill. The statement, as presented by the committee's chairman, read:

> The word "psychiatric" has taken on prestige value in social work for a long time though pioneers in psychiatric case work have fought this for years. Helen Perlman said that it is not "frosting on the cake." Ethel Ginsburg said, "In our simple-minded fashion, we try to explain that the 'psychiatric' in psychiatric social work does not mean that we know more psychodynamics than the other fellow. It just means that we know how to work as social workers in a psychiatric setting with psychiatric patients and their relatives, as partners in a team."
>
> And I repeat here Grace Weyker's statement that we presented at the meeting last year when our committee on similarities and differences between group work and group therapy made the first statement.
>
> "Psychiatric social work has gone through a series of stages which might be listed as (1) early recognition of a distinct self, (2) the play-by-myself age, and (3) the know-all, superior age. It seems to me that psychiatric social work should now be ready to enter a fourth stage, to be a stable adult member of the social work family. Probably one of the biggest blocks to such adult stability for psychiatric social work is confusion over the label. Much of this confusion is tied in with a mistaken connotation of glamor or superiority which has been accepted tacitly among groups who should know better.

[25] Harleigh B. Trecker, ed., *Group Work Foundations and Frontiers, op. cit.,* pp. 4-5.

"Psychiatric social work according to the official and accepted definition is simply 'social work practiced in direct and responsible relationship to psychiatry.' Part of the misunderstanding of psychiatric social work lies in the idea that a psychiatric social worker has some peculiar skill in working with people or understanding the dynamics of behavior. This should not be true. Certainly any social work training which aims to prepare people for case work or group work cannot be considered satisfactory if it does not include this understanding of behavior. Certainly the entire field of social work has taken over from psychiatry a great many concepts regarding personality development and causation in behavior. In other words, it would seem obvious that any practice of social case work or social group work would require a psychodynamically oriented social worker.

"A concept that met general approval was that psychiatric social work requires all of the equipment of the social worker and in addition, (1) a deepened knowledge of psychopathology and of the various settings in which mental and emotional disorders may be treated, and (2) a clear delineation of the social worker's place in and contribution to, the collaborative treatment of a clinical team. . . ."

We defined psychiatric group work or therapeutic group work as "the use of the social group work method in working with groups of patients in a psychiatric setting." In casework this is often designated as "casework in a foreign setting" and this applies to group work too. It was underlined that in such a setting the group worker is part of the psychiatric team and the responsibility is a medical–psychiatric one under guidance of the psychiatrist. In the general group work setting the group worker is primarily responsible for the work done. Much of what he does is also therapeutic.

Knowledge Needed: Both general group work and psychiatric group work are a social work method or working with people in groups. Basic to both of them are understanding and skill in working with individuals in groups.

Goal: Goal of the general group worker is the adjustment of the individual to the group and the group as a whole to society. Its focus is an educational socializing, democratic one—and is on individual growth *through* group growth. Psychiatric group work has the same goal of adjustment of the individual. Focus is on helping the individual move toward health and emotional development.

Diagnosis: Both are concerned with recognition of sickness and strength in the individual.

Role of the Worker: The general group worker moves from the central role as soon as possible, enabling the group to determine its own goals and leadership. The psychiatric group worker is the central figure in the group, often assuming the role of mother- or father-figure. He may always remain in this role.

Impact of Social Values on the Role of the Worker: The group worker in the general setting as well as in the psychiatric setting deals with social values. Yet a neighborhood group will be more influenced by neighborhood status values than a group in a psychiatric setting. The difference again is more and less, not in terms of not at all. One of the values of the group in a psychiatric setting is the possibility for the member to get away from established status situations and to start comparatively as a "blank" in relation to others.

In the general group setting the group worker has also a greater educational responsibility in terms of social values.

Type of Group: The group worker in the general setting works with formed or natural groups. The psychiatric group worker always works with formed groups.

Grouping: In general group work the agency determines groupings in relation to social goals and individual preferences. In psychiatric group work grouping is an important factor in helping the individual. The agency[26] determines and controls groupings on the basis of individual therapy needs only.

Duration of Groups: In general group work the group worker may work with a group over a long span of time helping the individuals and the group move into different projects and relationships according to their changing age group. In psychiatric group work the time limit is set in relation to the therapeutic goal determined by the psychiatrist and the rest of the team.[27]

While the impact of psychoanalysis on social work had been strong after World War I, group work accepted its insights somewhat critically and tempered them—partly because it entered the social work family at a time when psychoanalytic thinking had begun to change and partly because the underlying concepts of group work were derived from such early sociologists as Simmel and Weber.

The postwar years showed a great increase in research in small group behavior done mostly by representatives of a new specialization, social psychology. New insights also came from the field of cultural anthropology. These developments helped strengthen the integration of knowledge (which we will discuss in a following chapter); they also hindered the development of the group work method through

---

26 The committee meant hospitals or child guidance clinics although it was not spelled out in the original report.
27 Gisela Konopka, "Similarities and Differences between Group Work and Group Therapy," Report of the Group Therapy Committee, A.A.G.W., mimeographed, ST-451-8, undated; also in *Selected Papers of the National Conference of Social Welfare,* 1951, pp. 51-60.

the unfortunate phenomenon of "faddism" in our society. "Group dynamics," misunderstood as a form of method instead of "the study of forces underlying the behavior of groups," as clearly stated by one of its foremost experts,[28] became a mechanistic device in working with groups. In general, however, this development in the social sciences enriched group work and ultimately all social work, as seen in the recent Curriculum Study of the Council on Social Work Education.[29] Louis Towley foresaw this trend when he wrote:

> . . . Then came a dynamic kind of sociology—anthropology: the concept of status, role, casts, and pattern, and the influence of the situation on conduct. Social group work responded to these sympathetic, explanatory, group-rooted ideas. Many workers shared Cohen's belief that the social group work field is closer to these developments than is casework and therefore should bring the ideas to social work as a whole.[30]

The historical development of an approach to one of the basic problems of human society—such as relationship among people and their individual development over such a comparatively short period of time—cannot yet produce agreement among all those who practice group work. In her volume on the curriculum study, published in 1959, Marjorie Murphy tried to summarize some generalizations on social group work on which there is agreement at the present time. I will present only the first three points:

> 1. Social group work is a method of rendering service to persons, through providing experience in groups. Development of the person towards his individual potential, improvement of relationship and social functioning competencies, and social action are recognized as purposes of social group work. The worker functions within a framework of ethical and social values.
> 2. Social group work is a generic method which can be used in different settings.
> 3. The method includes conscious use of worker-member relationships, relationships among members, and of group activity. The worker simultaneously uses relationships with individual members and with the group

28   Leon Festinger, "Current Developments in Group Dynamics," mimeographed, undated, New York: A.A.G.W., p. 1.
29   Werner W. Boehm, Director and Coordinator, A Project Report of the Curriculum Study, Vols. I-XIII. New York: Council on Social Work Education, 1959.
30   Frank J. Bruno (with chapters by Louis Towley), op. cit., pp. 426-427.

as a whole. He works as an enabler with both, helping members and the group to use their capacities and strengths. He uses himself differently in accordance with specific objectives and his assessment of members' needs, interests and capacities.[31]

And, as previously stated, there is agreement that group work is a method of social work. Method is an orderly way to achieve an objective. Social work methods are helping processes. They cannot be separated from the function the profession as a whole sees as its own, from the specific purpose to be achieved in each case, whether individual or group, from the deep understanding of the one who needs help, from an understanding of oneself and from the total ethos and value base of the profession.

A helping method cannot be mechanical. It is the heart of the profession because only its competent use can truly fulfill the ends for which a humanitarian profession stands. For example, preventing recidivism among criminals may be a goal. The *way in which it is done* determines whether one follows the precepts of a humanitarian profession or those of another value system. One can, for example, shoot the offender or cut off his hand, certainly ways to achieve the goal of "preventing recidivism." The example is used to show the intricate and inseparable relationship between goal, function, philosophy and method. This makes the use of the group work method a professional effort which includes knowledge and judgment. It cannot be used mechanistically. There have been voices raised that social work should consider the goals more and should forget about methods. Yet one cannot supersede the other. Practice is the heart of the social work profession and this necessitates the use of a method congruent with the ends. No one said it better than Gandhi:

> . . . The means may be likened to a seed, the end to a tree; and there is just the same inviolable connection between the means and the end as there is between the seed and the tree . . .[32]

We traced the historical development of the concept of social group work and saw it change from the designation of a field, a movement, a goal to a social work method, part of the "means" of social work.

---

[31] Marjorie Murphy, *op. cit.*, p. 78.
[32] Gandhi in Rudolph Flesch, ed., *The Book of Unusual Quotations*, New York: Harper & Row, Publishers, 1957, p. 167.

To understand it today, we must therefore understand the goal and its function in society today as part of the function of the total social work profession.

Its present-day definition may be summarized as: *Social group work is a method of social work which helps individuals to enhance their social functioning through purposeful group experiences and to cope more effectively with their personal, group or community problems.*

BIBLIOGRAPHY

Bright, Sallie E., "Letting the Public in on Group Work Objectives," in Harleigh B. Trecker, Editor, *Group Work—Foundations and Frontiers*, New York: Whiteside, Inc. and William Morrow and Co., 1955, pp. 35-49.

Bruno, Frank J., *Trends in Social Work 1874-1956*, New York: Columbia University Press, 1957.

Cohen, Nathan E., *Social Work in the American Tradition*, New York: The Dryden Press, 1958, pp. 10-13; 144-145; 189-193.

Coyle, Grace L., "On Becoming Professional," in Harleigh B. Trecker, Editor, *op. cit.*, pp. 328-342.

————,"Social Group Work," *Social Work Year Book*, 1954, New York: American Association of Social Workers, 1954, pp. 480-486.

Fink, Arthur E., Everett E. Wilson, and Merrill B. Conover, *The Field of Social Work*, third edition, New York: Henry Holt and Co., 1942, pp. 500-528.

Follett, Mary Parker, *The New State*, fourth edition, New York: Longmans, Green and Co., 1934.

Freud, Sigmund, *A General Introduction to Psychoanalysis*, English translation by Joan Riviere, New York: Liveright Publishing Corp., 1935.

Hendry, Charles E., Editor, *Decade of Group Work*, New York: Association Press, 1948.

Kaiser, Clara A., "The Advance of Social Group Work," *Social Welfare Forum 1955*, New York: Columbia University Press, 1955, pp. 35-47.

————, "Group Work Education in the Last Decade," *The Group*, Vol. XV, No. 5, June 1953, pp. 3-10; 27-29.

Konopka, Gisela, *Eduard C. Lindeman and Social Work Philosophy*, Minneapolis: University of Minnesota Press, 1958.

———, "Group Therapy in Overcoming Racial and Cultural Tensions," *The American Journal of Orthopsychiatry*, Vol. XVII, No. 4, Oct. 1947, pp. 694-699.

———, "Group Work: A Heritage and a Challenge," *Social Work with Groups 1960*, New York: N.A.S.W., 1960, pp. 7-21.

———,"Knowledge and Skill of the Group Therapist," see "Group Therapy," Round Table 1948, Harry M. Little, Chairman, *American Journal of Orthopsychiatry*, Vol. XIX, No. 1, Jan. 1949, pp. 56-60.

Kunstler, Peter, *Social Group Work in Great Britain*, London: Faber and Faber, Ltd., 1955.

Lieberman, Joshua, Editor, *New Trends in Group Work*, New York: Association Press, 1938.

Lindeman, Eduard C., "Group Work and Education for Democracy," *Proceedings of the National Conference of Social Work*, 1939, New York: Columbia University Press, 1939, pp. 342-347.

———, "The Roots of Democratic Culture," in Harleigh B. Trecker, Editor, *op. cit.*, pp. 13-25.

Maloney, Sara E. and Margaret H. Mudgett, "Group Work—Group Casework: Are They the Same?" *Social Work*, Vol. 4, No. 2, Apr. 1959, pp. 29-36.

Murphy, Marjorie, *The Social Group Work Method in Social Work Education*, Vol. XI, A *Project Report of the Curriculum Study*, Werner W. Boehm, Director and Coordinator, New York: Council on Social Work Education, 1959.

Perlman, Helen Harris, *Social Case Work*, Chicago: University of Chicago Press (copyright 1957 by University of Chicago).

Phillips, Helen U., *Essentials of Social Group Work Skill*, New York: Association Press, 1957.

Richmond, Mary, "Some Next Steps in Social Treatment," *Proceedings of the National Conference of Social Work*, 1920, New York: Columbia University Press, 1939, pp. 254-258.

Schwartz, William, "Group Work and the Social Scene," in Alfred J. Kahn, Editor, *Issues in American Social Work*, New York: Columbia University Press, 1959, pp. 110-137.

Slavson, Samuel R., "Group in Development and in Therapy," *Proceedings of the National Conference of Social Work*, 1938, New York: Columbia University Press, 1938, pp. 339-349.

Trecker, Harleigh B., *Social Group Work: Principles and Practices*, revised edition, New York: Whiteside, Inc., 1955.

Wilson, Gertrude, *Group Work and Case Work—Their Relationship and Practice*, New York: Family Welfare Association of America, 1941.

———, "Social Group Work—Trends and Developments," *Social Work*, Vol. 1, No. 4, Oct. 1956, pp. 66-75.

Wilson, Gertrude and Gladys Ryland, *Social Group Work Practice: The Creative Use of the Social Process*, Boston: Houghton, Mifflin Co., 1949.

Woods, Robert A., *The Neighborhood in Nation Building*, Boston: Houghton Mifflin Co., 1923.

CHAPTER TWO

Social Group Work as a Part of Social Work

. . . that the conception of the field of social work should above all be kept fluid in order to maintain in this profession at least an open mind toward humanity's changing needs and the best methods for meeting them.[1]

In the course of history the term *social work* has meant a type of service, a certain function to fulfill, a method of practice, and a profession. Today we conceive it to be a profession just as we consider teaching. It is practiced in the large field of social welfare which encompasses all services whose defined social goal is to promote the social welfare of individuals and groups in the community. These services include, among others, public education, hospitals, and playgrounds, and they all require the skills of many different professions.

[1] James H. Tufts, *Education and Training for Social Work*, New York: Russell Sage Foundation, 1923, pp. 30-31.

23

The particular functions of these different professions are determined by the role society has ascribed to them, and they alter with the passage of time. We can see this in the profession of teaching, which has widened its function since the time it was limited to the teaching of simple skills such as reading and writing. It also has different functions in different societies; it varies according to the development and the culture of a given society. Teaching has broadened its scope from the education of a few belonging to the clergy and the nobility in the Middle Ages to practically every member of society in modern–day America. Social work too has changed its function during the course of history. It started with almsgiving (a function seen as its sole or major purpose in only a few societies at the present time). Today it serves all people regardless of their social or economic status and works on a wide variety of individual, group and community problems. The common purpose is "help with social functioning." Admittedly this encompasses a wide area of human behavior, but no wider than "physical functioning" which has been for a long time the main concern of the medical profession. Without question this social work function overlaps in part with the function of other professions.

In the complicated web of human society many efforts have been and are being made to replace its defective fibers. They are made to improve the environment as well as to help the individual. As long as human beings have existed, they have been striving to conquer nature and to improve man's relationship to his fellow man. These goals include the efforts of the common laborer, the artisan, and the highly trained professional. The more complicated a society becomes the more these efforts are separated according to the specific function they have to fulfill as well as according to the skill needed to fulfill them. They become increasingly specialized. In our present society each individual who is gainfully employed carries out a specialized function in his working hours. Yet, outside of these hours he engages in a large, undifferentiated range of human efforts and skills. He does this in his role of parent, of friend and of citizen in a democratic society. As a parent or friend he is physician, nurse, teacher, social worker, dressmaker, laborer, counselor, typist, baker, cook, etc. As a citizen in a democratic society, he is also legislator and policy maker. Any vocation or profession utilizes only a few of the functions which every human being can and must fulfill. It refines skill; it adds and uses specific knowledge. This applies to dressmaking and cooking as well as to nursing the sick, teaching the young, and helping the distressed. Every profession, therefore, must by necessity overlap at points with other professions and it *always* overlaps with certain functions every human being does. For far too long this has been of concern to the profession of social work as if it were something that should not be. Too often social workers were worried lest their functions were also carried out by others. This should not concern us. What social work has to offer—and this is true of every other profession—is specific knowledge and skill to be employed in one of the many areas other people are also concerned with.

Even if we do not concern ourselves with these grey areas of overlapping responsibilities, we must establish the "core" function of social work, and derive from this the goal of each individual professional effort in the profession. Otherwise the discussion of method is futile. Since method is an orderly way of procedure, it must have a specific aim. For a long time those aims were expressed in agency efforts, described, for example, as "giving relief" or "preventing juvenile delinquency" or "providing services to youth." Yet each of these goals involves the services of many professions. It is not easy to determine this core function. Herman D. Stein, professor of the New York School of Social Work, hastened to state in an address given at the Annual Forum of the National Conference of Social Welfare in 1961:

> I do not have the temerity nor the slightest intention of attempting to answer the question "What is the function of social work?" but will continue the process of addressing this central and never-ending question for our profession.[2]

The words of Dr. Tuft, written in 1923 and quoted at the beginning of this chapter, warn against a too early or too narrow definition. Early definitions, sometimes still used today, are often too limited.

The social worker is expected by society to be able (1) *to assess, clarify and help individuals with the integration of their inner motives and the demands of their social environment* and (2) *to help change*

---

2 Herman D. Stein, "Observations of the Function of Social Work: A Discussion Based on Dr. De Jongh's Paper at the International Conference of Social Work in Rome," Jan. 1961, p. 1, mimeographed. (Published version of this paper, contained in *Community Organization*, 1961, published in New York by Columbia University Press, 1961, does not contain this quotation.)

*social environment if it is detrimental to the social development of
individuals.* This is a far cry and quite different from an earlier concept of "social adjustment" which implied conformity and submission
to any demand of the social environment—a concept that stigmatized
the social work profession as primarily an effort to maintain the "status
quo," countrary to its tradition of social reform. What it does mean is
the assessment of the individual, his capacities and motivations as well
as his environment, and helping with acceptance or change of one or
the other, depending on who or what needs help. To repeat: professional responsibilities always overlap at the outer edges. Their core
practice, task, or function differs.

Two basic needs of the human being—besides the physical one of
survival—are the needs for self-respect and for "belonging," the acceptance of the "I" and the "you," the finding of the bridge between
these two. Only in this way can he live up to his greatest potential
and make his contribution to an imperfect society within the limitations of his particular capacity. This means the development of
many capacities: the capacity to fulfill different tasks at different
stages of development; to learn to accept frustration or to deal
with it in a constructive way; to postpone gratification—a difficult
art; to express anger and fear, yet to express them in a way that does
no harm to others or to oneself; to be able to work and play; to think
and feel and, above all, to love and to accept love. These capacities are
all learned only in interaction with others. In a healthy community
they are learned naturally in the family and through relations with
neighbors and friends. Yet modern society is complex. The demands
of the social environment bring many problems: increasing loneliness
produced in large urban centers, high mobility that does not always
allow easy access to friendship ("What is the use of making friends,"
a teenager said, "whenever we are close to someone, they move or we
do"). People must learn new skills; to make new friendships quickly;
to deepen the ones already formed, and to bear the frustration of loss;
to meet the members of groups that look at each other with suspicion
—racial, religious or nationality groups; to cope with economic deprivation, which means not only having no money but also experiencing
the agonies of failure and bitterness; to cope with marital problems;
to accept and adjust to the fast pace of modern life with the resultant
gaps of misunderstanding between generations; to maintain the wish
to succeed, but also to know the limits placed upon each person by

both internal and external factors, and much more. Sometimes these problems too can be worked out with the assistance of neighbors and friends. Often they need the help of the social worker, who will not always do the work himself, but might skillfully enlist the aid of members of the community. Social group work services therefore cover the wide range from individual to community problems, from working with healthy, capable leadership to working with the sick and rejected. Werner Boehm in his *Curriculum Study* classified the tasks of social work under "restoration" (work with a breakdown, either of an individual or a group or community), "prevention" and "provision of services," an indication of the widened range of social work functions.

The *group work method* is one of several methods used to fulfill social work functions whenever its particular approach is most appropriate. The matrix of the group work situation is the *group*, individuals in interaction. This differentiates the specific helping process from that of casework, another basic social work method. Helen Perlman designated the components of the casework situation as the *Person*, the *Problem*, and the *Place*. The group work situation is more complex: its components are the *Person in the group, the Group, the Problem*—sometimes of this particular person, sometimes of the particular group, sometimes of the total community—*and the Place*.

This complex situation includes also diverse "points of entry" of group work services:

1. Individuals in distress ask for help or are referred to group work services because of their problems. We find this in family services, mental health services, school social work, corrections, agencies working with the handicapped, and others.

2. Groups ask for help to better fulfill their members' needs and purposes. Such situations include groups discriminated against in the community, parents groups concerned with the upbringing of their children, community service and action groups wanting to find better solutions to community problems.

3. There is no specific request for help, either by a group or an individual, but the community as a whole has recognized needs for services to either prevent problems or promote a healthy group life. Examples of this are group work with street corner gangs, and youth work, which helps children and young people

with their developmental tasks. It includes also the still neglected services to people (children and adults) in institutions.

Overlapping functions with other professions have led to confusion in terminology and have, in turn, influenced group work practice. The most significant example of this is the confusion and conflict around the terms of *group work* and *group therapy*. They need clarification as part of the discussion of the function of social group work.

There are a few representatives of social work who use the term "group work" as a synonym for "recreation" or "informal education." For them, the terms "group work" and "group therapy" are completely separated, since to them group work is exclusively concerned with the leisure time needs of healthy children and adults. This concept of group work has practically disappeared. It is today a method of social work with its threefold functions mentioned above. Recreation and adult education are seen as fields of service in which group workers function as social workers with their group work skill.

If we therefore eliminate the outdated concept of group work as equaling recreation, the confusion between the terms "group work" and "group therapy" needs serious consideration. The following is an attempt at clarification:

Among board members of the American Association for Orthopsychiatry in which the major professions of the psychiatric team are represented (i.e., psychiatry, psychology, and social work), it was for a time a joke to suggest that one should have a meeting regarding "Who does What to Whom and Why and When" because of differences of opinion over who was qualified to perform what therapeutic duties. There is confusion also in terminology pertaining to individual treatment, as seen in the interchangeable use of "case work treatment," "case work therapy," "therapy," "treatment," "counseling." Yet this is multiplied when it comes to work with groups. This may have its cause in the more recent success of group work as a method for therapeutic treatment after many years of being considered an inferior tool by the helping professions—including social work. Corsini wrote that these group methods represent "a revolution in psychotherapy and may well be the answer for some up-to-now unsolved problems, . . ."[3]

    [3]   Raymond J. Corsini, *Methods of Group Psychotherapy*, New York: McGraw-Hill Book Co., Inc., 1957, p. 3.

Yet which group methods are we talking about? What is the definition? *Social group work*, as presented in this book, *is a method of social work which helps individuals to enhance their social functioning through purposeful group experiences and to cope more effectively with their personal, group or community problems.* This means that it is based on the competence a social worker develops in his training and education and that it is concerned with mental health and social problems. Its beneficiaries are both the sick and the healthy. The agencies in which it is practiced span the wide arc of health, education and welfare organizations. Its specific means and approaches will be discussed in detail in the following chapters.

What, then, is understood under *group therapy?* Corsini, who has given us one of the most comprehensive and clear presentations of the whole complex question of group therapy, starts out by confronting the reader of his book on *Methods of Group Psychotherapy* with the fact that there exists no simple, inclusive and yet exclusive definition. He states:

> What contributes to the confusion is that the term group psychotherapy[4] may be used in two specific ways. It may be thought of as a generic term, encompassing a variety of procedures. It may also be thought of as a name for a single procedure. If by group psychotherapy therapist A means method X and if therapist B understands that group psychotherapy means method Y, then it is obvious that the two are not communicating. The complexity of this problem becomes evident when it is realized that more than 25 specific methods have been described in the literature.[5]

Corsini points out that definitions can be too wide or too narrow. An example of the former is a statement he quotes from a War Department bulletin:

> In a broad sense any procedure which tends to improve the mental health of more than one individual is group psychotherapy.[6]

And the example of a too narrow one is, according to Corsini, the remark of one of his colleagues:

[4]   Corsini uses this term interchangeably with group therapy. This is frequently done in the literature.
[5]   *Ibid.*, p. 4.
[6]   *Loc. cit.*

This is not group psychotherapy, because the members do not sit in a circle and talk.[7]

Corsini's own definition is more inclusive and more precise:

Group psychotherapy consists of processes occurring in formally organized, protected groups and calculated to attain rapid ameliorations in personality and behavior of individual members through specified and controlled group interactions.[8]

One edition of the *Journal of Social Issues* was devoted exclusively to group methods in psychotherapy, social work and adult education; in it, Jerome D. Frank gave his definition of group therapy. It is a fairly elaborate explanation:

The term group therapy refers to all methods of treating psychiatric patients in groups under the leadership of a psychotherapist. Therapeutic groups may consist of children, adolescents or adults in or out of institutions who are in emotional distress presumably arising in large part from chronic disturbances in their relationships with other people. The goal of these groups is to ameliorate the suffering and improve the personal and social functioning of their members. The means to this goal are the emotional interactions of the members with the leader and each other. . . .[9]

If we compare the two definitions, we find that neither confines group therapy to the method of one profession alone, but leaves it open as to what kind of professional shall conduct the groups. They both stress the purposefulness of the action and the goal of amelioration of suffering or stress in individuals. Frank adds "social functioning" as a goal, but this may also be implied in Corsini's definition without being specified. The only difference between the two may lie—although this is not necessarily so—in some differentiation of clientele. Jerome Frank limits group therapy to psychiatric patients, while Corsini includes seemingly a wider group.

If we compare these two definitions with the one used for social group work, we realize that group work practice directed toward groups with emotional or mental problems would fall within the same def-

---

7 *Ibid.*, p. 5.
8 *Loc. cit.*
9 Jerome D. Frank, "Group Methods in Psychotherapy," *Journal of Social Issues*, Vol. VIII, No. 2, 1952, p. 35.

inition. The difference lies only in the fact that group work is also concerned with groups consisting of healthy individuals and with social action groups.

In recent years, two other attempts have been made to delineate and clarify terms which designate group treatment. Both show that practice of group work and group therapy are difficult to sort out. Differences are seen mostly in fields in which the methods are practiced, but in recent years these two overlap frequently. For example, group work—as well as group therapy—is practised in psychiatric hospitals.[10]

The logical conclusion seems to be that the terms used for purposeful use of the group are interchangeable, as long as the purpose includes—as Fritz Redl said once in a letter to the author—"a repair job"; that means some help with emotional or mental problems. That would mean *group therapy is practice which is aimed at ameliorating suffering and improving the personal and social functioning of its members through specified and controlled group interaction aided by a professional person.* This definition of the term "group therapy" does not limit it to any specific professional identification, nor to adherence to a certain technique. It includes aim and function. This is in accordance with the thinking of Corsini and Spotnitz. This is also the way the public understands the term "group therapy." Group work practice, therefore, when directed toward amelioration of personal and social functioning, may rightfully be called group therapy.

This does not mean, however, that the practice of the social group worker will be or should be the same as the practice of the psychiatrist. Corsini speaks about the fact that therapist A may mean a certain method X and therapist B, another method Y. These differences in group therapy methods occur within the same profession, according to differing theories or assumptions. Beyond this there is a difference in method related to the professional background of the group therapist. Ethics and professional discipline require of him that he stay within the framework of his own competence.

Increasingly, knowledge of individual dynamics and group process

10   See *Journal of Social Issues* mentioned above; see also Philip Zlatchin, Clara A. Kaiser, and Saul Scheidlinger, "The Group in Education, Group Work and Psychotherapy," Round Table, 1953, Harris B. Peck, Chairman; Edward D. Greenwood, Discussant; *American Journal of Orthopsychiatry*, Vol. XXIV, No. 1, Jan. 1954, pp. 128-152.

becomes common knowledge for several professions, yet in differing degrees and appropriate to their own tasks. The social worker, for example, learns them in the context of reality interactions, of cultural background and economic conditions; the psychiatrist learns about them in the context of medical knowledge and pathology. The twentieth century is caught in a dilemma: On the one hand, all sciences are becoming more and more aware of their interrelatedness, a trend requiring more people with broad, general knowledge. But on the other hand, since knowledge in each field of science has increased tremendously, more specialization and scientists with more specialized knowledge are required within each field. The only answer is close teamwork.

It is the purpose of team members to supplement one another and to constantly learn from each other. Each professional person is equally important if he uses his specific knowledge and skill and limits himself to the practice for which he has been trained, and when it is necessary to cross professional boundaries, uses consultation. Grace Coyle suggested that:

> the social group worker should refrain from interpretation of unconscious mechanisms to individuals in the group, although he may help group members to deal with conscious or preconscious material and to ease their fear or guilt through discussion or activity.[11]

Using interpretation of unconscious material for treatment is usually part of the practice of the analytically trained psychiatrist, rarely of the social worker. On the other hand, the understanding of environmental pressures and their meaning to individuals, the analytic knowledge of group process, and the skill in working with group process and interrelationships are within specialized province of the social group worker. This method requires a certain tolerance toward group behavior, whic his different from that encountered in individual-to-individual contacts. The analyst, Spotnitz, suggests that:

> a higher degree of emotional preparation is needed to conduct analytic psychotherapy comfortably in a group than in individual practice.[12]

---

11   Grace L. Coyle, "Social Group Work: An Aspect of Social Work Practice," *Journal of Social Issues*, Vol. VIII, No. 2, 1952, p. 29.
12   Hyman Spotnitz M. D., *The Couch and the Circle*, New York: Alfred A. Knopf, 1961, p. 227.

It is part of the preparation for social group work to gain, through supervised field work, this emotional preparation Spotnitz talks about.

Another aspect of the controversy between group work and group therapy should be discussed, namely the question of *status*. It seems unpardonable that in the field of human relations this problem of competition has added to the confusion and sometimes has prevented progress. For some reason—probably because of the high status of psychiatry on the North American continent—the term "therapy" seemed to indicate something more precious and more important than the term originally used by social work. This applies to both the individual and group approaches. Group work fought this prestige value from the beginning.[13] This was in accord with the value system of the social group worker who resisted any class system, even in the theoretical or interprofessional realm. To indicate that they were talking about the same method in the framework of their own social work profession and of equal importance and skill, regardless of whether it was practice with healthy or sick people in groups, most social group workers consciously avoided the term *group therapy* to describe their practice; instead, they called it *social group* work. The decision to do so has kept the unity of group work and has enhanced its general status. It has at times confused the public and, unfortunately, has led to confusing terminology in social work itself. Social workers trained in a period when group work was practiced predominantly in the field of recreation and who had not kept up with its changing focus frequently disregarded the specialization in group method developed within their own profession. They turned to other professions to learn group therapy or practiced it without help in handling a *group*. The confusion of terms grew. Such verbal monstrosities as "group case work" were added. Fortunately this period has practically passed. The social work profession sees social group work as one of its basic methods practiced in many different settings, directed at a variety of social-psychological problems. This writer will adhere to the term *social group work* to designate the identification with the profession of social work.

Summary

The function of social group work is seen as part of the function of social work and the agencies in which it is practiced.

[13]   See pp. 15, 16.

Social work's function at the present is not finalized. Its core tasks are (1) to assess, clarify and help individuals with the interaction of their inner motives and the demands of their social environment and (2) to help change social environment if it is detrimental to the social development of individuals. Functions of each particular agency in which social work is practiced are more limited and specific.

Social group work functions within the fields of health, welfare, education and recreation as a helping method used in groups with varied purposes and consisting of members on a wide scale from healthy to sick.

Functions of professions in a complex society overlap partially.

To clarify one of the major confusions in function and terminology, the relationship between group work and group therapy is discussed.

Definitions used in this text are:

> *Social Group Work* is a method of social work which helps individuals to enhance their social functioning through purposeful group experiences and to cope more effectively with their personal, group or community problems.
>
> *Group Therapy* is practice which is aimed at ameliorating suffering and improving the personal and social functioning of its members through specified and controlled group interaction enabled by a professional person.
>
> *Group Work* includes work with groups consisting of healthy as well as of sick individuals. When the group worker uses his particular professional training and skill to work with groups of individuals who have problems in personal and social functioning, he enters the practice of group therapy. He does it in his own way based on the extent of his particular professional qualifications.
>
> To avoid status conflicts and to clearly keep the identification with social work, this practice is called *social group work* (a parallel to social case work, another method of social work).

The summary would not be complete if the reader were not also reminded of the fact that there are numerous other terms for group work and group therapy, i.e., group counseling, group guidance. They are used interchangeably with the other two terms and, therefore, will not be discussed separately.

BIBLIOGRAPHY

American Association of Group Workers, "Definition of the Function of the Group Worker," *The Group*, Vol. XI, No. 3, May 1949, pp. 11-12.

Bruno, Frank J., *Trends in Social Work 1874-1956*, New York: Columbia University Press, 1957.

Corsini, Raymond J., *Methods of Group Psychotherapy*, New York: McGraw-Hill Book Co., Inc., 1957.

Coyle, Grace L., *Group Work with American Youth*, New York: Harper & Row, Publishers, 1948.

———, "Social Group Work: An Aspect of Social Work Practice," *Journal of Social Issues*, Vol. VIII, No. 2, 1952, pp. 23-34.

Festinger, Leon, "Current Developments in Group Dynamics," New York: *Amer. Assoc. of Group Workers*, mimeographed, undated.

Frank, Jerome D., "Group Methods in Psychotherapy," *Journal of Social Issues*, Vol. VIII, No. 2, 1952, pp. 35-44.

Konopka, Gisela, "Similarities and Differences between Group Work and Group Therapy," Report of the Group Therapy Committee, A.A.G.W., mimeographed ST-451-8, undated; also in *Selected Papers of the National Conference of Social Welfare*, 1951, pp. 51-60.

———, "Team Relationships and Operations in Social Group Work," Appendix C in Marjorie Murphy, *The Social Group Work Method in Social Work Education*, Vol. XI, *A Project Report of the Curriculum Study*, Werner W. Boehm, Director and Coordinator, New York: Council on Social Work Education, 1959, pp. 106-114.

———, *Therapeutic Group Work With Children*, Minneapolis: University of Minnesota Press, 1949.

Murphy, Marjorie, *The Social Group Work Method in Social Work Education*, Vol. XI, *A Project Report of the Curriculum Study*, Werner W. Boehm, Director and Coordinator, New York: Council on Social Work Education, 1959.

Spotnitz, Hyman, *The Couch and the Circle*, New York: Alfred A. Knopf, 1961.

Trecker, Harleigh B., Editor, *Group Work—Foundations and Frontiers*, New York: Whiteside, Inc. and William Morrow and Co., 1955.

———, *Group Work in Psychiatric Settings*, New York: Whiteside, Inc., 1956.

Wilson, Gertrude and Gladys Ryland, *Social Group Work Practice*, Boston: Houghton Mifflin Co., 1949.

Zlatchin, Philip, Clara A. Kaiser, and Saul Scheidlinger, "The Group in Education, Group Work and Psychotherapy," Round Table 1953, Harris B. Peck, Chairman; Edward D. Greenwood, Discussant; *American Journal of Orthopsychiatry*, Vol. XXIV, No. 1, Jan. 1954, pp. 128-152.

CHAPTER THREE

Theories of Man and His Life Cycle Underlying Social Group Work

"Every man is in certain respects
"a. like all other men,
"b. like some other men,
"c. like no other man."[1]

In this simple sentence, Kluckhohn and Murray have expressed their view of man as a being who has many characteristics in common with other men and yet who occurs in an infinite variety of patterns. The view of man underlying group work practice is derived from many theories of personality; it takes account of his human, natural and socio-economic environment, since it seems increasingly impossible to speak of the human being as an entity separated from all other influences. With the exception of the very unusual occasion of

---

[1] Clyde Kluckhohn and Henry A. Murray, "Personality Formation: The Determinants," *Personality in Nature, Society and Culture*, New York: Alfred A. Knopf, 1949, p. 35.

37

a hermitic existence, the human being must always interact with others, changing them and being changed by them. This concept of interaction in no way contradicts the concept of individuality and each person's essential difference.

The following is an attempt to present man's life cycle by integrating understanding of the individual with understanding of the natural group. Students of human behavior and dynamics are constantly trying to formulate a basic theory of this integration. Underlying this somewhat new and unorthodox view of developmental needs and tasks and the ways in which they are fulfilled are assumptions derived from a modified dynamic psychology, best expressed by Erik Erikson.[2]

The presentation omits a detailed discussion of assumptions underlying the understanding of the individual. This can be found in books presenting the dynamic psychology or psychiatry of Freud and writers who built on him. I will list here only a few of the most important concepts which help in understanding individual dynamics and which are used extensively in social work:

1. The importance of early childhood experiences in the development of personality.

2. The capacity of the human being to grow and change throughout his entire life (which refutes the idea that concept 1 is deterministic).

3. The acceptance of the existence of unconscious and preconscious motivation.

4. The capacity of the human being, despite concept 3, to act consciously and rationally. This capacity to act is a function of the ego, which may sometimes be weak or impaired, but which can usually be helped to act rationally.

5. The concept of ambivalence: the human being can experience two opposing emotions at the same time toward the same person or situation.

---

2   The reader is urged to read Erik H. Erikson, *Childhood and Society*, New York: W. W. Norton and Co., 1950, and social role theories, especially as presented by Richard A. Cloward and Lloyd E. Ohlin, *Delinquency and Opportunity*, Glencoe, Ill.: Free Press, 1960, and by Robert K. Merton, *Social Theory and Social Structure*, Glencoe, Ill.: Free Press, 1949. See also: Helen L. Witmer and Ruth Kotinsky, Editors, *New Perspectives for Research on Juvenile Delinquency*, Washington, D.C.: U.S. Dept. of Health, Education and Welfare, Social Security Administration, Children's Bureau, 1956.

6. The concepts of defense mechanism, projection, and sublimation —all of which are the ego's ways of dealing with inner drives and outer relationships.

Basic needs of human beings grow out of their physical, mental, emotional, and spiritual natures. They cannot be separated. The theory of the Greeks, which hypothesized a soul within but separate from the body, is no longer acceptable. Even the recent concepts of dynamic psychiatry, which rest on the assumption that the human being is a whole but separate entity, are no longer completely acceptable. Our present theory holds that the individual is *not a separate entity* but is a *whole individual interrelated with others.* Man's need for food and shelter, for love and tenderness, for accomplishment, and for fulfillment of his thirst for knowledge, are all dependent on the interaction of man with man. Next to the biological necessities, man's deepest longings are to be loved and to be important—important to someone; it is from these that all other needs spring. An inseparable connection exists between self-respect and a freely-given relationship with someone else. All his life, man struggles to gain or to retain this sense of self by reaching out to the *you*—to the one who gives importance and warmth and tenderness to his own self. When this bridge is built he can give love to others and can accomplish whatever he is capable of doing. At that point he can feel fulfillment and achieve sacrifice. But without the bridge between the *I* and the *you*, the human being crumbles. He may either destroy himself or others in subtle or glaring forms. It is the assumption of social group work that human beings have not only the basic need to be loved, but the capacity and strength to love in return. But this is not achieved without constant struggle to overcome other tendencies and to counteract environmental forces which may prevent, suppress, or diminish this capacity.

A second assumption made in social group work is that the individual achieves healthy development through a healthy and appropriate group life throughout his life cycle. It is important to clarify what is meant by a healthy group life. A healthy group life has the following ingredients:

1. Provision for the identification with equals.
2. Provision for the warmth of belonging to more than one per-

son. Fear of the threatened loss of the one and only beloved person is always present and becomes overwhelming if a wider relationship is not established in the course of life.

3. Freedom to be and to express one's self and to be different in the presence of others.

4. Freedom to choose the friends one prefers combined with a responsibility to accept others if they need to be accepted, even though no close friendly relationship has been established.

5. Opportunity to try out one's own individuality while at the same time permitting the enjoyment of the uniqueness of others.

6. Opportunity to exercise independence and to be allowed to be dependent when this is necessary and indicated, as in childhood or in distressing situations in adulthood.

It is only in very early infancy that the human being is not related to or has no need for such a group situation. In the first weeks of the human being's life he responds only to the warmth and protection of an individual stronger and more powerful than himself—the mother or the substitute mother, which includes any other member of a healthy family. The infant certainly has an impact on the family group situation, but he himself is involved only with one person. If the basic need for a one-to-one relationship is not fulfilled at this period, the child will be an exceedingly disturbed person in later life. It is then impossible to give help through the medium of the social group work method. The only help, as far as we know, can come from an intensive therapeutic one-to-one relationship. Fortunately, these situations are comparatively rare.

Very early in the life cycle individuals begin to interact with others, not just with single persons outside the mother, but in group situations as well. The characteristics of this interaction, though, show as much change as any other characteristics of the developing human being. In the healthy development of a child, the family provides this early satisfaction of group needs. The earliest group experience of interaction within the family circle gives the child a valuable mental and emotional learning experience which he begins to apply as he grows and begins to reach out beyond the intimate family group to peers. Comparatively recent psychological observation has shown that even at an early age a child needs to reach out to contemporaries, even though his predominant need at this stage is his need for adult protection and care. He is too young to tolerate a large group or to enter into a complicated group relationship, but even the two-year-old shows increased animation and delight when he discovers another "baby" and reaches out to him. This is the beginning of his need to relate to his contemporaries. His greatest need is still for adult protection. Yet, different from what was thought only a few years ago, the need to "participate" starts very early in life.

With increased awareness of the *I*, the child's need for interaction with persons outside the family group (i.e., with peers) increases and gradually becomes more complicated. At the same time, however, he must look to the adult, specifically to his parents, both mother and father, to provide a sense of security and protection for the whole period of childhood. The child's sense of importance, then, develops through the influence of these two sets of relationships: his relationships with family members and his relationships with contemporaries outside the family group. Two-year-olds frequently play "alone together," enjoying each other's presence, but rarely relating closely to each other. Three- and four-year-olds, however, interact with each other and try out their own personalities and a whole range of conflict-solving in group situations. The provision of a healthy group life both within and outside the family becomes essential to healthy development. Dynamic psychology has stressed for years the importance of family relationships and the working out of interpersonal conflicts and dependencies between parents and children. It has stressed the way these influence the child's identification with societal values and his development of trust and self-respect. The helping methods of psychiatry and social casework have been founded on an understanding of these relationships. Social group work also bases the theory of its understanding of the human being on the importance of the parent-child relationship, but it goes beyond this and recognizes that this relationship plays only one part in producing the healthy or unhealthy development of the individual, that group life outside the family also influences the development of the child.

Case histories of disturbed or delinquent children too frequently omit any reference to such group associations. It is the opinion of this author that only by taking them into consideration can additional light be shed on the understanding of such children or adults. For too long the family has been credited for all positive development or blamed for all shortcomings in the mental health of children. Without question the climate of the family group is a very important factor, but it is not the only one. A handicapped child, for instance, who is exposed to the torments of his little neighbors can be only partly protected by his family group—he may still suffer serious emotional disturbance as a result of his contacts outside the family. If the knowledge of these outside contacts is not available to those who want to help this child at a later stage, treatment may be based on the wrong factors and the experts will be puzzled because they cannot find the reasons for the disturbance in the close family environment.

Social group work is making a real contribution to the understanding of individual dynamics by insisting upon the importance of group life outside the family group. "I had my first seizure on the playground when I was nine years old," recalled an adult seizure patient; "I woke up and saw the kids staring at me and heard them shout, 'Ida had a fit! Ida had a fit!' Mother rushed out and held me in her arms, and she has supported me ever since, but I can only see the kids! I never felt I was worth anything." "Don't ever get a child that looks like me," said a pretty dark-skinned ten-year-old Negro child to her beloved Caucasian group worker. She had a loving family, but she had experienced the cruel selectivity of a society that discriminates against Negroes. Both these children had experienced not only hurt, but also a breakdown of their self-esteem. In each instance this had occurred through harmful group experience outside the family. Help with this could come only through *experience* with positive relationships in another kind of group situation.

"You know that I had a terribly weak mother, and a father who did not care one hoot about his family," said a young man who enjoyed at this time his own wonderful, warm and loving family and was carrying a responsible position. "But I will never forget what it meant to me to have friendships in my youth group, to have your understanding (this was directed to the group worker) and to be able to do things that made me not only forget my dismal home, but gave me the feeling that I was an important being, not just someone on this earth to be slapped around." Here the group life outside the family provided the necessary ingredients for a healthy development, in spite of family breakdown.

The importance of group experiences increases at the time the child enters school. It is not purely an accident that school life usually starts when the child no longer has an intense need for parental protection. In general, he can move into a wider circle of outside relationships, although the adult remains his most significant object of identification as well as his protector and stimulator. Emotional and intellectual growth occur in part through group interaction and in part through stimulation emanating from inanimate objects and play. Stimulation through things and activities occurs throughout the human life cycle, from early childhood to old age, but it is especially significant in the early school years. The concern with these objects is rarely expressed in solitary occupation; more often it is expressed in games with other children or in efforts directed toward other human beings, as in gift-giving or in demonstrations of accomplishment: "I made this; look at me!" The group worker's efforts in working with children in the latency period, whether they are healthy or sick, are based on this particular characteristic of that age. The group worker's efforts will include a great deal of use of materials and activities in the context of group relationships. In general, children of this age involve less verbal interaction than they do at a later age and less direct human interaction than in the preschool years.

The importance of group life is probably strongest in adolescence. This is closely related to the physical maturation process and the movement away from adult protection. To become an adult himself the adolescent must find his way toward independence from those who have sheltered, protected, and taught him. At this period of his life he cannot yet give these up completely. Family ties actually mean a great deal to the adolescent if he feels that they are not interfering with his attempts at independence. The insecurity at this age is almost pervasive. The biological change is dramatic and the youth must come to terms with the fact that biologically he is a full grown man or woman while emotionally and socially he is neither ready nor permitted to fulfill this function. This alone is an immense task fraught with conflict and anxiety. Doubts of one's identity increase with the awareness of adult responsibilities while one is still a child. Even the healthy, well-balanced adolescent goes through this period of fear of adulthood's demands while at the same time thrilling to the prospect of the privileges which come with emancipation. Mentally, insecurity and confusion are expressed in the re-evaluation of values which seemed absolute at an earlier age. While identification with parental values seemed achieved during the latency period, doubts about their validity arise in the adolescent period. Some adolescents express their doubts by completely rejecting parental values; others, by constantly questioning them.

This pervasive insecurity needs some balance, and it is found usually in identification with and relation to the contemporary group: other adolescents are not only "co-sufferers," they are also mirrors that help one to learn about one's own image. They are people with whom one can share everything, even feelings of degradation, guilt or shame, without losing one's self-respect because they, too, are living through these same emotions. They give support to one's own development of individuality despite the influence of the previous generation which by necessity wants and must try to mold the young in its image. They provide an outlet for the wide swings in mood so frequent in adolescence. They cry and laugh with one another when to do so would seem silly or exaggerated to anyone outside the in-group. Association with other adolescents also permits actual "trying out" of unexplored territory and fulfillment of the consuming thirst for adventure. Sometimes this appears in forms tolerable to society and sometimes, in forms dangerous to it. Yet, adolescents must be provided with this "trying-out period," which Erik Erikson calls the necessary "moratorium." The society which does not provide for it invites the development not only of a docile, unimaginative and conforming youth population but of a hostile, seriously delinquent one as well. Modern society, with its tight rules, is in danger of doing this. The rigid authoritarian system of Nazi Germany is a classic example of a society which made for conformity and hostility. With no room for the harmless trying out of adventure, with no toleration of mistakes, the feelings of young people brought up under this regime became hateful and anti-social. The diabolical psychological understanding of the Hitler regime understood this and nurtured it: German youth, impressed by the doctrines of racism, were sent into Jewish homes to destroy property and to torture and abuse the adults; they were provided outlets for promiscuous sex relations which were reserved for those selected by the state.

In recent years, the fear of "permissiveness" has created in the U.S.A. and in some other western countries an atmosphere of fear of youth and a tightening of rules related to adolescents that might easily lead to rebellious hate. In fact, some forms of delinquent behavior can be traced back directly to this disregard of the youthful need to experiment. Yet, untempered permissiveness itself is not the answer.

Youth looks to adults to set standards. It is important, however, that the standards be presented and enforced by the parents—who ordinarily protect the youngster—and not be too frequently made matters of "law" (e.g., curfew); that adults insist upon correct behavior and punish inappropriate behavior, but do so with the realization that some things can be learned only through the process of making mistakes. This again rules out the constant involvement of public authorities in each case of juvenile misbehavior; that adults themselves adhere to the same code of behavior expected of young people (as not cheating, being considerate of others, and so forth), and that a far more imaginative network of outlets for the youthful adventuresome spirit be created. There could be more opportunities for exploration, for travelling, for channelling the spirit of adventure into acceptable outlets. How many youngsters yearn for a trip to strange and unknown places! A walk around the corner no longer has much meaning. How different it would be to offer swimming youth hostels on the rivers of this large country or even a trip across the ocean. An enterprising group worker assigned to a settlement house in a deprived neighborhood capitalized on this spirit of adventure by arranging for her group to make an exchange visit with a group from a French Canadian neighborhood house. What an experience it was! The American group talked for a long time about the thrill of having crossed a border and of having heard a foreign language!

With adolescence, the child enters the arena of wider societal group relations. He begins to consciously experience group acceptance and/or group discrimination. He may experience discrimination by or exclusion from a group because of his belonging to a particular racial, religious, economic or social status group, and the experience may create deep scars and resentment. He may see his legitimate ambitions thwarted for the same reason. If acceptance cannot be found, rejected adolescents will band together not only to find some sense of security and worth, but also to openly defy or undermine the adult world which stands against them.

During adolescence, the need for intensive group life reaches its peak. Adulthood has not as strong an emotional drive for this since developmental tasks are not as much in the foreground then as they are during childhood. It is a mistake, though, to assume that developmental tasks are ever completely fulfilled.

By necessity, psychology in the twentieth century had to focus on the child; the adult was usually seen as a finished product with only remnants of unfinished childhood traits to be ironed out. At the present, psychological theory underlying social group work views adult life, including old age, as a continuous developmental process. The process is slower than in childhood and does not involve as much an active helping person. Yet, there always must be a growth-conducive climate in the community and outlets for the constant need to belong and to participate.

Most adults find partial fulfillment of these needs in the family; this time, however, they function in a role different from that of childhood. They are now in the responsible position of forming a healthy group life in their own families. Dependency needs, which never completely cease, are fulfilled by the marriage partner, a person chosen from outside the previous intimate circle of the first family constellation. The need to contribute can be fulfilled in responsible care of children and in participation in wider community groups.

In general, the healthy group life of the adult pivots around these two major group constellations. With the increase of the small family unit in our western society, limited to parents and children, adults increasingly long for an additional group constellation, the friendship group outside the family circle. The wider family in other cultures, and in some parts of our culture, provides for the continued need of friendship, of relating intimately to people of one's own sex and one's own age group. If relatives do not provide this, the adult needs such friendship groups outside of the family circle. Such relationship gives him an opportunity, when it is necessary, to move away from the demand for competency, for status, or for responsibility. This need to be a "child" at times or "to let down one's hair" is again fulfilled frequently by the marriage partner. But most adults need another second such outlet. This is especially important for those adults who are not married or who have lost their spouse. The need for adult friendship was too frequently overlooked in individual psychology. It is not a need for large or for high activity-centered groups. A businessman in a small community expressed it best by saying, "We feel so alone when we have only our family or acquaintances based on prestige and business association. What can we do? We run to psychiatrists because we can't have friends." Our culture at present offers comparatively good opportunities for outlets for the need to participate and to gain importance in adulthood, but it provides little fulfillment of the need to belong outside the narrow confines of the family. A solution certainly will not lie in the formation of "friendship clubs"; it will lie more in the direction of a *cultural acceptance of the friendship needs of adults, an emotional recognition of the right of adults to be "dependent" as well as independent,* and provision for opportunities to "belong."

The interdependence needs of the aged fall into the same range as those of the adult in general. There was a time when it was assumed that the aged wanted only to be dependent and this desire was accompanied by a withdrawal from others. It has become evident that these assumptions were false. At no time in his life cycle, with the exception of the very first weeks of infancy, does the human being want to be completely dependent. Dependency realistically may increase because of decreased physical or mental capacity, but it never again becomes emotionally satisfying in the normally developed adult. The aged continue to want to be active and to participate and "belong" to a community of people. If all his other faculties remain intact, an elderly person continues to be a developing, learning, and contributing member of the community. This is only impossible if the community climate does *not* allow for such continued creative effort. The aged whose faculties are not intact, either physically or mentally, has the same needs but they are tinged with deep anxiety and a feeling of frustration.

Group work services for the aged are shaped increasingly by this changed understanding of the aged.

Summary

Group Work Practice is based on a concept of man as a constantly developing human being in necessary and significant interaction with other men. He is shaped by others and is shaping others. He presents an inseparable unit of physical, mental and emotional forces, again in interaction with others.

Development does not cease with childhood but continues all through the life cycle. The basic needs beyond the biological ones are the needs to belong, to be an important individual and to participate.

In the life cycle these needs must be fulfilled in a variety of changing small group associations. These associations have specific characteristics in different age periods. At each stage of development individuals must find fulfillment through qualitative group associations or they will be damaged in one way or another.

No individual goes through the life cycle without some damage. Human beings have various capacities to deal with dissatisfactions and frustrations on their own. They need help at different stages of their development with their developmental task or with overcoming hurdles to them.

Group work practice is directed towards provision of such help and takes as its rationale the use of its method from this view.

Because of its strong emphasis on viewing the individual in interaction and therefore the importance of qualitative group life, its practice is also based on a thorough understanding of the dynamics of face-to-face groups. This will be presented in the next chapter.

BIBLIOGRAPHY

Erikson, Erik H., *Childhood and Society*, New York: W. W. Norton Co., 1950.

Kluckhohn, Clyde and Henry A. Murray, "Personality Formation: The Determinants," *Personality in Nature, Society and Culture*, New York: Alfred A. Knopf, 1949.

Konopka, Gisela, "A Healthy Group Life—Social Group Work's Contribution to Mental Health," *Mental Hygiene*, Vol. 45, No. 3, July 1961.

———, "Resistance and Hostility in Group Members," in Harleigh B. Trecker, Editor, *Group Work—Foundations and Frontiers*, New York: Whiteside, Inc., 1955.

Northen, Helen, "Interrelated Functions of the Social Group Worker," *Social Work*, Vol. 2, No. 2, Apr. 1957, pp. 63-69.

Wilson, Gertrude, "Human Needs Pertinent to Group Work Services," *Proceedings of the National Conference of Social Work*, 1942, New York: Columbia University Press, 1942, pp. 338-360.

CHAPTER FOUR

Theories of Group Process Underlying Social Group Work

Self-respect—the survival of the soul
Spranger.

In the helping process of group work the client is not only a client, but also a *group member*. This additional role changes the psychological climate fundamentally from the one in a one-to-one relationship. In the individual interview, the person who needs help is confronted by the "strong" and "capable" one, with a psychological "distance" between him and the helper. Helen Perlman wrote:

> Whatever the nature of the problem the person brings to the social agency, it is always accompanied, and often complicated, by the problem of being a client.[1]

A similar relationship exists between the individual group member and the group worker, but at the same time the client is surrounded by equals, by people "in the same boat." The relationships of the

[1]   Helen Harris Perlman, *op. cit.*, p. 37.

49

members to each other have much meaning. They are never static. They change in time, and in relation to specific situations, even if a helping person such as the group worker is not present. This changing movement is called the group process. Marjorie Murphy defined it as "the totality of the group's interactions, developments and changes which occur in the group's life."[2]

As in the preceding chapter, where an attempt was made to integrate understanding of individual dynamics with the changing group needs during the life cycle, this chapter will try to integrate our knowledge of group dynamics with an understanding of the individual. This will not and cannot be achieved perfectly, since such integration must come from the concerted effort of many disciplines. There is increasing drive in this direction, as symbolized in the rise of social psychology. Muzafer Sherif, one of the early investigators of social process, began to build such a bridge in his book *The Psychology of Social Norms*.[3] Erich Fromm's *Escape from Freedom*, was perhaps one of the deepest integrative efforts of combining psychoanalytic theory with an understanding of group relations and group needs.[4] The following presentation must be short—by necessity. It is based on concepts derived mainly from the older sociologists—Simmel, Eubank and Durkheim; on research done by Kurt Lewin and his followers, and on writings by representatives of group work as Coyle, Wilson, Trecker, Somers and Konopka (see bibliography at the end of this chapter). The theories and "key ideas" presented will always be placed within the context of the kind of groups the social group worker encounters.

Before we describe those concepts theoretically, let us see some short "snapshots" of the impact of group relations:

Example

Janie, an 11 year old girl had been referred to the group in a Child Guidance Clinic, because of her excessive silence, almost amounting to muteness. Individual interviews could not reach her. In the first meeting the girls were discussing why they had come to the clinic in an informal way, while they were doing

2   Marjorie Murphy, *op. cit.*, p. 32.
3   Muzafer Sherif, *The Psychology of Social Norms*, New York: Harper & Row, Publishers, 1936.
4   Erich Fromm, *Escape from Freedom*, New York: Holt, Rinehart & Winston, Inc., 1941.

some handicraft. When one of the girls told about her feelings of being odd, different, Janie burst out with a "You think you are crazy too?" She had seemed completely detached from the group until this moment.

Identification with another group member had freed Janie to speak up.

Example

"I can't go out. I have no skill," said an older man in a group of long hospitalized mental patients which had been formed to help them to move back into the community. Other group members protested, and pointed out his great skill in gardening. He still looked doubtful, but somewhat pleased. The discussion turned to others. Shortly before the end of the session he suddenly looked around and said slowly, "Did you guys really mean it, about my gardening?"

The group had given support and a beginning new self-concept.

Example

Johnny was only five years old. He was intellectually far above this age level and was treated like a 10-year-old by his family; in fact he was constantly pushed toward more achievement. He was hostile to other children, destroyed what they cherished and attacked them. His group associations, chosen by his parents, were always with older children. The group worker suggested a group of his age. He first wandered around, seemingly forlorn and incapable of relating to the active play of the four- and five-year-olds. No pressure was placed on him, either by the group worker or the other children. He idly joined two children exploring a plant. The sure, gentle hands of one of the children took the leaves apart without breaking them. "How do you do that?" came from Johnny. The two began to work on other plants. After awhile they started to race, to laugh. Johnny became a little boy among others, he relaxed.

The group had given back the opportunity to be a *child* in his natural social relations.

There could be many more such examples in which we can see and observe the strength of the group process. The dynamics in this process are the relationships of the members with one another, produced by the individuality of each member and changing him in the process while changing others too.

The groups with which the social group worker is concerned are *face-to-face groups which allow for individualization*. No specific size can be given, because the number of people who can make up such a group depend on the age of the members (younger children cannot relate to as many persons as adults), on the capacity for relationships among the members (emotionally deprived people can relate only to very few at a time), and on the content of the group meetings that might prove most significant to the members (intimate discussions will require fewer members than will active work on projects). We must distinguish a "group" from the concept of "mass," which implies parallel action, but not interaction among the members. It must also be distinguished from a loose, small or large assembly of people who happen to be in the same place. *Interaction* and some *feeling of common goal* or *concern* are attributes of a group. A simple collection of people can change into a group under certain circumstances.

Example

At the beginning of a flight in a commercial airplane, the passengers were isolated individuals, who only happened to be in the same plane. There was little or practically no communication. Then a propeller stopped and the plane had to make a forced landing. During the wait for another form of transportation, the unrelated passengers became a group. There was interchange of feelings—what they had thought when the pilot announced the necessity to land; interchange of concern for what meaning the delay had for each passenger. Strangers tried to find solutions for those who were seriously inconvenienced by the delay. There was a shared appreciation of the pilot's skill and a wish to express this. When he boarded the bus that was to take the passengers to another airport, all those aboard spontaneously cheered him.

A group had emerged under the pressure of a common strong experience.

The original *formation* of groups does influence group relationships and group behavior. Often group workers work with groups that existed before they met them. It is necessary to know each group's formation to be able to understand its present needs. Sociologists have distinguished between *natural* and *formed* groups. Natural groups are those formed by the members themselves; formed groups, those brought together by a person outside the group membership. The primary natural group is the family. Other examples of such groups are friendship groups, gangs, and professional groups. Formed groups are therapy groups or groups brought together for educational purposes, such as a school class. Inside such groups, natural sub-groups may emerge.

Most natural groups form around causes, traditions, or people. Yet the purpose for which such groups were originally formed may change in time. If a social group worker is called upon to help with an ongoing group, the knowledge of its original purpose may be an important clue to the group's present functioning:

Example

A group worker was asked to work with a neighborhood group of adults which met regularly once a week in a settlement house. It was a *social group* whose members constantly fought with each other and with everyone else in the house. Members of the group had a powerful influence in the neighborhood and succeeded in fanning hostilities. The behavior of this group was puzzling until the group worker learned that it was originally not a social group, not a friendship group, and that it had been formed around a *cause*—the improvement of the neighborhood—a number of years prior to its assignment to the group worker. Members had met with high hopes and enthusiasm, but they encountered many difficulties and received no help. Their frustration turned into resignation and, finally, they gave up the cause. Several strong members refused to disband the group and so it continued to meet without a specific goal and held together only by a diffused hostility.

Knowing this, helped the group worker to approach this group differently from the way he would have worked with it had it always been a friendship group.

In the context of social work or its host agencies, such as courts, hospitals, and clinics, groups are *formed* according to the helping purpose. There is a large variety of common denominators around which group formation has proved itself effective: groups may be built around specific symptoms (groups of eneuretic children), or certain behavior (groups of highly acting-out children or groups of withdrawn ones), or diagnosed illness (groups of diabetics or multiple sclerotics), or specific forms of treatment (patients who receive shock therapy). Groups may be formed around the common concern of people for others: parents seeking or needing help with problems of their children, relatives trying to understand their mentally sick spouses or parents, citizens working on specific community problems such as the need for housing, playgrounds, old age homes, better mental health facilities, and so forth.

Group constellation influences vitally group process and may mean the difference between a helpful, ineffective or harmful group.

The dynamics of the group process are determined by the *kind and quality* of the *interaction among members*. To understand this network of relationships—to be helpful to individuals in it—we must understand this constantly changing process. What we observe in a group is the basic and immense power human beings have over one another. It is the power of acceptance or rejection, of pulling a person into the circle of the group or leaving him at the rim or outside, of making him feel himself to be a valuable being or someone to be shunned, ignored or mishandled. By knowing the position of a person in the group or the role taken by him or assigned to him, we do not yet know the "why" of this position, but we do have a valuable observation which might lead us to the "why," and in this way determine the kind of help needed. Sometimes an understanding of the network of relationships in the group is sufficient to gain insight into a certain position of an individual and his actions—yet most of the time we must combine this knowledge with an understanding of him as an individual. The reverse is also true: it is impossible to understand the individual without knowing his position in groups that are significant to him (i.e., the family, the work group for an adult, the play group for a child).

Moreno developed a way of taking a "snapshot" of relationships in a group, of drawing the acceptance-rejection pattern; it is called the sociogram.[5] It is a graphic way of becoming more aware of the constellations in a group: the *subgroups*, the *leader*, the *isolate*. It must be understood that the sociogram gives only the picture of a given phase in the group process—only a moment in time. The picture is constantly changing. It cannot give the reasons for the observed phenomena. Action—helping intervention—cannot simply follow out of the observation. It is an instrument for observation; it is not intended for use in making decisions in regard to treatment.

Most groups show the phenomenon of *subgroups*. They are part of the natural workings of the group process. Rarely will we find a group where all members have exactly the same relationships, qualitatively and quantitatively, with all other members. This does not even exist in the primary group, the family. The parents form by nature a separate pair—a subgroup distinguished from the rest of the family. Beyond this, every family, even the happy and healthy one, will have some additional subgroup formation, changing in time. The Freudian concept of the Oedipal situation is an example of a changing subgroup in the family. Freud surmises that at a certain age a child strives to form a pair—a subgroup with the parent of the other sex—but that this changes when the child enters another stage, the one of identification with the parent of his own sex.

Subgroups may consist of two (pair or diad) or three (triad) or more members of the group. Aside from the diagnostic value their recognition has for the one who works with groups, the emotional acceptance of the inevitability and legitimacy of subgroups is a prerequisite for good and skillful group work. If this is not forthcoming, the group worker who works against the subgroups usually loses the whole group. People working with groups used to assume that a "good" group must do everything together and must show equally strong bond among all members. They—the group leaders—became tense when subgroups emerged. Teachers, for instance, began to relax in the school room and became more effective when they accepted and recognized the subgroups in their class rooms and began to work *with* them instead of *against* them. Subgroups may enhance the quality

5 See Jacob L. Moreno, *Who Shall Survive? Foundations of Sociometry, Group Psychotherapy and Sociodrama*, revised edition, Beacon, N.Y.: Beacon House, 1953. See also use of the sociogram in the context of working with delinquents in Gisela Konopka, *Therapeutic Group Work With Children*, Minneapolis: University of Minnesota Press, 1949, pp. 42-45.

of the total group when they feel part of the group and contribute to its strength and growth. Examples of this are the divisions in professional organizations or specializations in professional practice.

Subgroups may become dangerous to the group—and to their own members—when they begin to separate themselves out of the group. These are the subgroups with "walls," frequently called cliques. Work with such subgroups for the purpose of integration is difficult. Sensitivity to their beginning before they develop into full-blown entities is part of the preventive task of the group worker.[6]

Most members of a group belong to one or another subgroup. Yet there are two *group positions* or *roles* which need special attention: the position of the *isolate* and the *leader*. The isolate is a member either neglected or highly rejected by the group, yet present in it. The *neglected isolate* is in the most lonely situation. He is tolerated by the group, but he is surrounded by a glass wall. He may be seen, and he may see through it, but there is no communication, no bridge. We find such isolates frequently in groups that are formed by necessity, as living groups in institutions, school classes, work groups of adults in prisons. He is there, but not of his own volition. Yet we do find him also in voluntary groups where he could leave, but he stays and comes to each meeting. Why? The answer will be different in each case. It must be found in the individual *and* the group situation. Most isolates suffer desperately. They are frequently people who are most in need of group acceptance; they yearn for nearness to others. They have a low self-concept and they cannot reach out. They find tenuous satisfaction in just being tolerated by the group or in pretending to themselves that they are truly a part of the group.

Example

In a group discussion, Miss A. described how she had never felt comfortable in a group. She had always belonged to some —"I could not just be by myself all the time"—but she could not remember that she ever talked to anyone or that anyone talked to her. She had always pretended she was quite busy

---

6   Administration deals to a considerable degree with group behavior. It is not the task of this book to go into detail regarding this. It should be mentioned here, however, that this distinction between subgroup and clique often becomes vital in the administrative process.

when she was in those groups, she had helped in the kitchen at parties or had done just what the others did, but nobody seemed to see her and nobody ever met her outside the group. She always felt like crying. One of the members asked, "Why did you not start talking?" "I could not," said Miss A. "Why the heck did you come back?" "I was afraid to be alone, and, sometimes I thought I was just imagining all this, and everything really was all right. . . ."

Miss A's overwhelming need to be with others because she could not tolerate herself, made her choose to stay with the group even in the uncomfortable position of the isolate. This was less painful than being alone. And she had found an additional way out: to pretend everything was all right. And why was she in this isolate position? Group members expressed their disgust with her "footmat" quality. In this particular group the need of all members for attention was great, and their capacity to reach out spontaneously was limited until they began to talk over some of their problems. Similar dynamics may have been present in other groups Miss A. had joined. This is also an example of why conscious help with these relationships is so necessary.

The *rejected isolate* is more actively involved in the total group situation. He usually reaches out to other members of the group or to the group as a whole, but finds himself rebuffed. The reasons for this may be again inside the rejected individual, as for instance the boy who provokes others, who never wants to do what the others want to do, who starts fights, etc. It may also lie in the specific group constellation and the group "climate." A sensitive artistic boy may become the rejected isolate in a group of little "he" men. The person who violates the mores of his group, willingly or unwillingly, may find himself in this position. Examples of this are the eneuretic child who "smells," the camper who has head lice, the youngster who "tattled" on some planned illegal activity of the street corner gang, or an adult who stands for racial integration in a neighborhood group opposed to it. The rejected isolate sometimes becomes the *scapegoat* of the group. He is not rejected for something he is himself, but something the group projects on him—group projection frequently being as unconscious as individual projection.

Example

Carol was constantly attacked by her club, a group of 14 and 15 year old girls, because she was, according to them, "a bad girl," and "over-sexed." The girls were themselves very curious about sex. Unconsciously they envied Carol's mature figure.

The irrationality and usually unconscious motivation of "scapegoating" makes work with it especially difficult.

Leadership in a group is perceived differently today from the way it was perceived in the early days of social group work. Early textbooks characterized the leader as a person possessing a certain list of qualities which made him a leader in every group. Today, however, leadership is seen as being related to the purpose and the situation in the group. Leadership may change in the same group in the course of development of a group. Personalities who take on leadership roles in groups cover a wide range. The young man who fires the imagination of his community action group in the discussion of an effort to work in a high delinquency area and stimulates the carrying through of a plan is a different personality from the slow moving, hesitant, soft-spoken woman patient on the mental hospital ward who always succeeds in coaxing her copatients into some active involvement, thus keeping alive in them the spark of sanity. Both are leaders in their particular groups.

Helen Jennings, in her early investigation into leadership and isolation, described in her book of the same name[7] several personalities who showed completely different characteristics, yet who were clearly accepted as leaders in the institution for girls that she studied. They fulfilled different needs of the group. Jennings found only one quality they had in common: they were more interested in others than they were in themselves. Even this characteristic would not apply to all leaders in groups. We need only to think of the highly authoritarian gang leader, whose interest is frequently only in himself and who uses the group members as a tool for his own advantage.

The indigenous leader grows out of the group. He is accepted by group members as the leader because he fulfills the purpose of the

[7] Helen Hall Jennings, *Leadership and Isolation, A Study in Personality in Interpersonal Relations*, New York: Longmans, Green and Co., 1943.

group, because he can be helpful to them, or because he has usurped power and is ruling by fear. The social group worker is *not* considered and must not take the role of the leader in the modern concept of group work. He is an outsider who *helps* the group and each member, including the leader. At times he must help a group to become strong enough to withdraw from an authoritarian leader or to help him change into a different form of leadership.

Leader, isolate, member of a subgroup are all positions the individual takes in the group by virtue of his interaction with others. In recent years the concept of *role* has been added to the understanding of individual behavior. It indicates the *expected behavior of an individual in a group*, usually defined not by himself, but by the group and by the culture in which he grows up. Each human being is expected to perform many roles, often simultaneously. A young adult must be parent to his child and at the same time, child to his own parents, two highly diverse roles, difficult to hold at the same time, and frequently a cause for conflict. Yet to become what is expected of him, he must be able to learn to combine those roles, and many additional ones. He may have to be learner in one group context—an evening class, for instance—and a teacher, either to his own children or as a professional, in another. The capacity to carry roles of often very different nature competently and without great inner conflict is part of a healthy personality. One of the attributes of a healthy society is to make demands on its members that are not too contradictory. Yet, few do this. The present culture of the U.S.A., for example, asks for highly divergent role behavior among women, ranging from the role of wife and mother, with focus on the home, to the one of breadwinner and citizen, with active participation in the affairs of the country. Where these expectations are not regarded as mutually exclusive and where the women can accept the role appropriate to her own specific situation, no breakdown occurs. Some women can combine all these roles successfully. When the role expectation is such that it allows no flexibility and where a particular subgroup (i.e., the family, the profession, or the neighborhood) insists upon the exclusive value of one or the other role, the girl or woman may then develop feelings of guilt or conflict.

Role conflict may also be produced by an individual's faulty perception of what is expected of him.

Example

In a group of parents discussing mental health needs in the family, Mr. D. constantly injected complicated terms and their definitions. The group became increasingly impatient with him, and finally "told him off." Mr. D. was bewildered. "I thought it was expected of me to bring in my knowledge," he said. (He had worked in a mental hygiene clinic.)

Mr. D. had not realized that, by joining the group of parents, the others expected him to participate as the father of his children, not as a teacher.

Helen Padula described dramatically how role expectation can influence behavior so strongly that it prevents recovery:

> Patients may reflect the expectation that they are sick as long as they are in a mental hospital. Throughout many years of hospitalization, a young man in a V.A. hospital was never known to walk forward; he always navigated backward. A nurse ran into him on the street, on his first trial visit. He was walking forward, quite normally. Amazed, she asked him, "How come?" "Oh," said he, "outside you are not allowed to walk backward."[8]

The concept of role is a valuable one in adding to the understanding of the individual as well as of group mores. It must never be used rigidly, though, and it must always be used with the full knowledge of the great variety of roles an individual can and must play, as well as the many cultural differences expressed through role behavior. Much harm has been done by stereotyped assumptions of roles based on preconceived value systems or limited understanding and experience with the richness and variety of many roles human beings can take.

A group becomes a group—more than the sum of its individuals—when it develops a certain relationship, a tie, a force that gives the

---

[8]   Helen Padula, "Releasing the Human Potential in Chronic Mental Patients through Social Work Services," paper presented at Workshop conducted by Ontario Department of Health, May 25-26, 1961, mimeographed; subsequently published in *The Social Worker*, Vol. 29, No. 4, Canadian Assn. of Social Workers, October, 1961, pp. 13-25.

individual a feeling of belonging. This feeling of belonging is called the group *bond*. Bond may change in time; it may become stronger or weaker. Natural groups usually start with some bond; formed groups frequently have no feeling of bond in the beginning, but develop it in the course of treatment or work together. A group cannot exist for long without bond. This does mean, however, that a strong bond is always beneficial to group members or that a weak one always indicates a poor group experience.

In post-World War II Germany, a young American tried to discuss with a group the great importance of *Gemeinschaft*, group with a bond; he extolled its virtues. He could not understand why his audience froze. He learned later that this had been one of the major propaganda slogans of Nazi Germany: the Nazis had fostered a strong bond among Germans to enhance the exclusiveness of the German "Aryan" and to bind them closely to one another. Bond in itself does not present a value. It can serve constructive or destructive purposes. A delinquent gang may have a strong group bond. The purpose of the group—stealing—is well served by this. Group work with the gang may mean help with a change of its purpose while keeping the bond strong; yet it may also lie in helping to dissolve the bond, depending on the dynamics of a particular gang. In a therapy group, the worker usually will help the group to develop some bond, otherwise the individual shells cannot be broken. Yet he will be wary lest the bond become too strong and the group not allow its members to join other healthy community groups even if they are capable of this. He will have to use his skill to help diminish bond when the group has served its limited purpose. He must be aware of the great emotional significance of bond among members and not force them to give it up abruptly: this has been done too frequently when group dynamics were overlooked in the treatment and the group was regarded as a collection of individuals. He will have to help the group members to be "weaned" from the bond among themselves, just as the baby is weaned, by allowing for some pleasure and substitution in the process. This may mean referral to new satisfying groups or a conscious return to groups that had meaning to the patient prior to his sickness.

Bond can also become damaging when its strength prevents members from seeking any associations outside the group.

Example

In one of the Y's, the group worker encountered a group of middle-aged women who had met since they were teenagers. They enjoyed their meetings. They guarded their relationship so strongly that any member who had tried to break away was considered a "traitor." The women had stayed unmarried and had made no friendships outside this club.

One may argue that these women apparently were enjoying the life they wanted—which may be true. It was apparent, though, that the strong bond had severely limited their horizon. A similar dynamic can sometimes be observed in professional groups or in agency staffs which are proud of their strong sense of unity, but it severely limits members to their own particular group. The members interpret a movement away from the group—a change of profession or agency affiliation, for example—as a rejection of the total group; they react toward anyone's leaving with hostility and a complete severance of relationships.

The group worker's aim is toward a bond that gives warmth and security to its members and which allows them to move with relative freedom to or away from the group. The degree of strength of the bond must vary according to each individual group's constellation and purposes.

The move into a group which has developed a bond is not easy. The position of the *newcomer*, the one who enters an already formed group, needs special attention. It is a basic law of groups that the total "Gestalt" of the group changes when a new person enters. This applies also to the family, the primary group. Any additional child changes the total family situation. The smaller the family the more intense is this change. Groups react to the newcomer in a way different from the way they react to any other member. At entrance into the group the newcomer becomes the receiver of the group's hopes or its anxieties or hostilities. The exaggerated acceptance which an "expert from far away" (for instance, the American consultant in a foreign country) usually experiences is produced largely by his being "the stranger in the group." If he has high status all expectations and hopes are thrown upon him. He does not enter the daily concerns of the group—their more intimate relationships—and therefore he is exempt from certain strains and stresses among the members. He enjoys a "moratorium" in group relationships, thus making him very effective for a limited time, but excluding him from real acceptance. Only when his "feet of clay" are allowed to show, does he become a member of the group. If a consultant or expert is not aware of this, he may have the wrong idea of his true capacities and get a rude awakening.

The anxiety and hostility are usually encountered by the newcomer who has no high status introduction. This occurs often in children's groups—especially in institutions where group composition changes frequently—if no special help is given to change this damaging aspect of the group process. Since the newcomer, whether adult or child, is usually insecure and afraid when he must enter an already formed group, such help is a necessary function of group work. The newcomer is not only afraid of the others he will meet—he is afraid of himself and whether he will measure up to his expectations of himself.

Example

John had been on a trial visit to the treatment center and had met the other children. That day he had moved in "easily," almost with bravado. At noon he arrived to stay. He ate little. The other children—very occupied with themselves—either ignored him or showed a certain coldness. In the rest period after lunch I found John lying on the floor of his room with his head sticking out into the corridor—he was obviously trying to hear what others were saying and yet did not dare to join them.

Each individual in the group changes constantly through his interaction with others. Most people feel a healthy ambivalence in regard to this. They wish to be involved, but at the same time they resist change and desire to keep their identity as it is. This struggle in the individual between status quo and change has its parallel in the processes *of conflict and solution* in the group. A group that shows no conflict (this includes again the family) is a dead one, indicating either an extinction of its member's individuality or a pretense at it—with underlying deep cleavages. A group that is in constant conflict with no way of solving it is a sick one, giving no satisfaction to its members and keeping them in a state of insecurity and hostility. Conflict solving is a major task of groups, whether it concerns the sharp clash between inmates in a penitentiary, the hurting differences in a family, the gang fights of teenagers, the racial conflicts in a neighborhood, the nagging accusations in a secluded group of institutionalized people, or the differences of opinions in a community leadership group. The various types of conflict solving can be classified as follows:

1. *Withdrawal* of one part of the group. Examples of this are the "We don't play with you any more" in a children's group or desertion in a family.

2. *Subjugation*, a willful silencing of one part of the group either by the leader of the opposition or by a subgroup. This can be accomplished through violence, including death, or through threat, ridicule, or any display of superior power on the part of a particular subgroup within the total group.

3. *Majority rule*. This is also a form of subjugating the minority, although it is not quite as arbitrary as other forms of subjugation.

4. *Minority consent to majority rule*. Here the factor of "subjugation" is ruled out since deliberations must have preceded the final solution and the minority has agreed to abide by the majority decision.

5. *Compromise*, neither side gets full satisfaction, but each agrees to the limits to be set on its own suggestions.

6. *Integration*, a rare and highly complicated form of conflict solving which presupposes thoughtful deliberations with a desire on both sides to arrive at a common decision, even though the final decision may be quite different from that originally proposed. Integration occurs, for example, in Quaker meetings where the required period of silence is a recognition that each side must somehow work through its own desire to be "victor." (Being human, they do not always succeed).

These solutions lie on an ascending scale of capacity in conflict solving. Group maturity can be measured partially in the way a group solves its conflicts and arrives at decisions; conflict solving and decision-making are similar processes since both involve a choice between alternatives.

The group worker in his helping role must use this knowledge to give to the individuals in the groups he works with an opportunity for conflict solving and decision-making. He must recognize that deprivation of this opportunity can bring about or increase pathology within any group. This is evident in hospitalized mental patients, particularly those in the less progressive institutions.

Example

In adapting to the insular mores of the mental hospital the patient loses his capacity to deal with the world outside. Already afflicted by dissociative and depersonalizing influences inside himself, he is exposed to a culture in which these very symptoms are powerfully reinforced. Conditioned by a sick, empty and routinized world; *deprived of any necessity or right to make decisions* [italics by author]; enervated by monotony; separated from family, friends, and normal associations, the patient is gradually shorn of whatever courage, capacity, and resources he ever had. He becomes socially crippled in addition to, or in place of, his illness.[9]

The problem of deprivation also exists in prisons, which rarely give an opportunity for decision-making in a group. (And this in a population that particularly needs learning in this area!)

When a group moves away from irrational behavior in the way it makes decisions and learns a new—and more rational—way of solving conflicts, the individual in the group begins to feel an inner strength and a pride in himself as well as in his group. "Self-discipline" does not grow out of the effort an individual makes alone; it is helped through group interaction. Thus discipline is no longer felt by the individual as rigid confinement, but rather as a breath of freedom from overwhelming forces.

Summary

The *dynamics of the group* are deeply intertwined with the dynamics of each individual in it. The movement of the group—the group process—is seen in the relationships between its members. It changes in time; its quality depends on the degree of health and the maturity of its members and on the purpose of the group. The group worker must understand group formation. He must understand the necessity for subgroups and assess their place in the total group. He must know about the positions of members as *isolates, leaders* or *members of subgroups*, for the role of each member is related to the expectations of the group and to its values and mores. He must rec-

9   *Ibid.*, p. 1.

ognize *bond* as a vital part of every group and realize that its degree is intrinsically related to *group formation* and *goal*. Finally, he must recognize *conflict-solving* and *decision-making* as specific functions of groups, with a strong impact, in turn, on individual development.

BIBLIOGRAPHY

Adler, Dan L., Ronald Lippitt, and Ralph K. White, "An Experiment with Young People Under Democratic, Autocratic and Laissez-faire Atmospheres," *Proceedings of the National Conference of Social Work*, 1939, New York: Columbia University Press, 1939, pp. 152-158.

Baxter, Bernice and Rosalind Cassidy, *Group Experience: The Democratic Way*, New York: Harper & Row, Publishers, 1943.

Borgatta, Edgar F., "What Social Science Says About Groups," *Social Welfare Forum*, 1957, New York: Columbia University Press, 1957, pp. 212-235.

Bernstein, Saul, "There are Groups and Groups," *The Group*, Vol. XIII, No. 1, 1951.

Bradford, Leland P. and Ronald Lippitt, "Building a Democratic Work Group," *Personnel*, Vol. 22, No. 3, 1945.

Cartwright, Dorwin and Alvin Zander, Editors, *Group Dynamics—Research and Theory*, Evanston, Ill.: Row, Peterson and Co., 1953.

Cooley, Charles H., "Primary Groups," in A. Paul Hare, Edgar F. Borgatta, and Robert F. Bales, Editors, *Small Groups—Studies in Social Interaction*, New York: Alfred A. Knopf, 1955, pp. 15-20.

Coyle, Grace L., "New Insights Available to the Social Worker from the Social Sciences," *Social Service Review*, Vol. XXVI, No. 3, Sept. 1952, pp. 289-304.

————, *Social Process in Organized Groups*, New York: Richard R. Smith and Co., 1930.

————, *Studies in Group Behavior*, New York: Harper & Row, Publishers, 1937.

Durkheim, Emile, "Division of Labor," in Hare *et al.*, editors, *op. cit.*, pp. 5-9.

Festinger, Leon, "A Theory of Social Comparison Processes," in Hare *et al.*, editors, *op. cit.*, pp. 163-187.

Fromm, Erich, *Escape From Freedom*, New York: Holt, Rinehart & Winston, 1941.

Haiman, Franklyn S., *Group Leadership and Democratic Action*, Boston: Houghton Mifflin Co., 1950.

Hendry, Charles E., Editor, *Decade of Group Work*, New York: Association Press, 1948.

Inkeles, Alex, "Personality and Social Structure," in Robert K. Merton, Leonard Broom, and Leonard S. Cottrell, Jr., Editors, *Sociology Today*, New York: Basic Books, Inc., 1959, pp. 249-276.

Jennings, Helen Hull, *Leadership and Isolation, A Study in Personality in Interpersonal Relations*, New York: Longmans, Green and Co., 1943.

———, *Sociometry of Leadership*, Sociometry Monographs No. 14, 1947.

Kendall, Katherine A., "New Dimensions in Casework and Group Work Practice: Implications for Professional Education," *Social Work*, Vol. 4, No. 4, Oct. 1959, pp. 49-56.

Konopka, Gisela, "Social Group Work: A Social Work Method," *Social Work*, Vol. 5, No. 4, Oct. 1960, pp. 53-61.

———, *Therapeutic Group Work with Children*, Minneapolis: University of Minnesota Press, 1949.

Lewin, Kurt, *Resolving Social Conflicts*, New York: Harper & Row, Publishers, 1948.

———, " 'Subjective' and 'Objective' Elements in the Social Field: The Three-Step Procedures," in Hare *et al.*, Editors, *op. cit.*, pp. 95-98.

Lippitt, Ronald, "Applying New Knowledge about Group Behavior," *Selected Papers in Group Work and Community Organization*, Raleigh, N.C.: Health Publications Institute, 1951, pp. 7-17.

Merton, Robert K., *Social Theory and Social Structure*, Glencoe, Ill.: The Free Press, 1949.

Newstetter, Wilber I., "What is Social Group Work?" *Proceedings of the National Conference of Social Work*, 1935, New York: Columbia University Press, 1935, pp. 291-299.

Sherif, Muzafer, *The Psychology of Social Norms*, New York: Harper & Row, Publishers, 1936.

Simmel, Georg, "The Significance of Numbers for Social Life," in Hare *et al.*, Editors, *op. cit.*, pp. 9-15.

Somers, Mary Louise, "Four Small Group Theories: An Analysis and Frame of Reference for Use as Teaching Content in Social Group Work," D.S.W. Thesis, Western Reserve University, June 1957.

Tyler, Ralph W., "Implications of Research in the Behavioral Sciences for Group Life and Group Services," *Social Welfare Forum*, 1960, New York: Columbia University Press, 1960, pp. 113-126.

CHAPTER FIVE

The Value Base
of Social Group Work

What can I know?
What ought I to do?
What may I hope?[1]
I call the World a moral World in so far as
it may be in accordance with all the ethical
laws—which, by virtue of the freedom of
reasonable beings, it can be, and according
to the necessary laws of morality it ought
to be.[2]

All intervention of a professional nature is goal-directed, regardless of whether it is dealing with inanimate objects or with human beings. An intervention which is called upon to deal with human relationships must consider ethical values in determining its purpose. The helping process of social work is strongly influenced by the profession's values and its view of the people with whom it is concerned. Social work has struggled through its history with its goal direction. It has gone through a period, which is not yet completely over, where it tried to take over the goal orientation of medicine, whose key con-

---

[1] Immanuel Kant, *Critique of Pure Reason*, translated by J. M. D. Meiklejohn, New York: John Wiley Book Co., 1943, p. 451.
[2] *Ibid.*, p. 453.

cept is "health," and which, when related to physical medicine, has a certain objectivity or tangibility. Yet the moment any profession is concerned with aspects other than the purely physical ones, the concept of "health" becomes more complicated and begins to include culturally determined ethical values. This value system—the "philosophy" of social work, as it is frequently designated—is the same for the whole profession:

> That philosophy . . . is not different when the activity happens to be skillful leadership of groups, the casework method of helping troubled people, or a project in community organization. Indeed, the philosophy of social work cannot be separated from the prevailing philosophy of a nation as to how it values people, and what importance it sets upon their welfare.[3]

The key values of social work are ethical ones, since they concern themselves with interpersonal relations. They are "justice" and "responsibility" combined with a less defined, but somewhat different, value of "mental health." "Justice" means the basic acceptance of the dignity of each human being regardless of any specific attribute, such as race, sex, economic status, intellectual endowment, physical prowess, and so forth, that might differentiate him from others. Justice does not imply that all people are the same or require that all be treated the same; it implies only that all be accorded the same consideration, the same acceptance, the same love, and the same opportunity.

"Responsibility" includes the awareness of the interdependence of human beings, of the acceptance of the rights of others as well as of one's own, and of the concept of the brotherhood of all people—the concept that each is his "brother's keeper."

"Mental health" signifies the understanding that the human being must have a sense of inner satisfaction and inner strength to be able to give to others.

These values are *a priori*; they are the axioms of professional practice. They are imbedded in the value systems of a large number of human cultures. Great religions, occidental and oriental, have incorporated them, and humanists have accepted them. They do not

---

[3]   Bertha C. Reynolds, *Social Work and Social Living*, New York: Citadel Press, 1951.

belong to one profession or to one discipline alone. They belong to all citizens in all human societies. The professions that work with individuals and their relations to each other must at every moment in practice come to terms with these questions of values, for they constantly deal, as Eduard C. Lindeman once said, with "facts infused with values." Social workers have hesitated at times to use such terms as "right" and "wrong" or "good" and "bad" when it comes to human behavior; they have wanted to avoid becoming "too judgmental." Yet we must face the fact that we actually use these judgments in every aspect of our work with individual clients and groups.

Why should we help a youngster to learn not to steal cars? Only because we want to avoid his being caught? In that case perhaps someone can teach him to steal cars better. Why do we ask for humane treatment of patients in mental hospitals? So many are not yet curable, and the cheapest way to take care of them is to herd them into some large congregate institution and forget about them. The *dignity of each individual* as a value is the only answer to this. The idea of a "valueless" practice of social work hardly ever existed. When it was advocated it was more an attempt made to ward off *arbitrary imposition* of values. This idea had haunted social work practice from the beginning, especially in the field of public relief when people from comfortable middle-class backgrounds tried to impose their kind of living on others tortured by poverty and a life that could not conform to the totality of middle-class values.[4] The social worker had much to learn about understanding people and appreciating the cultural differences between them while at the same time, maintaining clarity about ethical values. Eduard C. Lindeman, one of the few philosophers in social work, helped by his distinction between *primary* and *secondary* values, the first ones representing basic ethical demands, and the latter ones growing out of cultural mores which change in time and place. They are not easily separated or recognized in practice.[5]

Among social workers there is no common agreement as to the origin of the two primary values—the dignity of each individual human being and the responsibility of human beings for each other.

---

4 An illustration of this is a bitter book, *Lilly Crackell,* by Caroline Slade, Cleveland and New York: The World Publishing Co., 1943.

5 For a more intensive discussion of the philosophy of social work see Gisela Konopka, *Eduard C. Lindeman and Social Work Philosophy,* Minneapolis: University of Minnesota Press, 1958, especially Chapter V.

Those social workers who come into the profession with strong religious backgrounds see them as values derived from a spiritual being, God; those who represent a more secular background see them as derived from ethical law. In spite of the difference of opinion in regard to their origin, the acceptance of these values as the basis of the profession is general. They are recognized as absolute values by the profession and axiomatic to its practice. Certain translations of these values into practice are commonly agreed to by practitioners, regardless of the method they use.

1. All social group workers agree on the importance of *positive relations between people of different color, creed, national origin and social class*. This is an important goal in group work practice even where it is under sectarian auspices. A social work practitioner using the group work method in a Catholic, Protestant or Jewish agency will always make an effort to help members to learn to appreciate and live with those of other religions. It is one of the basic tasks of the use of the social group work method to help change the culture of racial discrimination through a learning of inner acceptance of people of different backgrounds. (Application of the value of "dignity of each individual".)

2. All social group workers agree on the *value of cooperation*. In the framework of a highly competitive society the social group work method consciously includes provision for positive experience in cooperating with each other. (Man's healthy striving for individual recognition may destroy the value of "responsibility for others.")

3. The value system of the social group worker includes the importance of *individual initiative*. Social group work practice must enhance individual initiative in the framework of creative cooperation. (Application of both primary values.)

4. Another accepted value derived from the basic ones is *freedom of participation*. The dignity of the individual must be expressed through his freedom to express his thoughts and ideas and his right to participate in matters concerning himself and his community. This concept is so basic to the group work method that it distinguishes its practitioner from the entertainer or authoritarian leader. Those roles are legitimate ones in other human endeavors, but they must be avoided in the helping process of social group work. This value also raises the demand for one of the most difficult processes of social group work, namely the encouragement of participation of each individual

in *decision-making*. One of the greatest skills of the social group worker is to help individuals in different stages of development and with different capacities to participate in a given group situation. It is also one of the most gratifying accomplishments of the use of this method.

5. Agreement also lies in the value placed on high *individualization in the group*. One of the basic characteristics of the social group work method is individualization in the group. Although some activities can be conducted without it, they do not belong in the practice of social group work. The emotional satisfaction felt by people through mass events may have an important place in human society. However, such events do not use the social group work method, for the social group work method always includes individualization.

There is certainly far less agreement in the area of *secondary values*. If they are values relating to cultural mores without major ethical implications, as questions of taste and aesthetics, they usually do not present serious problems to the practitioner. If the group worker has enough insight into his own personality, he recognizes quickly his own bias and is capable of either letting members decide differently from his own taste or of honestly presenting to them the reasons for his preferences. More difficult to handle are the secondary values which do include ethical considerations, for they are not as clearly outlined and not as commonly agreed upon as the previously named five primary values.

For instance: Should a delinquency institution be co-educational? Must every mother stay at home and not accept gainful employment? How compatible with good practice is the use of rewards? These questions are answered differently because of four factors influencing the practitioner: his own cultural and family background; the precepts and demands of given groups to which he belongs—his church, his professional or social groups, demands which sometimes create conflicts within the individual; personal experiences such as illness, experiences in groups at earlier times in life, and so forth, and differing theories regarding human behavior.

A first step toward not arbitrarily using one's own values lies in the willingness to examine honestly and conscientiously the base of one's own values.

The profession of social work places upon the practitioner the stern demand to investigate constantly the source of his secondary values. It does not mean that he has to reject them—on the contrary, he will be an effective human being only if he maintains standards. But he must be willing to reject them if they are not compatible with the demands of his profession or be able to understand his group members if their values are different from his own.

To understand his own cultural and family backgrounds and to realize the way they influence his values, the social worker should gain some knowledge of differing cultures. An anthropologist once remarked that people react to their own culture in the same way they react to their own drinking water. While their own has no flavor, they readily discern a peculiar taste in water from other regions. It is impossible for a person to understand and look objectively at his own cultural background if he has no exposure to others. This exposure must include a real *experiencing* of the other culture, not just a cold observation. It must become evident to the social group worker that others consider their particular values just as desirable as the group worker considers his own. This cannot easily be learned in the actual group work situation because of the helping role of the group worker. In this role he cannot "experience" the other culture in the genuine way one can only truly experience it: by being an equal and a friend. The demand therefore for insight into another culture is not an easy one to fulfill. It may be achieved before the start of professional education, either by belonging to organizations which offer an experience with a wide variety of people of different cultural and social backgrounds, or by conscious effort in liberal education to let the student vicariously experience this through literature, theater, and the arts. It may be done in professional education by giving students opportunities to meet other students and to discuss openly and freely their differing values. Because of the importance of the value component in group interaction, social group work education places great emphasis on this. This will have to be done more than ever because of increasing stratification in present society.

Yet exposure to other groups alone does not lead to critical evaluation of one's own value system. It only provides the necessary prerequisite to do so. The social group worker must realize that he cannot be a responsible practitioner without involving himself in such self-evaluation. He can only fulfill his helping role if he, for example, understands that swearing does not have the same meaning to children from a certain neighborhood that it may have to him if he comes from a different background. He need not accept swearing in every case as "right," but he must learn to understand its meaning and not see it only as a moral issue.

The same investigation must apply to values which are derived from the precepts of significant groups or personal experiences. Group demands can be very stringent, but the group worker must distinguish whether they are demands related to the basic ethical values of his profession or to a segment of the society in which he lives. To illustrate this: a professional group worker who belonged to a religious order accepted clearly the precepts of her religion which demanded daily church attendance. Yet in no way did she consider it right to make this same demand on the members of the groups in her charge. She had learned to distinguish between the demands and precepts of her group which were binding on her, but which were not necessarily so for those with whom she worked—even if she considered them desirable. Only if values are clearly understood can the worker distinguish between those which are indispensible to social work practice and those which may be desirable but must not be imposed.

The values growing out of specific personal experiences are often as deeply ingrained in a person as those originating in parental attitudes. A group worker argued vehemently with every reasoning available against a camping season of longer duration than two weeks. When she became aware of the rigidity of her rejection of longer camping periods she began to realize that it related to her own painful experience of a long separation from her parents. Only then did she understand that it might have a different meaning to others.

All forms of social interaction in a given culture are expressions of certain values. Some of these violate basic ethical demands, as previously discussed; among them are: discrimination or enforced segregation or the withholding of opportunities from individuals because of their race, color, creed, nationality, or social class. The social worker is obliged to work toward change in individuals as well as in the environment. There are other forms of social interaction which also require active change, although they do not violate ethical values; rather they are harmful to the emotional or mental health of individuals. One example of this is presented here because the social group worker is especially concerned with it:[6] the threatening disappearance of friendship in our present culture.

In the post World War II years, the United States has experienced

6   See also p. 47.

an increased growth of urban living combined with a general rise in the standard of living and an almost pervasive middle class. These changes have been accompanied by a loss of intimacy among people. Friendship in the sense of warm, giving relationships outside the family circle has become rare. There are numerous group associations, but usually they are on a rather superficial emotional basis. Many suffer from the fact that they have no friends with whom they can openly discuss personal problems.

The fear of losing "status" prevents many from sharing their feelings of joy, anger, or distress with others. Association with others may serve professional or vocational purposes ("business contacts") or purely recreational or intellectual ones. A happy "front" is required which prohibits discussion of any personal problem. The relationships among people are usually friendly but casual. In case of a major catastrophe, which is socially acceptable (i.e., a natural death of a family member or physical illness), colleagues or neighbors rally and help. But problems which involve feelings of unhappiness or inadequacy usually are avoided. The same applies to the genuine sharing of deep satisfactions—success may arouse envy. Thus the human being is deprived of the vital contribution friendship makes to life. Yet he cannot live without this support.

The loss of intimacy among adults outside the family circle has serious effects on young people. Some withdraw into serious emotional isolation; others develop only shallow relationships with people. Many of them can conceive of a comfortable and giving relationship only in marriage, hence they rush into marriage without ever having experienced a close and secure friendship with contemporaries previous to it.

Professional services, whether given individually or in groups, are only poor substitutes for real friendship. The social group worker may encourage friendship between group members and create an atmosphere of trust in the group with which he works. He also works consciously on cultural change by drawing attention to the loss of a most valuable form of human relations.

Summary

The line between justified use of values in social work practice and of arbitrary imposition on others is fine. As usual, when human beings are confronted with such a dilemma they may fall into one extreme or the other. The fear of imposing one's own values has led at times to an unprincipled laissez-faire attitude in practice. On the other hand, the fear of becoming too permissive has led to an imposition of values and the creation of a dogmatic group climate. The clear acceptance of primary values and of the demand of honest investigation into the social worker's own value system are basic to social group work practice.

BIBLIOGRAPHY

Addams, Jane, *Democracy and Social Ethics*, New York: Macmillan Co., 1902.

Cooke, The Reverend Terence J., *Thomistic Philosophy in the Principles of Social Group Work*, Washington D.C.: The Catholic University of America Press, 1951.

Coyle, Grace L., *Group Experience and Democratic Values*, New York: The Woman's Press, 1947.

Hall, L. K., "Group Workers and Professional Ethics," *The Group*, Vol. XV, No. 1, Oct. 1952, pp. 3-8.

Kaiser, Clara A., "Social Group Work Practice and Social Responsibility," *Social Welfare Forum 1952*, New York: Columbia University Press, 1952, pp. 161-167.

Konopka, Gisela, *Eduard C. Lindeman and Social Work Philosophy*, Minneapolis: University of Minnesota Press, 1958.

Murphy, Marjorie, *The Social Group Work Method in Social Work Education*, Vol. XI, A *Project Report of the Curriculum Study*, Werner W. Boehm, Director and Coordinator, New York: Council on Social Work Education, 1959.

Pumphrey, Muriel W., *The Teaching of Values and Ethics in Social Work Teaching*, Vol. XIII, A *Project Report of the Curriculum Study*, cited above.

Reynolds, Bertha C., *Social Work and Social Living*, New York: Citadel Press, 1951.

Tillich, Paul, "The Philosophy of Social Work," *The Social Service Review*, Vol. XXXVI, No. 1, Mar. 1962, pp. 13-16.

Wilson, Gertrude and Gladys Ryland, "Social Classes: Implications for Social Group Work," *Social Welfare Forum 1954*, New York: Columbia University Press, 1954, pp. 168-186.

CHAPTER SIX

Assessing and Establishing Objectives in Social Group Work (Diagnosis)

The faculty of judgment . . . must belong to the learner himself: and in the absence of such a natural gift no rule that may be prescribed to him for this purpose can insure against misuse.[1]

After discussing the concepts of the individual and the group, and clarifying the value base of the group worker's approach, we can now develop the helping process of social group work as part of the general function of social work as discussed in Chapter II. Let us return once more to the three points Marjorie Murphy presented in the Curriculum Study, on which there is agreement in regard to the group work method:

---

[1] Immanuel Kant, *Critique of Pure Reason*, translated by J. M. D. Meiklejohn, New York: John Wiley Book Co., 1943, p. 451.

1. Social group work is a method of rendering service to persons, through providing experience in groups. Development of the person towards his individual potential, improvement of relationship and social functioning competencies, and social action are recognized as purposes of social group work. The worker functions within a framework of ethical and social values.

2. Social group work is a generic method which can be used in different settings.

3. The method includes conscious use of worker-member relationships, relationships among members, and of group activity. The worker simultaneously uses relationships with individual members and with the group as a whole. He works as an enabler with both, helping members and the group to use their capacities and strengths. He uses himself differently in accordance with specific objectives and his assessment of members' needs, interests and capacities.[2]

Points 1 and 2 show the range of purposes for which group work help is needed and include a large range of agencies fulfilling such purposes. They fall clearly into two distinct categories:

1. Those groups which serve the "development of the person toward his individual potential, improvement of relationship and social functioning competencies," as most youth groups and all groups with therapeutic intent, and

2. Those groups which need help with "social action," frequently consisting of highly capable people in leadership positions in their communities who want to become effective combatants of social problems.

There has been and still is some controversy among social group workers as to whether these two categories fall within the province of social group work. Gertrude Wilson distinguished between "growth oriented" and "task oriented" groups, and was frequently attacked because she seemed to say that "task oriented groups" do not fall within the province of social group work.[3] To this writer the differentiation between "growth oriented" and "social action" oriented groups seems a clearer one, although perhaps some day a better and more refined classification can be found. "Task orientation" seems to this author too wide, since this may include groups in a factory with the task of finishing a piece of machinery (obviously not in the orbit

[2] Marjorie Murphy, op. cit., p. 78
[3] Gertrude Wilson, "Social Group Work: Trends and Developments," Social Work, Vol. I, No. 4, Oct. 1956, pp. 66-75.

of social group work, although anyone working with such a group may gain from it a knowledge of group process and dynamics). It may include a group of severely handicapped people consciously working on the task of learning to move into normal society from which they may have been cut off for a long time—obviously falling within the orbit of social group work. If we distinguish between "growth oriented" and "social action oriented" groups, however, we stay clearly in the area of social group work and we have a classification of different groups, although a very rough and not highly differentiated one, but nevertheless necessary for determination of the differential use of social group work skills. Both these categories demand problem solving; both relate to social problems; both demand group work skill through individualization in face-to-face groups; both need the understanding of individual and group dynamics; both require the same translation of values into action, which in this case is the helping process. Yet they are distinguished from each other by the fact that the individual in the "growth oriented group" needs direct help with his own development and problems, while the individual in the "social action" directed group needs help with becoming effective on behalf of problems not necessarily rooted within himself or in his relationships with others. Not every social action group needs a social group worker, but many do. This author also includes in this term staff committees of social agencies which try to work on such things as the improvement of practice, adult committees in neighborhood houses, and so forth. It must be understood, of course, that there may be individuals in such groups who need specific help for themselves and that it is part of the group worker's general responsibility for individualization to spot this. But individual treatment is not the purpose of social action groups, and turning them into "therapy groups" (i.e., growth oriented groups) or constantly searching for "sick people" among the members is a misuse of the helping function in such groups.

It would be desirable if we had a more refined system of classifying groups. This is not yet available.

In spite of the absence of a clear classification system in the total social work profession, the group worker must be able to assess individual members as well as the group as a whole so as to establish objectives for doing purposeful work. In working with individuals social workers have frequently used psychiatric classification systems, yet they become increasingly aware of the fact that these are not sufficient for the social work orientation of seeing the individual in his interaction with others and his environment. Much of what is called "diagnosis" in social work is not a diagnosis in the medical sense. It is more a summarized recognition of the individual in his group situation. It is an assessment of it in the light of theory and a resulting establishment of goal-directed work. It often changes in the course of social work treatment, because of changing conditions or the influence of new experiences and knowledge on the social worker and the client or members.

The absence of diagnostic categories lies in the nature of the phenomena with which the group worker works. This was early recognized by those who worked in child guidance clinics:

> We have little sympathy with the idea that an individual or his problem can be really known through 'an examination' and a labelling process— it requires, rather an *examination into* what makes him what he is and makes him do what he does. It can only be lack of experience in studying life careers that leads anyone to believe otherwise. . . .
> . . . Important whole groups of facts are not taken account of in any ordinary investigation; for example, the powerful but formative influences of mental life that are always active in home and other associations beneath the surface of observable exteriors.[4]

Clarity of assessment and establishment of purposeful objectives is a prerequisite for competent help and for critical evaluation of goals reached. Without such assessment the work of the group worker either becomes vague ("I just work with this group," a young group worker in training said. "What is the purpose of your being there? What is it that you try to help with?" "I don't know; I am just there.") or it becomes sterile with a stereotyped kind of "recipe" approach ("I always use an observer and recorder. I always let the group be completely free to decide to do whatever it wants to do.")

Objectives are not determined by the group worker alone. They are determined by the group members' conscious needs which bring them to the groups, the purpose of the agency which provides the service and the group worker's understanding of the individual and the total group, including frequently a recognition of needs not conscious to the members. The latter does not mean that the group worker "always knows best" and that he constantly searches for meaning exactly opposite to what members express. This tendency to never interpret an

[4] Judge Baker Foundation, *Case Studies*, Series 1, No. 1, Sept. 1922, p. 3a.

expressed emotion or thought as real was an unfortunate by-product of a misunderstood Freudian approach. It has seriously harmed the work of the human relations professions, because the knowledge of pre-conscious or unconscious motivation was used in an almost punishing, or omnipotent, way and allowed the group member or client no recourse when he disagreed with the professional. This was then chalked up as "resistance." It often distorted understanding into a fanciful guesswork, instead of helping to determine what the person *really* wanted or felt. The group worker must know about the pre- and unconscious; he must understand that many needs are not explicitly known to and often are not expressed by the group member even if known, hence he must take seriously the *expressed* needs and consider them as strongly as those not expressed.

The three goal determinants—the member's expressed needs, the agency's purpose and the group worker's understanding—may coincide, supplement or contradict each other. Let us look at some examples of this:

Example 1

Several adult patients in a mental hospital joined a group, because they hoped that group discussions would help them get better.

The purpose of the mental hospital is to help the patient get better and the discussion group was formed for this purpose.

The social group worker, together with other members of the hospital team, had selected those patients whom he considered capable of involving themselves in group discussions which would help them get better.

In this example the goals of all three goal determinants coincide.

Example 2

Youngsters in a delinquency institution participate in an activity group because they find it enjoyable. They want fun, stimulation and satisfaction in accomplishing something with their hands.

The institution's goal is to help these youngsters to cease their delinquent behavior and to get satisfaction from "lawful activities."

The group worker also wants to help them enjoy non-delinquent activities. In addition he wants them to experience positive solutions to group conflict, which inevitably occurs in such groups; to experience a positive relationship with an adult in authority and to learn to live with it; to have an opportunity to speak frankly within the group about their problems and to gain direct help with them through the instrumentality of the group worker and other group members.

In this example the goals of the three goal determinants partially coincide with each other and partially complement each other.

Example 3

A gang of boys meets at the street corner to hang around and plan occasional thefts.

The agency in the neighborhood sends a group worker to work with the gang to prevent serious delinquent behavior.

The group worker has the same goal as the agency. Because of the situation of these particular boys a specific task is to help them feel more positively toward school.

In this example agency and group worker's goals contradict those of the group members.

The latter situation is the hardest one to work with. Since all group work is practiced in a reality situation, reflecting not only on past or future action, but on present action as well, such divergence must be faced frankly from the beginning.

A helping relationship must be built on trust. The group worker therefore cannot "manipulate" a group in the sense of working toward his or the agency's goal, even if well-meant, without letting the members know about this and working it through with them. Not every step of his method must be consciously shared with them or explained, but the intent must be made known. A social worker once reported that his agency (a Department of Public Welfare) asked him to work with a group of men on relief, who had shown little responsibility for their families or had deserted them, and made no effort to look for gainful employment. He felt embarrassed to share with them the concern of the agency and did not inform them of the actual purpose of the group in order to help them to take on more responsibility. He told them that he was working on a research project to find out what they were thinking. This is "manipulation" and not permissible in social group work. The group worker could have shared in an honest and yet respectful way the actual purpose of the agency by stating that the agency was concerned with the situation of the men and their families. To be helpful to both of them, the agency needed to understand their own point of view, their own thinking and maybe work out, together with the men, a possible solution. This was the actual intent.

Social group work is *application* of knowledge to *specific* situations. To help group members—young, middle-aged, old; some deeply troubled and incapable of reaching out; others highly aggressive and full of hostility; some unaware of inner pain, but inflicting it on others; others struggling with the daily tasks of growing up or with the limits imposed on them because of a racial difference—the group worker must first and above all try to *understand* and to feel deeply involved with each of them. He must realize that each member and each group is different from everyone else and from any other group, in the past, present or future. *Individualization in the group*—individualization, not singling out—is one of the first and basic principles of social group work and the prerequisite for its particular helping function. No teenager can be to him "another teenager," no Golden Age Club, only "one of the many." Each person and each group must be seen in its uniqueness and work with them must be in accordance with this. The theories of individual and group dynamics offer a framework. They present *possibilities* of human behavior and its explanation; they present *averages*, but they never present the actual human being as he is. This must be underlined and fundamentally understood. Too often, theory is used rigidly with the assumption that it will give the explanation for every single person. Surely, being late to group meetings may indicate resistance (this possibility is indicated by the knowledge of dynamic Freudian theory) but it may also simply indicate that John always gets into a quarrel with his father whenever he gets ready to leave the house. Ella's persistence in wearing blue jeans on every occasion may indicate masculine preferences and rejection of her femininity; it may also be her way of trying to defy the adult world or it may indicate actual yearning for feminine adornment on the part of a girl who does not have the means to fulfill her dreams. All these possibilities, and many more, must be considered. Theories are indispensable; they open the practitioner's eye to vistas he could not always see by himself and could not find by pure intuition. They also help to order impressions and they often give meaning to seemingly unrelated observations. Yet the group worker must know that they are generalizations and that in practice he always must look for the *particular*.

How can one human being understand another one? What are the *media* the group worker can use to achieve this? His professional tool box does not include objective mental tests, x-rays, encephalograms, blood tests, etc.—although he may obtain the results of such tests from other professionals, if this is indicated. His tools are:

1. The general theories of individual and group behavior, as discussed in Chapters III and IV, enlarged and intensified. When he works with disturbed people, he needs additional psychiatric knowledge. He must add knowledge of the particular culture in which he works and from which the members of his group come.
2. Listening.
3. Observation.
4. Empathy.

The text will enlarge further on the last three tools.

Listening

In general, people listen little to what others have to say. In a group of ADC mothers the most voiced complaint was that people did not listen to them, that they had made up their mind what the mothers should do, how they should handle things before they themselves could say anything.

In a group discussion with delinquent girls the bitterness of the girls was directed mostly against adults who never listen to what "we have to say." A ten-year-old boy in a residential treatment center wrote, "Most important: The counselors must listen to us." This cry for being heard is the cry of the individual wanting to be understood. It is his need and his right. Effective help cannot be given without true listening. The group worker must listen carefully to *what* is said, to *how* it is said and to *whom* it is said. All this has meaning and helps in better understanding:

Example

It was visiting afternoon in camp. The children spoke eagerly about their parents' or other relatives' coming. John (12 years) said casually, turning to no one in particular, "There is too much to do in the fields these days. Nobody of my family will come, but it does not matter much." The casual way in which he spoke, his refusal to look at anyone revealed clearly his fear, his longing, his fierce wish "not to be found out"—his desire to be a "man." The group worker felt he must respect this boy's struggle and yet let him know that he was understood. He said, almost casually and to the whole group of boys: "Yes, I think, some will have no visitors. It is harvest time. I guess that is a bit tough on the parents. Why don't we write to those who could not come?" John looked up eagerly, some others crowded around.

We see how sensitive the group worker was, not only to the content of the words, but also to the way in which they were spoken and to the feeling behind them. He then used his understanding to help John —not sentimentally by commiserating with him, but by respecting his effort to be "grown-up" and by giving him at the same time an outlet in action; this helped others in the group too.

In "I Am Lazarus," a short story describing sensitively the feelings of a young mental patient, Anna Kavan describes so well the non-listening and what it does to a person,

Example

The young man stood still and picked one of the grasses and brushed it against his cheek. It touched his skin lightly, prickingly, like the electrified fur of a cat in a thunderstorm. He picked several more grasses.

Suddenly he was aware of a presence. The gym mistress cycling along the path had approached noiselessly . . .

"Why, Mr. Bow, what are you doing with those?"

The young man laboriously assembled words in his head. He wished to explain that the grasses turned into a soft furred cat and arched its back under his hands.

The gym mistress did not listen to what he was trying to say.

It was not the fashion at the clinic to listen to what patients said. There was not enough time. Instead, she put out her hand . . . and took the grasses away from Thomas Bow and threw them down on the path. . . .

"You don't want those," she said. "Nobody picks grass. We could pick some flowers though, if you like." She reached down for a handful of moon daisies and offered them to him. "There, aren't they pretty?" She was very good-natured about it.

Mr. Bow unwillingly accepted the flowers. . . .

. . . When the gym mistress was not looking he dropped them and trod on them with his brown shoes.[5]

Mr. B. was not helped—he only felt misunderstood—and the person who had not time to listen missed a golden opportunity to find out more about the mysteries of thinking and feeling in this particular patient: Perhaps just hearing about his love and delight with the soft, furry things might have given some insight into his state of mind and his fears.

The listening a social group worker must learn is different from the listening we usually do in our daily lives. We are used to listening through the screen of our own preoccupations, our own thinking. For instance, observe group discussions on a social evening: most of the time each person presents only his own ideas with a disregard for what anyone else has said. More often, then, these are interrupted monologues rather than true "dialogues" which require an interchange of ideas and a building upon one another's thoughts. "Listening" is an art involving conscious self-discipline to consider truly the *other one*, not just oneself. If one seriously does this, one might find sometimes the unexpected, as in the incident reported by Helen Padula which occurred in a mental hospital:

Example:

An old man complained persistently to his wife that although he received the ice cream she ordered for him, he had to eat it in the bathtub. His wife apologetically brought the complaint to the social worker's attention. She didn't think there was anything to it—but her husband was so emphatic! The social worker agreed

5   Anna Kavan, *I Am Lazarus*, London: Jonathan Cape, Ltd., 1945, p. 11.

it sounded too absurd to be true, but she would inquire. It *was* true. The man's ice cream happened to be delivered at the same time his bath was scheduled. No one had thought to rearrange the one or the other![6]

Aside from the almost incredible bureaucracy seen in this illustration, we must also realize the frustration of the patient to whom no one had listened: even his wife did not take his words seriously! It is to the credit of the social worker that she did not simply dismiss what he said as a figment of the imagination of a sick mind; she listened and she investigated, and she found that the patient's complaint was valid. *All social workers must listen to what their clients say*; otherwise they may miss the salient clue to a purposeful, goal-directed solution.

Let me cite one more example to illustrate the many facets of this capacity to listen:

Example

A young woman group worker worked with a group of teenage girls in a settlement house. Her fiancé usually picked her up after the meetings. One day, after the girls had seen him several times, they crowded around the group worker and asked her when she planned to get married. She replied, "June 27th."

The group worker in this case had not listened well; she had heard the words, but she had missed the content: she had not felt the eager concern of teenage girls about dating and what it meant to *them* and whether it always must lead to marriage. She had not listened with the sensitivity of someone attuned to the concern of the *other* one. By simply stating the wedding date, she had cut the youngsters off from an opportunity to ask questions dealing specifically with their own areas of concern.

Observation

Observation is similar to listening, but it includes awareness of non-verbal expressions of feelings and thoughts. Much of the action and communication in groups is of such non-verbal nature. This is one of

---

[6] Helen Padula, *op. cit.*, p. 3.

the reasons why the group work method is so appropriate in working with people who are not highly intellectual or introspective (i.e., young children or youngsters and adults who come from cultures that are not given to much discussion). Many such persons cannot discuss their individual problems within the confines of an office or put into words their anguish or sufferings, but they can act them out. Thus the unique value of observation. Consider the following:

Example

There were only three boys in a group at a newly established child guidance clinic. All three had been referred because of low achievement and other difficulties in school. John, at the age of ten, was considered "hopeless." He hardly spoke and, when questioned, answered only in monosyllables and with great reluctance. He lived with a grandmother to whom he clung fiercely at the slightest indication by authorities that he might be better off in another environment. He absented himself from the home whenever he pleased; he slept in parks; he truanted. All attempts at the clinic to involve him in some friendly discussion had failed.

One day the group worker prepared paper, pencils, water colors, crayons and clay for the boys to work with, whatever their preference. Erik quickly reached for the water colors and worked rapidly with broad strokes and somber colors; aggression and fear practically stared out from the paper. Jim drew tiny, timid lines with pencil on white paper; they bespoke aimlessness. He did not need to speak; the way in which he worked and used the materials spoke as clearly as words of his guard against intrusion and his feelings of defeat and inadequacy. John just sat there, sullenness all over his face. When Eric reached for a fresh sheet of paper, John glanced at his design, guardedly, almost furtively—the first clue to the group worker that John was aware of the others. John's hand opened, then closed—a sign of a wish to do something and yet not wanting to give in to this wish. The group worker reached for the clay, rolled it in her hands to form a ball, and then, smiling at John, rolled it casually over to him. John caught the clay ball, rolled it back and forth, and then made a dent in it here and there. When the group worker stopped looking at him, he began to work with it intensely and without looking up. In this hour John suddenly bloomed forth, producing little works of art—miniature cars and animals and houses and trees, exquisite in all details. Nobody had ever known of this gift before.

We see in this example the power of observation and the way that facial expression, choice of material and the movement of hands all became meaningful to the sensitive observer. And we can see how the group worker reacted quickly and appropriately to these signs to help all three youngsters, but especially John, on the road toward a more satisfying life.

Just as important as the observation of individual behavior in the group is the observation of relationships: Who chooses whom as friend? What members usually arrive together for a meeting? (Note that the group worker must always be in the meeting place before the members arrive.) What members leave together?

Example

In the treatment center, Ella, 15 years old, always sought to protect the younger children. The group worker's problem was to determine whether this effort at protection represented a feeling for the younger children or simply an identification with them against the adult world. She had to observe Ella's facial expressions, the way she planted her feet so firmly on the ground, the manner in which she moved her body—all these were indices which helped in understanding her.

Empathy

The Minnesota Indians have a proverb that says, "Never judge a man until you have walked a moon in his moccasins." No picture can express more beautifully the need for empathy in understanding another person. One has to "walk in his shoes," and not just for a short time, but "for a moon." Nor is it sufficient to try them on while sitting down. One must do the "walking."

Students living in the Quonset hut villages near some college campuses are usually poor—they experience poverty. Yet they still do not live through the same kind of poverty that the person on relief experiences. The college student's poverty exists for a limited time; he has hopes of finding work, once he completes his education, which will amply compensate him for this period. The person on relief, however, has no definite limit on the duration of his period of poverty. He has less hope.

We cannot—as social workers—walk in the moccasins of all our clients. We cannot live through all the desperate pains of abandonment by parents or spouses, of unemployment, of discrimination, of mental or emotional sickness, of imprisonment, of crippling physical handicaps, or of utter hopelessness. Somehow we must learn to understand and to feel these things. Bertha Reynolds once said, "It is the sensitivity of the socially vital layman raised to the nth power which makes the difference between amateur and professional skill in working with social relationships."[7]

There was a time in social work when the idea was advanced that only students with happy family backgrounds should be accepted in schools of social work. Some even went so far as to suggest that any applicant motivated by some strong personal experience of suffering, be it physical, emotional or social, should not be accepted for fear that this might indicate a neurotic identification. This, of course, is nonsense. There is always the possibility of neurotic use of human experience, but this may relate to happy experiences, too. In fact, a too shallow, undemanding life will not usually produce a good social worker.

Saroyan spoke of a man who came to see him to ask whether he could become a great writer:

> As he read I felt that there was a good man, and yet I could not help wondering what would come of his writing of poems. For he was very faraway from the dirt and anxiety of the world.[8]

This again does not mean that every social worker must have lived through great tragedy or that he must have pain inflicted on him during the educational process. It does mean that he must open his mind to the many anxieties people encounter and not shy away from a closer look into the problems of life. A comfortable withdrawal into the four walls of an office cannot keep empathy alive. The group worker who works with the bitter teenager who is out to "make money

---

[7] Bertha C. Reynolds, *Learning and Teaching in the Practice of Social Work*, New York: Farrar, Rinehart, Inc., 1945, p. 51.
[8] William Saroyan, *op. cit.*, p. 5.

quickly" may read in books about "lower class culture and its different values," yet he cannot help the youngster if he does not learn to *feel* what it means to live in a teeming tenement house, to see no beauty, to hear day and night the noise of quarrels, to be chided in school for not having worked his lesson when the needed book is not available in the home. This understanding of the teenager's lot may help the group worker to better appreciate his need to "make money quickly," and enable him to work with him on the basis of understanding and empathy. The group worker may even come to question the textbook theories of differing values between "lower" and "upper" class when this teenager, and others like him, begins to trust him and to talk shyly about his "sissy" dreams of a clean home, of love, even of learning. He may also learn to look behind the facade of "middle" and "upper" class homes in search for the same naked hunger for things and the drive to "make money quickly."

And most important of all the group worker must feel what *injustice* means to a person, whether it is belonging to a minority group or not having as much intelligence as someone else or not being as physically attractive as others or whatever. Injustice, whether it be really inflicted or only felt as such by an individual or an entire group, leads to many different forms of behavior—teen-agers, for instance, as a group frequently feel they are unfairly treated. Some forms of this behavior may be constructive—a determination to break through the barrier by participating in community life or by becoming more understanding and tolerant of others; some forms may be destructive and manifest themselves in delinquency, the creation of hate groups, or withdrawal. The group worker cannot be effective if he is only a cold onlooker. And yet, while he must try to feel and understand the problems of those he wants to help, he should not, like the actor, become completely identified with these persons while he is fulfilling his professional role. The social worker must feel simultaneously like the person or group with whom he works, and feel differently—like the *helper*. He must understand the objectives of the group members as well as those of the agency; he must understand the function of his profession. The group worker cannot join the gang as a delinquent, even though he feels the strength of the pull on the youngsters. He cannot help men defy authority in prison, although he must understand why they feel like doing so. He may feel deeply the pain of the growing adolescent who must postpone fulfillment of his mature physical urges, but he must help him to counteract them in a meaningful way and thus help the adolescent acquire a consideration for others.

Empathy—"identification" with clients and members—has sometimes been looked upon by members of the social work profession as dangerous to good social work practice. On the contrary, it is indispensable if it is combined with the discipline of the *helping role*.

The three media of understanding—listening, observation and empathy—are centered in the personality of the social group worker; they are not "objective" tools. The group worker, then, must realize that he sees others through the screen of his own personality and his own life experiences. "Phenomenology," a psychological system widely accepted in Europe, stresses this fact. Without placing it into a total system, social work practice has taken this into account. This is the reason why a social worker must develop enough insight into his own personality to be conscious of at least the make-up of his own particular "screen." This helps him to come closer to understanding the members and groups he works with and to take account of his own bias even though he cannot completely eliminate it.

A combination of an innate capacity for empathy with heightened awareness of oneself and one's value system, and constant patient exercise in sharpening the powers of observation and listening are needed for the particular "fact-finding" process of social group work. The knowledge of individual and group dynamics then contributes to the ordering of the facts and their proper assessment. The group worker's fact-finding tools are not always sufficient for all the group situations he encounters. His professional integrity then demands consultation and help from others in such related professions as psychology, psychiatry, education, and so forth.

Let us look at the fact-finding, assessment and objective setting processes in practice, by presenting a few examples:

Example 1

A neighborhood friendship group of 15- and 16-year-old girls who had met in each other's homes had asked to come to the agency. They had accepted the agency's policy of having an adult worker meeting with them. None of the girls had previously participated in any activities at the Neighborhood House, but the families were known, because of participation by younger brothers and sisters, and because the agency had been asked to help in some instances with brothers who had been on probation or parole.

At the first meeting Judy came early and alone. She looked unusually mature, physically, but seemed to get much pleasure from going around the room with the group worker, touching everything and keeping close to her in the manner of a younger child. Four other group members came together; two others followed, also together. During the meeting there appeared little difference between the two latter groups. Judy remained an isolate although she was outspoken in her comments in the group discussion. Her comments remained usually "in the air" and were not picked up by the others. On the surface she seemed not to notice this.

The girls expressed dissatisfaction with their club's activities. They did not know exactly what to do. When the group worker asked whether this was the reason they had decided to come to the agency, there was first a quick "yes," then much giggling and finally an outburst of hostility against "those kids in school" who had given them a "black name." They wanted to do something about this. "Those kids" had accused them of letting themselves be picked up by boys at any time and of being "easy." They expressed hurt and anger at being "maligned." The group worker wondered whether they knew how such rumors may have started. There was immediate sensitivity as to any possible implication that there may have been any truth in this (although the group worker had tried to avoid this) and sharp denial of the slightest interest in boys. The group worker let them know that such an interest was quite normal and acceptable at their age. This opened a flood of virtuous accusations against other girls, none of whom were present. Joan and Violet vehemently denounced all men as being "no good." Judy, Sue and Violet, too, discussed their brothers, who were then in training schools, and expressed bitter feelings against them, saying that they were the cause of their "bad reputation." They seemed almost forlorn. They spoke, sometimes angrily, sometimes almost tearfully.

They hated school and spoke with distaste of teachers and classes. Some complaints seemed genuine; some were said with an eye on the group worker, obviously to provoke her.

At one point, Sue said to the group worker: "You don't say much. Do you think you can stand us?" The group worker said that she would like to get to know them, that she knew it was important for girls to talk about the things that concerned them, and that she was looking forward to working with them. Sue turned around saying, "News that someone cares." It was said flippantly, yet somewhat wistfully. . . . With hope?

The girls talked about clothes, again expressing dissatisfaction with and some envy of others. The group worker suggested that at another meeting they could make colorful felt cut-outs to decorate their simple skirts (a teenage favorite at that time), while continuing to talk. This aroused excitement, a lively discussion and some random planning, interspersed with laughter and much running around the room.

The group worker asked whether it was all right for her to visit each one of them before the next meeting so that she could get to know them and their families. This was accepted—to the group worker's surprise—with actual enthusiasm, and the girls suggested several times when it would be best for her to come.

What were the facts the group worker gained from this meeting alone that would help her to determine the objective of her role with this particular group?

This was an adolescent girls' group with many of the normal interests of most of them: boys, clothes, activities. Yet they felt they had to deny one of these basic interests.

They were, or they felt themselves to be, deprived and rejected by other girls. They had the same aspirations as the "good" girls, but felt hampered by their family reputations—at least three of them expressed this.

The remarks of two of the girls seemed to point toward poor relationships with their fathers, although this was not certain.

They disliked school.

They seemed to have an eager wish to be accepted by an adult (see the reaction to the offer of the home visit), but Sue's remark and the apparent acceptance of it by the others of "News that someone cares" showed that they did not expect much from adults.

As a group they seemed to be closely knit, with one person a neglected isolate. Reasons for this were not yet obvious in this meeting.

The group worker had not yet many facts pertaining to individual girls. Judy's isolation and the discrepancy between her physical development and her social maturity pointed toward her need for special attention. Sue might be the spokesman for the group and the most aggressive, and yet she might prove to be the girl with the greatest need for closeness to an adult.

First meetings usually yield only impressions of individuals and they must be cautiously interpreted. Only when a more trusting and close relationship is established can one expect members to be free to reveal themselves.

The understanding derived from this first meeting is not complete, but it is considerable. By knowing the neighborhood where the girls come from, by visiting them and their families in their homes (a very important and indispensable part of group work in neighborhood work) and by using the information known to the agency, the group worker can acquire valuable knowledge pertaining to each individual girl and to the entire group.

Her group's summary, the diagnosis and establishment of purpose, read:

> This is a group of teenage girls from low-middle class backgrounds in a neighborhood and school district which includes high income families. School activities involve at times a considerable amount of money.
> Five out of the seven girls come from home backgrounds with family difficulties (desertion, alcoholic fathers, brothers in delinquency institutions), two girls come from fairly stable families, but with money worries.
> All of the girls have truanted at one time or another and all had poor scholastic records. None of them tested below average. All of the girls date, some of them had been sexually promiscuous with boys. All of the girls are hungry for acceptance by adults and yearn to be "like others," have the same status as other girls. They have a "fighting spirit" and revolt against what they see as injustice, the higher economic status of others, their own low acceptance.
> Though the group looks like one with a close bond, each girl is actually very preoccupied with herself, and uses the others as a crutch. This is also the reason why they cannot be "bothered" by Judy.
> *Objective:* To help the girls gain satisfactions for themselves so

that the bitterness diminishes and they can begin to actually relate to each other.

To help them talk out their concerns with the aim of finding acceptable ways to change some of the situations (for instance discuss with the school the problem of too expensive activities) and to help them see their own part in their problems and motivate toward change (as school attendance).

To provide the girls with a warm and accepting and understanding adult so that they feel wanted and important as individuals and learn that such a relationship is possible. This should hopefully be transferred then to other adults too.

To help the girls have experiences of achievement and carry through responsibilities to raise their self-confidence and to strengthen them to live with certain home situations which cannot be changed. Consider referral of and enlist community resources for those with family problems which do not receive any attention at present and help them to get ready for this.

The above is only a summary of the goals for this group. The way of carrying them through is the next step of the group work process.

Only one individual diagnostic summary is given to show the specific way in which the group worker pulls together his knowledge of an individual and establishes objectives in working with her. They are never established *for* the individual, but always are worked through *with* the individual:

Example

Judy, 15 years, 9 months, is the second of four children, all the other children are boys. The oldest one is in a training school. Judy's father is an alcoholic; he is frequently abusive to his wife and the boys but he shies away from Judy when he is drunk and tries to make her his "ally" on the rare occasions when he is sober. Judy detests him and is ashamed of him, but fears him less than the rest of the family. She is aware of her power over him, especially when he is drunk. She is the adult in the family and has often shielded the younger boys and her mother. She is protective of them, but hates the older brother whom she identifies with the father.

The mother is a tired, frightened woman, prematurely old, who gladly lets Judy take over.

The family lives on the sporadic earnings of the father, who is a window washer, and has some additional support from a brother of the mother. Judy does occasional baby sitting in the neighborhood. Judy is one of the girls in the group who had occasional sex relations with boys. "I don't care much for them," she confided to the group worker, "It was just something different. I have not done it for a long time."

Judy's isolated position in the group seems to be caused by her surface affectation of indifference. She participates, but without any emotional involvement. She avoids close contact with any particular girl. Teachers report that her indifference is "maddening."

Two signs point toward much more inner involvement than Judy wants to admit: her tenacious and regular attendance in the group, in spite of group rejection and her habit of coming early and discussing her situation with the group worker.

Many of Judy's needs are the same as those of the other girls. The group worker must be available to Judy for those individual interviews she seeks out. Judy can accept this relationship only because it is not a highly formalized one, because she can "withdraw" into the group when the meetings begin. This must be allowed her until she asks for more help. Later she may either accept more intensive individual help, or, if the other girls are ready too, she may be encouraged to bring her concerns to the group. Judy also must be helped to be a "younger child" in the group to allow for all the child-needs she could never fulfill and the too adult role she continues to carry at home.

The group worker can be of help to Judy by presenting a strong mother person, whom she misses. If possible—also for the sake of other group members—a male worker should later join the group. Judy must be helped to allow herself to show emotions, positive and negative ones. She needs warmer relationships with other girls, and this involves work with the total group as well as with Judy. If possible, help should be given to the whole family, using the group work approach to overcome suspicion among family members.

Example 2

The long-range objective for this group of men who were for
many years in a mental hospital, was set by the staff—release
from the hospital. Yet little was known about these men and so
the immediate targets of the group had to be changed according
to the best understanding of the social worker. The "group" consisted of 37 men at Hilltop, a mental hospital.

This was their community and these were the members:[9]

The men slept in three long narrow wards, none with an outside
door, on unpainted cots with broken springs. The single bathroom boasted barely enough equipment for a medium-sized
family, and not a single facility was enclosed. There was only
one six by nine inch mirror. In place of towels, a sheet was
thrown across the door. In the dining room were wooden tables
and benches. There was no kitchen. No cooking was done in
Hilltop; food was brought over in open pails from the kitchen in
nearby Hillcrest.

Privacy was an unknown commodity. A few shelves in a small
closet served the needs of all. Any patient fortunate enough to
own personal belongings stuffed them into his pants pockets, or
hid them under his mattress.

A single attendant ran the building, into which other hospital
personnel seldom penetrated. The physician assigned to it made
rounds sporadically. The only "luxuries" were a small television
set and a water cooler, donated by a volunteer group from nearby
Catonsville, who in very recent years visited the men and served
refreshments one evening a month.

Hilltop, like its tenants, was neglected, rejected and withdrawn.
But its tenants are harder to describe. My first impression was of
a faceless mass of mechanized robots. As I gradually became better acquainted with them, they became 37 individual men, each
with his unique share of physical and emotional ingredients. I
want no more convincing evidence of the resilience of the human
personality. The Hilltop men wore, in a fashion all their own,
the shabby, faded, wrinkled, often soiled, uniformly gray hospital

---

[9]   Pansy K. Schmidt, "Assignment: Democracy's Scrap Heap," *Journal of Social
Work Process*, Vol. 12, 1961, pp. 73-93.

clothes. Many wore long winter underwear, vests, sweaters, jackets, and heavy trousers throughout the year, regardless of Maryland's famous summer temperatures. Since belts were traditionally not issued to them, they held up their pants with rope, or with suspenders tied by string to the belt-loops on their pants. They tucked their shirts into their underwear, and many didn't bother to put even the most essential buttons into buttonholes. The clothes were not their own in any personal sense. They went from Hilltop to the hospital laundry, came back to Hilltop, and were distributed without regard to individual size or preference. The men cared for themselves in a crude way. They worked, ate, slept, needed little attention, rarely got into difficulty. They were stoic, mute nonentities, known only to the attendant in charge— and not even he knew all by name. The majority, like sheep, followed the few who knew when to get up in the morning, when to wash, when to come to meals, and go to and from work. Those who could not shave were shaved. Those who did not know how to bathe were bathed, or went dirty.

They did not talk to each other. Some had not spoken a word for years; a few could not speak English. Though they spent their lives side by side, at meals, in bed, in the showers, in the fields, they hardly knew one another. This was no group, but an indistinguishable mass. They didn't live; the tide of bare existence had ebbed for them as they moved to Hilltop, and never risen again.

Their faces were as institutionally anonymous as their baggy hospital pants . . .

How to get started? The obvious point of departure was the men's hospital records. They weren't much help, beyond the barest facts of admissions dating from the days when everyone admitted to a mental hospital was expected to spend the rest of his natural life behind locked doors. (Much later I learned that not even these "barest facts" were to be trusted; one man, hospitalized for 23 years, had been "ashamed" to tell his name to the police bringing him to the hospital, and had been admitted under a pseudonym he selected on the spur of the moment!)

Fairly typical was Abel Monou's record:

"1905: Committed to Spring Grove. 1923: The *first* "progress" note. "He is well adjusted, cleans attendants' quarters in the

criminal building, delivers papers to various employees in and
near Hilltop." 1955: After half a century in the hospital, Mr.
Monou was performing the same tasks, but the note adds, "he
has become somewhat sloppy about his work and person."

More helpful than the records was a series of meetings to "staff"
all 37 patients. Dr. Ward, Mrs. Padula, Hilltop's attendant, and
I—what a sad, sorry parade of men sat down with us, one by one,
for discussions to evaluate the potentialities of each. We talked
about leaving the hospital—but of all 37, only five could be
tempted into any expression of a desire to leave.

The members refused, but the objective stood. It seemed best
to separate the group, to interview each man alone:

My next step, it seemed to me, was to find an office—just space
enough for a desk and two chairs—where I could arrange weekly
individual interviews with my new clients. The contrast between
that peaceful, conventional mental picture of my operations, and
the way I actually operated, is ludicrous. Fortunately my search
for an office, though frantic, was futile. There certainly was no
space in Hilltop. An attempt to use Hillcrest was doomed to
failure, because the men went into panic as four grim barred
doors were locked behind them on their way to the office Dr.
Ward found for me there.

Weeks later I came to know that an office, which to me was not
only familiar, but essential, would have been a foreign object to
these patients. I am quite sure that many of them would have
adamantly refused to sit across a desk from me. My search for
an office had a happy, though unexpected ending, as I held my
individual sessions with the men hunched over a familiar wooden
table in their own dining room. And by then I knew that most
of my preliminary work would have to be done, not with individuals, but with the group—also in familiar surroundings, their
own dingy day-room.

And the first group meetings?

In spite of my years of experience of working with the mentally
ill, I became anxious, even panic-stricken, when my calling of
their names echoed back from a wall of silence. It was a sad
silence: many had forgotten the sound of their names; others had
not heard themselves addressed by name for many years. They
knew, as did the attendant, that they would never leave the

hospital; and as I reminded them that I was here to discuss plans for leaving, they didn't even hear me, let alone understand my words.

The "sound of silence" mounted until it thundered in my ears, and I could see in their eyes the fear of cornered animals, defenseless against their fate.

Beating a hasty retreat from the discussion I had planned, I started talking about things they could understand: the broken bed springs, the need for a paint job to spruce up the drab walls and furniture. Wouldn't they like to have towels to dry their hands on, instead of that sheet? Didn't they sometimes wish there was more than one mirror? Wouldn't some pictures on the wall look pretty?

I was encouraged as a quarter of my audience gradually joined me in discussion. One asked for plastic glasses instead of heavy cups from which to drink their milk or water. Another, bolder, spoke up for transportation to and from the movies held weekly in the hospital auditorium—the four-mile round-trip was too far to walk after a day on the farm.

Seven men agreed that if I invited the doctor to our next meeting they would request his help in winning some reforms. Though timid and fearful at first, these patients heard themselves criticize the authorities at the meeting. The right to complain—inalienable even though it's *not* included in the Bill of Rights—gave them some sense of their individuality. At a later meeting, they reached the more advanced point of criticizing me and my function . . .

The objective had to be changed—at least for the time being. Before the patients could be prepared for release from the hospital they had to learn to be *people* again with the capacity to have opinions, to contradict, to make suggestions, to participate with others. Only the exercise of such capacity, carried out over a long period of time, could help the patients, or at least some of them, to become ready to leave. The original assessment of this situation was not easy because of the wish to fulfill the agency's request and the human resistance in everyone at taking small steps when one had expected to take big ones.

Summary

The assessment of the group and the establishment of objectives (group diagnosis) is one of the first steps in the group work process, parallel to the assessment of and establishment of objectives for each and with each individual member in the group (individual diagnosis).

The social group worker works with two large categories of groups: "growth oriented" and "social action" groups.

Each group is unique and must be treated as a unique entity.

The tools of assessment the social group worker uses are: (1) knowledge of individual and group dynamics; (2) knowledge of social environment and its meaning; (3) listening; (4) observation; (5) empathy.

The group worker must enlist the help of other professionals wherever indicated.

Three of these assessment tools—listening, observation and empathy —are part of the group worker's self. They therefore are not wholly objective. To diminish the element of subjectivity, the group worker must combine self-awareness with sensitivity toward others.

BIBLIOGRAPHY

Cohen, Nathan E., "Services to Groups and Individuals in Groups," *Social Welfare Forum 1957*, New York: Columbia University Press, 1957, pp. 15-20.

Judge Baker Foundation, *Case Studies*, Series 1, No. 1, Sep. 1922.

Klein, Alan F., "Individual Change through Group Experience," *Social Welfare Forum 1959*, New York: Columbia University Press, 1959, pp. 136-155.

Kolodny, Ralph L., "A Group Work Approach to the Isolated Child," *Social Work*, Vol. 6, No. 3, July 1961, pp. 76-84.

Konopka, Gisela, "Group Therapy in Overcoming Racial and Cultural Tensions," *American Journal of Orthopsychiatry*, Vol. XVII, No. 4, Oct. 1947, pp. 694-699.

————, *Group Work in the Institution, A Modern Challenge,* New York: Whiteside, Inc. and William Morrow and Co., 1954.

————, "The Method of Social Group Work," in Walter A. Friedlander, Editor, *Concepts and Methods of Social Work,* Englewood Cliffs, N.J.: Prentice-Hall, Inc., 1958, pp. 116-200.

————, "Resistance and Hostility in Group Members," *The Group,* Vol. XVI, No. 1, Oct. 1953, pp. 3-10.

Lifton, Walter M., *Working with Groups; Group Process and Individual Growth,* New York: John Wiley and Co., 1961.

Osborn, Hazel, "Some Factors of Resistance which Affect Group Participation," *The Group,* Vol. XI, No. 2, Jan. 1949, pp. 3-11 (with discussion by Harriet Young, pp. 12-18).

Philips, Helen U., Editor, *Achievement of Responsible Behavior Through Group Work Process,* Philadelphia: University of Pennsylvania School of Social Work, 1950.

————, "Social Group Work, a Functional Approach," *The Group,* Vol. X, No. 3, Mar. 1948, pp. 3-7.

Polansky, Norman A., "On the Dynamics of Behavioral Contagion," *The Group,* Vol. XIV, No. 3, Apr. 1952, pp. 3-8; 21; 25.

Reynolds, Bertha C., *Learning and Teaching in the Practice of Social Work,* New York: Farrar, Rinehart, Inc., 1945.

Reynolds, Rosemary, "Services to Individuals within a Group Work Setting," *Selected Papers in Group Work and Community Organization,* Raleigh, N.C.: Health Publications Institute, 1951, pp. 32-42.

Schwartz, William, "The Social Worker in the Group," *New Perspectives on Services to Groups: Theory, Organization, Practice,* New York: N.A.S.W., pp. 7-29 (with discussion by Ruth Smalley, pp. 30-34).

Sherif, Muzafer and Carolyn, "Psychological Harmony and Conflict in Minority Group Ties," *The American Catholic Sociological Review,* Vol. XXII, No. 3, Fall 1961, pp. 207-222.

Shiffman, Bernard M., "Effecting Change through Social Group Work," *Social Welfare Forum 1958,* New York: Columbia University Press, 1958, pp. 190-202.

Sloan, Marion B., "Factors in Forming Treatment Groups," *Use of Groups in the Psychiatric Setting,* New York: N.A.S.W., 1960, pp. 74-86.

Sullivan, Dorothea F., Editor, *The Practice of Group Work,* New York: Association Press, 1941.

————, *Readings in Group Work,* New York: Association Press, 1952.

Trecker, Harleigh B., Editor, *Social Group Work: Principles and Practices,* revised edition, New York: Whiteside, Inc., 1955.

Weiner, Hyman J., "Group Work and the Interdisciplinary Approach," *Social Work,* Vol. 3, No. 3, July 1958, pp. 76-82.

Wilson, Gertrude, *Group Work and Case Work*, New York: Family Welfare Association of America, 1941.

———, "Social Group Work: Trends and Developments," *Social Work*, Vol. 1, No. 4, Oct. 1956, pp. 66-75.

———, and Gladys Ryland, *Social Group Work Practice*, Boston: Houghton Mifflin Co., 1949.

Wittenberg, Rudolph M., *The Art of Group Discipline*, New York: Association Press, 1951.

———, *So You Want to Help People*, New York: Association Press, 1947.

CHAPTER SEVEN

The Helping Process of Social Group Work (Treatment)

True influence over another comes not from a moment's eloquence nor from any happily chosen word, but from the accumulation of a lifetime's thoughts stored up in the eyes.[1]

The term "treatment" was taken over from medicine into the social work vocabulary, as was the term "diagnosis." Mary Richmond, whose famous *Social Diagnosis* heralded the beginning of professional casework, had worked closely with physicians in Baltimore and had learned from their systematic approach to problems. With the influence of psychiatry on social work, the term "treatment" became more and more associated with the idea of treatment of emotional personality problems, something Mary Richmond had not

[1] Thornton Niven Wilder, *The Woman of Andros*, New York: Albert and Charles Boni, 1930, p. 128.

intended. Social group workers often shy away from the term because of this connotation. It is an appropriate term, though, if understood as "the act, mode or process of treating anything, as a raw material, substance or product"; that means a conscious and purposeful way of acting. It means also for social group work, in certain agencies at least, the "management of illness by the use of drugs, dieting or other means designed to bring relief or effect a cure," with an emphasis on "other means."[2] We must remember that the general goal of social group work is help with the basic needs of individuals to be important and to participate and the basic need of the total human society—expressed in the small group—for interdependence.

According to the function of the particular agency in which the social group worker works and the specific individuals and groups he is called upon to serve, the helping process must be modified according to the degree of health or sickness present. It must be modified, but the major processes used are the same because of the given frame of reference (see Chapters III and IV) and the underlying philosophy (see Chapter V). No single profession can encompass *all* helping media. In a group of inmates, for instance, a certain member needs not only the experiences which can be provided in the group, but dental care as well; his decayed teeth, besides being physically damaging, have a negative emotional impact on him. The group worker recognizes "dental care" as part of the treatment. It is his responsibility as a social worker to use all available resources to provide the care he himself cannot give.

The major helping media available to the social group worker are:

1. The purposeful, warm, understanding, professional relationship between the group worker and the group member;

2. The relationship among group members—the group process;

3. Verbal communication—discussions, "talking";

4. Non-verbal communication—program, play, experience;

5. Purposeful choice and creation of environment.

In the following we will illustrate the group worker's use of these through case material.

    2 Definitions taken from *Britannica Dictionary*, Vol. 2, Part I, New York: Funk and Wagnalls Co., 1956, p. 1389.

1. Relationship Between Group Worker and Group Members

Rudolf Wittenberg called relationship a "transmission belt" between human beings.[3] It makes communication possible and its quality determines whether treatment is effective or not.

Help can be given only in a relationship of trust and mutual respect. Yet this frequently does not exist from the beginning. The group worker is always the "outsider" in the group. Nothing significant can happen until the members have learned to trust him. Relationship between group worker and members is characterized by the group worker's attempt to understand—the empathy that was discussed previously—combined with his professional responsibility to help in whatever way necessary. The group worker must find the strength in the members and add his strength to theirs. Social action groups, for instance, or professional committees, frequently feel discouraged when they do not see immediate success. To help them continue their work, the group worker recognizes the discouragement, its explicit cause or, at times, its irrational source. His responsibility is to appraise the probable capabilities of the members so that they can move toward better solutions. He is not *Pollyanna* pretending everything is well, but he cannot become part of their despair. His helping role demands the mobilization of their strength. In the growth oriented group this means a serious working through of the forces that prevent the members from using their strength, a talking-out or an acting-out, and a testing of new-found capacities. Relationship means that the *intent* of the group worker is not only present in him, but that it is felt and accepted by the group members. The establishment of such relationship is a difficult task. Many people try to help others and mean well, but the recipients of their efforts do not feel served and do not really accept their help.

Quality [margin annotation]

Example

The new gym teacher in the training school complained, "I do everything possible—I even bought new balls. The boys need more exercise, need to get out, but they don't budge!"

[3] See Rudolf Wittenberg, *So You Want to Help People*, New York: Association Press, 1947.

He had to learn that it took time to establish a relationship of trust between himself and the boys before they would involve themselves in anything he thought was "good for them." Yes, they liked to play ball, but they also distrusted anything offered to them by an adult; they assumed a trap and constantly tried to preserve their shield of hatred that allowed them to continue feeling bitter about the adult world in general.

Example

The girls were incredulous. It was just not possible. The "mean" police women had collected money and bought a TV set for the cottage. They refused to write a "Thank you" note, they could not explain why.

It was obvious to the group worker that any admission of recognizing this gift meant to them that they could no longer blame those "mean police women" for everything, and that they would have to look into themselves for possible answers.

We see here how emotions block the acceptance of help, of relationships, because of the fear of introspection—yet change can come only when this is possible.

Helen Perlman wrote that "The identifying mark of a professional relationship is its conscious purposiveness growing out of the knowledge of what must go into achieving the goal."[24] Diagnosis and treatment are closely related. Relationship in group work is uniquely characterized by the fact that it is not a one-to-one relationship between the helping person and one client, but a relationship between the helper and individuals in a group and with the group as a whole. This has significant meaning. The group worker does not establish relationships with individuals one by one. He creates an atmosphere of trust and give-and-take with the whole group. This often means slow development and the acceptance of the fact that, as a group, members can be far more resistant than as individuals. In a group members support each other; they are not alone in the face of authority.

Social workers, psychologists, and psychiatrists, who are accustomed to working with individuals in a face-to-face relationship, always

4   Helen Harris Perlman, *op. cit.*, p. 68.

marvel at the greater temerity clients show when they are in a group.

Relationships in group work also cannot be as formalized as in the individual interview. This greater informality is especially obvious in activity groups, but it is also part of discussion groups, even therapy groups. A psychoanalyst describes this when talking about the group sessions he conducts:

> Functioning hour after hour as a shadowy figure in a dimly lit room with one patient at a time shuts out a lot of living; that is one of the occupational disabilities of the psychoanalyst. In the group, I felt much more of a human being—a more sociable and lively one. The situation was more challenging. It required qualities of leadership as well as technical skill and the ability to keep track of several lines of communication at a time. Yet the brighter atmosphere and more spontaneous emotional processes were at one and the same time more relaxing and more invigorating. The dramatic spirit of the interaction, the repartee and the intensity of the feelings coming to the fore made more of me come alive in the group sessions.[5]

In the reality of group interaction the group worker can never be aloof. He is not a *detached* observer, although he must be capable of sharp observation. He is active in a way appropriate to the group situation or to an individual member's needs. His helping role includes support and demand, often at the same time. His basic respect for each individual demands acceptance of each person, even if he does not agree with his views or actions. His responsibility demands intervention in damaging actions or feelings while still accepting each member. This means that the group worker is neither "permissive" nor "authoritarian-directive." Acceptance and limit setting are not considered contradictory in the use of the group work method, but are used according to the assessment of the group members' needs and the situation in which they find themselves.

In groups that are highly emotional—therapy groups, for example, or parent discussion groups—or in work with youth groups, the social group worker encounters the phenomenon of *transference* so well known in individual treatment.[6] In the group, transference is directed not only from the group member to the group worker, but also from

---

5 Hyman Spotnitz, *The Couch and the Circle*, New York: Alfred A. Knopf, 1961, p. 19.

6 Transference is understood as the unconscious displacement to the therapist of emotional attachment and reactions to a person in the client's past.

one group member to another. It is not part of the group work method (as in psychoanalysis) to provoke transference. The reality situation in the group partially counteracts this. However, the group worker must be able to recognize transference and work through it, if it occurs.

Example

Mr. Bell was one of the members of a group of former mental patients, young men and women. Mr. Bell had needed only short hospitalization, but was still unable to work. He was married and had two children. His mother was living with the family. Mr. Bell participated lively in the group, but only on an intellectual level. After the third meeting he told some of the members angrily that the group worker seemed to pick on him and he did not like to be chided because he had not yet accepted employment. Actually the group had discussed employment problems with little reference to Mr. Bell.

In the course of the next meeting, Mr. Bell said, for the first time showing more emotion than usual, "I can just see what you think, Mrs. Hare (the group worker). I resent the way you look at me. I am no bum." Another member tried to reassure him. The group worker held back realizing that Mr. Bell finally showed emotion and needed to work through this.

During the fourth meeting, Mr. Bell avoided any direct addressing of the group worker. He was back in his role of the intellectual, trying to "explain" some of the feelings of others and getting much hostility from other members. At the end of the meeting he said angrily, but with some control, "You people have no spine. You always side with her, just because she is in the driver's seat."

In the fifth meeting, Mr. Bell blew up. He gave the group worker a good "dressing down." She was just like all those females, always feeling superior, always "knowing better." But she was not so "hot" herself, had she not forgotten to bring the book for Miss Chandler she had promised (she really had forgotten it and apologized), she was not doing her job.

Mr. Bell seemed elated when he came to the eighth meeting. He said that he had discussed with his wife the problem of having his mother stay with them. He then was able to talk this over with his mother and make reasonable plans for another arrangement. It felt like a weight off his shoulders. Then he added sheepishly,

"And I could have never spoken up to her (the mother), if I had not told you off first, Mrs. Hare."

Mr. Bell had been allowed to work through his transference. The group worker did not give interpretation. Her skill lay in recognizing and accepting the hostility as a transference phenomenon. This helped Mr. Bell to work through his problem. It also helped him that the group listened to him, that he could complain to others "in the same boat" without being forced to directly attack the group worker who stood for the person he resented and feared. The group situation gave him an "out" before he could attack directly. He also was allowed to take his time: he was not forced too early into working through the transference. He needed a "pause" of several meetings without his continuing the attacks, when he took again the "adequate" intellectual role instead of the child desperately trying to grow up.

Example

Tilly, four years old, was referred to the Child Guidance Clinic and accepted on an emergency basis, rather unusual for a child that young. She had made several attempts to kill the newborn baby-sister. The parents were afraid to leave her or the baby alone for even a minute.

Tilly was tiny for her age, beautiful and very bright. In spite of her unusual verbal capacity she did not talk with anyone at the Clinic. Her play in the psychiatrist's office was guarded, covering up feelings. Tilly was referred to a small pre-school group of four children at the Clinic. In the beginning of the group meetings, there was little interaction, only parallel activities. The children were drawing. Susan was starting to draw on a light blue square of paper. Tilly had chosen a red one. Suddenly Tilly jumped up, tore Susan's paper away from her, and pushed her hard.

It was significant that she chose Susan, the smallest and youngest child in the group. The "guard" Tilly had kept up when meeting adults broke through when confronted with another child who stood for the hated new sister.

When Tilly was offered the same kind of drawing paper as Susan, she violently refused it. Nothing would do for her except Susan's own paper. Yet Susan was not the baby for which she stood; she was not helpless. She resisted. The group process—left alone—would have led to a violent fight with both children being hurt, not only physically, but also psychologically. Tilly probably would have won, triumphing over the "sister" and taking it for granted that this must always be the outcome. Susan probably would have lost and learned that "the strongest wins," thus making her stand up less for her rights than she was already capable of.

The group worker recognized the needs of *both* children; she also recognized Tilly's reaction to Susan as one of transference. She put her arms around both girls and held them closely and warmly. Tilly needed to feel that being confronted with a "new baby" meant no loss of tenderness. The group worker told them in a soft voice that it was tough to have sisters; she used simple words for Tilly's feelings. She did not force Tilly to give up the paper, but neither did she let Susan feel that she *had* to give it up. She reached for the whole stack of blue drawing paper and placed it before the girls. "There is enough for all of us (the *Us* is important!); just use it." Susan reached for another paper; Tilly tore three sheets apart (the inner rage was now directed toward a "thing") and then began to draw. The big stack of paper had symbolized love—a love large enough to be shared without loss. Some weeks later Tilly's mother told the caseworker, with whom she had interviews, with tears in her eyes, "Look in the waiting room where Tilly is waiting for the group to start. Just look!" There was Tilly placing a baby doll carefully into a doll carriage, cooing over her—Tilly, who had not touched a doll since the birth of her baby sister!

2. Relationship Among Group Members

This latter example has moved us already from the discussion of the relationship of the group worker to the individual member to the constant involvement of the group worker with the relations of

members with each other—his not only being aware of the group
process but of his responsibility to work with it. Group work is not
work with an individual against the background of a group. It is
individualized work with group members in and through the group.
The group worker's role is to forward the relationships of its separate
members and to make this relationship the most significant one. This
is one of the most important attributes of the group work skill. It is
also one of the frequent sources of frustration to the beginning group
worker who complains, "I can't always say I have helped with this or
that—the group members do so much for each other!" This becomes
in the long run his greatest pride and satisfaction: to have helped
members to help each other instead of becoming dependent on him.

There frequently have been discussions as to whether the group
approach or the individual interview is the more helpful method to
people who need assistance with their social functioning. This kind
of discussion is senseless, just as senseless as the indiscriminate use of
the group approach simply because it has become a "fad." Most people need at certain times help through either one or the other method
or both together. Neither one is auxiliary to the other. Each is to be
used when it is appropriate. Both methods in social work—casework
and group work—have many media in common. Purposeful and
voluntary relationship is the major tool of both methods, but each
method has certain unique characteristics with different meanings to
the individual client or group member. What, for instance, is unique
in the casework situation, that does not exist in the group work situation? It is the complete attention that the helping person gives to a
specific individual at a given time. The client may know that there
are others who also receive the caseworker's attention—he might even
resent this at times—but at the given time he receives full and un-
divided attention. He can also rely completely on the confidentiality
of whatever is discussed because of the caseworker's being profession-
ally bound to this. These are two important and unique aspects of the
casework situation (or any other individual-to-individual treatment
situation).

What, then, is unique in the group work situation that is not
found in the casework situation? It is being surrounded by others "in
the same boat," by equals, by being not only a client, but also a
"member." It allows for a feeling of identification that is impossible to
achieve on an individual basis with even the most accepting social
caseworker, because of his role—known to the client—as the helping

person. It allows for reassurance, but it also confronts the group member with people who are not bound by the professional principle of "acceptance." They will therefore express themselves and relate themselves to others on the level of "equals"; they will express hostility, anger, or disgust as well as love and tenderness, and express it on a personal level. This they experience as in life outside the group meetings, but with the help of the group worker.

The relationship with the group worker must always be shared with others in the group, hence it is not surprising that sibling rivalry is frequently relived and worked through in groups.

Confidentiality, important in certain groups with which the group worker works, is not a matter of certainty as it is in the casework process. It must be established by a special and voluntary effort on the part of group members; they must each be involved in the responsible action demanded of them through a specific act.

Awareness of the unique aspects of each method will help ease the tension of rivalry and will permit the approach to be employed that is best suited to the needs of the particular people who come for help in a given situation.

The relationship among members becomes important in the group for both diagnostic and treatment purposes. Tilly could not work through her sibling rivalry without meeting a real Susan, but she had to meet her under the protection of the group worker.

Example

A young adult coed group had met in a local YMCA for a long time.

George said he wished he could have more poise. He always felt like an outsider wherever he goes and has never really belonged in any group. Sue asked whether he felt part of this one. He said he thought he did belong, since everyone asked where he had been if he missed a meeting. But he wanted to tell them something today. For a long time the group members had been going to a coffee shop after meetings. Recently he had started going with them, but he never ordered anything. Last week one of them offered to buy him some coffee. He wanted them to know that he has the money and could order coffee, but he is always anxious that he is too clumsy and will spill it.

Janet said, "You sound like me. I'm always spilling things."

Ernest said, "Come on along today. If you spill coffee, I'll knock over the nearest chair and nobody will even notice you." Everybody, including George, laughed. Later George joined the group in the coffee shop.

We see the comfort derived by the admission and sharing of what was for one member a painful feeling of inadequacy. This is possible only if the group has experienced this kind of sharing as a part of its work and play together. We see the help that comes from one group member's helping George to feel that he is not so alone in this feeling of being "clumsy" (Janet) and how another one (Ernest) helps by promising active support and by allowing for the feeling that this is not as serious a defect as George thinks. Laughter is one of the greatest human assets, if it is well-meaning and not derisive. It occurs frequently in groups, because of the informal situation and the interaction with equals.

But group members also can pose demands; they do not allow for easy withdrawals from problems. Here is the excerpt from a record of a group of women patients in a mental hospital.

Example

The group had been talking about crying. Bertha said, "I can cry, but what's the use?" W. said, "Crying is certainly an acceptable way of telling someone that you're angry, isn't it?" Again Bertha said, "What's the use?" She began going over her life story with the other patients. They commented, asked questions and tried to help her understand more clearly what she was saying. Miriam said, "But don't you see? These are only the problems you are facing now, but they're not the cause?" It was interesting to note the patience and understanding that Gert demonstrated in trying to lead Bertha into some kind of acceptance of the fact that these were the effects rather than the causes. At one point Bertha ran out of the room to get her Bible, and said, "See, I just want to show you I'm trying to get better by reading helpful Bible passages." Ina said, "Reading the Bible may help, but it is no substitute for dealing with your problems yourself with the help of your doctor."

Bertha is not allowed to run away from responsibility in relation to her problems. Gently, but firmly, other group members let her know this. It will be harder for her to shrug this off than the remarks of a person in authority whom she regards as the "healthy one" who might not understand. Her own co-sufferers hold her to the need to work on her problems.

There is always a blending of the group worker's efforts with those of the members. And there is nothing more therapeutic, satisfying or growth-producing than to experience the knowledge that one can help another person. The *mutual* helping process of members is possible in the group, while it is not possible in the worker-client relationship. It is a vital part of the group work method to enhance opportunities for this.

Example

A group worker recorded: Although the men went as a group, we split up on reaching the shopping center (to reduce the conspicuous aspect). We gathered again as a group later and returned to the hospital as a group. But each had had an individual experience. And each had also had a sharing experience. Mr. Kidd was wrapped up in his problem when we started out. As the group split up, he and Mr. Eisen went with me.

We passed a book shop. I noticed a new book with a huge swastika on the cover. Knowing that Mr. Eisen had spent years in a concentration camp, I watched him as he approached the book. He stood for a long time in front of it, then shuddered and uttered a disgusted sound. He said, "It's awful." Mr. Kidd had become fascinated by a lighted globe and was twirling it on its stand. I walked over to him with Mr. Eisen and asked Mr. Eisen where he had come from. He said, "Berlin." Finding this on the globe, I also found Baltimore, and showed, with spread fingers, how far he had come. He looked up and smiled broadly. Mr. Kidd stood at his side and muttered, "Gee . . ." Later, in the coffee shop, Mr. Eisen began to shake violently. Other people in the restaurant were looking in our direction. Mr. Kidd reached over and placed his hand lightly on Mr. Eisen's arm and the tremors subsided. When Mr. Eisen began shaking again, Mr. Kidd repeated his remedy, with the comment, "It works," and then smiled softly at Mr. Eisen who smiled back.[7]

7   Robert Neubauer, "Agency Function as a Dynamic of the Social Group Work Process for the Realization and Enhancement of Change in the Long

What deep satisfaction for Mr. Kidd to discover that "It works" and that the "it" is he; what a powerful way of pulling him out of his self-concern! And what comfort to Mr. Eisen to experience this human kindness, spontaneously given, after he just had relived the horrors of his past.

Support

Sometimes group members need much support to be able to respond to others, and it must come first from the group worker. The following example presents work with a group of Bluebirds (9 year-old girls), as recorded by the group worker:

Example

Everyone was very busy and I had a little time to talk with Katie. I realized that Katie had so little relationship with anyone in the group that it would be necessary for me to develop a strong relationship with her to make her feel that she had support in me. The opportunity for talking with an individual youngster is, of course, really difficult in such an active group, but since everyone was so busy and occupied right now, I sat down near where Katie was threading beads and started a conversation. I asked her what we had here she liked best.

"Beads," she said laconically. She showed me her chain. Beading was fun, I agreed. What else did she think was fun? She stared down on her work.

I told Katie that the reason I was here in this club was so I could help the girls to have fun. That didn't mean you had to do something all the time. It was all right to do nothing, if you liked this. But I was here so that when ever anyone needed me, they could come to me. Katie looked at me seriously, said nothing, but did not move away. I went on to say that I was wondering if it was a little hard when you come into a new club and meet new people. She looked at me very gravely. Still she did not speak. I said that it was always that way when we met new people and came to a new place. After awhile when you get used to people, it's easier. At this Katie nodded and smiled a bit. Apparently this little talk had helped. Not ten minutes later, Katie engaged in conversation with other children, something which she had not done so far in this meeting or in the last.

Hospitalized Patients in a State Mental Hospital," unpublished thesis, University of Pennsylvania, School of Social Work, 1961.

The group worker showed Katie that she understood the difficulty of being a newcomer and an isolate. She responded to the tangible interests of a little girl, but helped her to feel free to move toward others. Her concern was more on relationships with other members, although she foresaw the possibility of involving herself more with Katie than with the others. And she also helped Katie to feel free to drop an activity, if she so desired. Apparently this made it possible for her to move toward the other children.

Yet member-to-member relationships are not always helpful. Human beings have the capacity to love and support each other, but they have just as strong a capacity to hurt each other cruelly, either in deeds or words. Group relations in themselves are not always helpful. Those who completely rely on the natural course of the group process and advocate a complete non-interference, as some theorists have done, are not really aware of the strength of this process that can destroy people. I remember vividly one such group that I observed conducted under this theory:

Example

One boy, the leader in his group, used the others to torture one of the group who apparently was selected as his victim. They jeered at him and taunted him when he began to tremble with rage, frustration and fear. They chased him and poked him. When one of the boys refused to follow the order of the leader in this cruel game, the leader threw him down, sat on him and thumped this boy's head against the floor. During all this time the person who conducted the group made no move.

The children not only harmed one another physically, but they carried with them the conviction that this kind of acting-out was all right since it was done under the eyes of an adult. This is not group work. It is part of the social group work method to combine the use of *limitation* with acceptance. The judicious use of limitations can be guaranteed only through the process of understanding and diagnosis, and must never rely on dogmatic attitudes. At times, many outbursts of hostility must be accepted—even provoked, if this is the only way for the group member to work through those feelings. Yet he must be helped to do this in a way that is not harmful to others or to himself. Personal needs are always balanced by the needs and rights of others.

Let us look at an example which occurred in a group of delinquent boys in an institution:

Example

. . . It was a hot day, and the wind was blowing without relief. This weather seemed to make itself felt with everyone, and the boys were restless. Things went all right, however, until Ned and Larry got into a fight. Neither boy had any self-control, but Larry had a real fit and was dangerous. He threw stones and took up the scissors and a large pole. Fortunately, he is not very quick, so W. could get hold of him. W. held both his arms, talking in a soothing voice until he relaxed under her hands. The difficulty was that Ned did not let him alone, but again provoked him. Larry's rage mounted once more, and besides physical force he used terrible language. Again he reacted to the holding and the soothing words like somebody coming out of a trance. He then lay down on the ground, completely exhausted, sweat standing on his forehead. When he had rested a little, W. asked him if he wanted to draw and write out all his anger. He was perfectly willing to do this, and Ned immediately asked for paper too.[8]

The group worker understands the rivalry between the two boys, she knows of their backgrounds and of Larry's constant frustration because of his comparatively low intelligence. She realizes the influence of the environment, the weather. This understanding dictates the non-punitive attitude of the group worker, but it also demands her active interference in the fight: she knows that these boys can physically harm each other. She then tries to allow the anger to continue coming out, but through a less dangerous channel, thus not overstressing the pressure and helping the boys to experience less destructive ways of expressing their feelings. Another example of necessary limitation, because of possible psychological damage, is seen in the following excerpt:

Example

Phyllis, 6 years old, had a tragic history. Her father had died before the child was born. Mother had been hospitalized for a

8   Gisela Konopka, *Therapeutic Group Work With Children, op. cit.*, pp. 56-57.

long sickness over several years when Phyllis was two years old. She was left with a woman who "took care" of her by strapping her into a chair for the whole day, taking her up only when she was too soiled. No one had known about this or interfered until the mother returned to the home. By that time Phyllis was almost mute. She began to learn to walk quite rapidly, but was extremely hostile toward her mother and let her touch her only reluctantly; she kicked and bit her whenever possible.

Phyllis was placed in a group at the child guidance clinic because any undiluted contact with an adult alone provoked violent outbursts which could not be handled for hours.

When Phyllis saw the other children, she stood still, then glanced around and walked slowly up to them. She saw the table covered with pencils, drawing paper, clay, and dolls. With one sweeping movement everything was thrown to the floor. The group worker said quietly, "You can play with all those things, Phyllis. You can use them, no one will take them away from you." Phyllis looked surprised at this unexpected reaction and bent down to collect the dolls. But the fear of "losing" was again overwhelming. She lifted her skirt like an apron and dropped everything into it. Then, straightening up, she began to run around the room holding on to as many of the things she carried as was possible. She screamed like a wounded animal. At this time the group worker could feel that "acting out" was no longer a release, but an increase of pain, and also frightening to the other children. She opened her arms and caught Phyllis almost playfully. Phyllis began to sob. The group worker comforted her, but released her quickly since she knew about Phyllis' fear of women. She turned to the other children and said that Phyllis had never had many toys and had had a hard time. Would they like to bring her some of the dolls that had fallen down? With the compassion so common to children who have suffered, Ellen and Rachel quickly picked up some dolls for Phyllis and then offered her some of the cookies prepared for a snack. Phyllis was in this way relieved of the adult presence and could get used to it with the help of the other children.

The group worker had set a limit to strong acting-out behavior. The way in which it was done was dictated by her understanding of the individual and the group situation, using herself, interaction among the children and "objects" (e.g. the dolls, etc.).

In adult autonomous groups the problem of help with relationships among group members is often more difficult than with children. The group worker respects the right of members to determine their group association, and yet must help particular individuals not to be harmed either by being censured by others or by being removed from the group, especially if they seem to need the group and if the group can carry them.

The following example is an extract from the records of a group meeting in a community center. The group consisted of adults suffering from muscular dystrophy; its purpose was to provide a normal social outlet for the members:

Example

After Jim's election to the vice-presidency and his resignation, his relationships in the group deteriorated once more to a point where the question of expulsion from the group was raised.

At the 24th session, Louise said she wanted to raise something with the group.

"Jim shows no interest in this group," she said. "He makes no effort, he just carps and criticizes and is displeased all the time but he is quite willing to ride along and take, take, take and give nothing . . . I think it is about time we called a halt. Maybe he just takes this group for granted."

Allan said, ". . . frankly some of us are not interested in carrying him on our backs any longer."

Ernie said, "On this, I'm forced to go along with Louise and Allan. This man has demonstrated that he has no interest in the group, only in himself. . . ."

Jim cried out, "Whatever I do is no good. If I talk it is no good. If I keep quiet it is no good."

Allan said ". . . He feels he has us over a barrel because we accept the group idea and he doesn't. But if we get tired of carrying him and rebel, then he hollers 'unfair.' How much of that can you take?"

Ernie said, "What do you want to do about it?"

Louise said, "What does Jim have to say?"

Jim said, "You're against me because I'm wealthier than you."

Ernie said, "You always pull in that money talk. You never try to get into the group. You back away from us. You consistently disagree and criticize. What is with you?"

Louise asked, "Are you interested in coming here at all?"

Jim said, "I just want to be quiet here. You didn't make me vice-president with a full heart."

Ernie said, "I'm here only 6-7 months but I've seen the deals you pulled. Can't you make an effort in our direction . . . ?"

Allan broke in and said, "It isn't as though this is the first time. It has happened countless other times . . . I don't consider him a member. He's just something we carry on our back."

Ernie said, "It's true, Jim. You pull your backside away from us all the time. You wheel over to the window and turn your back on us. If I go over to talk to you, you pull away. Tell me, if you sit on your fat prat with your back toward us, how are we supposed to know what is bothering you?"

Allan said, "I propose we give you a rest period away from the group. Otherwise we won't solve the problem."

Ernie said, "That would have to be put up to the whole group."

Jim said, "If you want to throw me out, throw me out but give me back my quarters I put in for dues."

Ernie said, "There you go with the money bit again . . . We are willing to give you a hand up. But if this keeps up, we'll bump you for sure. As I see it, you're on probation now . . . If things don't get better, if you don't straighten out and fly right, you're kissed off."

Allan said, "You are really giving him another chance. Then we'll have the same thing, over and over again."

Ernie said, "I do believe that every man has an inherent right to another chance."

Louise said, "Up until Jan. 15th. Then if he doesn't have an interest, he's through."

Ernie said, "Let's put it to a vote. Either he improves or he is bumped."

Allan said, "But we did that before, last year, and he improves for a little while till the crisis is passed and then it is the same thing again."

Ernie said, "As president, I will accept the responsibility of enforcing this by Jan. 15. If Jim louses up again, I'll have to take the responsibility of putting it up to the membership to vote to expel him." Then Ernie turned to the worker and said, "Do we have the right to expel a member?" W. said, "Yes, the group has the right to do so."

Ernie said, "Then I call for a vote. Either Jim shows a desire to be part of the group by Jan. 15th or out he goes." He went around the room for the vote. Ten were present. Anna and Ruth were absent. Louise voted yes; George, no; Bert, yes; Harry, yes; Sue, yes; and Allan, yes. Ernie who was president and chairing the meeting did not vote. Jim did not vote and Roger was asleep. (I had a feeling Roger was playing asleep as a way of not participating in the proceedings. Roger has fallen asleep on other occasions too but it hardly seemed likely he could have slept through the ruckus of this discussion. He fights Jim on a personal basis but he doesn't participate in any joint criticism of him.) This was the first time Bert and Sue had voted yes in a direct censure of Jim.

Ernie then turned to Jim and said, "I know how miserable it is to be censured publicly. But we had no choice. You have forced us to this. But I want to know. Do you understand what we have been saying? Do you understand our vote and do you accept the decision?"

Jim said (and it was amazing after all the rejection and caustic punishment he had taken), "I accept the decision." It is clear that Jim will hang onto the group on any basis as long as he can. During the next few months Jim obviously made an effort to control open incidents of hostility to group members. He did not call people names or attack them in a biting way. He participated to some extent in a number of group efforts and even began to speak to Allan though he continued to hold his distance from Louise whose sharp tongue he feared. Jan. 15th came and went and nothing about Jim was mentioned.

On March 19th Ernie announced that he had been asked to raise something by Jim.

He recalled that back a number of months ago the group had censured Jim and put him on probation till Jan. 15th. If he improved and handled himself as a group member, fine, otherwise the president would raise it and the group could consider dropping him as a member. Ernie said he had not raised it but Jim had raised it with him and said he wanted to know where he stood, whether he was still on the hook or off. Ernie said he had not raised it because he felt that things were going along OK but Jim wanted to know.

The worker said that Jim had a right to know.

Louise asked Ernie for the floor and he gave it to her. Louise said, "I think Jim has shown a lovely improvement . . ." then she added, half in a joke, but half in accumulated resentment, "put him on trial for another year. . . ." Allan started to make jokes and kibbitz and Ernie took a few of them and then told Allan to cut the comedy, that this was serious business . . . When Allan saw that Ernie was annoyed and wanted this handled on a different level, he said with some seriousness, "Let's forget about the probation." Everyone in the group concurred.

Ernie said, "Then that's settled." I asked for the floor. I said that I was glad that Jim had raised it because it showed that Jim was concerned about his role and relationship in the group. I said that everyone was aware that Jim had made an effort and that when he had stepped out of line in the group, he had taken the criticism that came with it and handled it in a different way in the recent period.

I felt that what had been proved in this whole episode was that the people in our group felt that relationships were important and were willing to struggle not just to maintain relationships but to maintain them in a certain way, with some dignity and standards about the way people live together. I felt that in the past Jim had seriously provoked the people in the group, almost to a point where there was little reason to feel he could use a group experience. That the people in the group had been able to insist on certain changes and that Jim had been able to meet those demands, and had valued his being in the group enough to want to change, meant that the value of people in our group had a top priority. I felt that the people in the group had achieved an important human thing in salvaging and developing a relationship.

Ernie said, "We feel good about it too." Ernie then turned to program arrangements . . .[9]

9   Morris L. Eisenstein, Project Director; Fannie P. Eisenstein, Group and Research Worker, Excerpt of Records taken from Fourth Annual Report of the Muscular Dystrophy Social Group, Sept. 1958—June 1959, Process Record, 48th Session, Brooklyn: United Community Centers, undated, mimeographed.

No dramatic "personality change" had occurred in Jim. Yet the group pressure—and the willingness of the group to work things out with him—had helped him change the behavior that had previously hurt others and himself.

The group worker had let the group act. These were adults and they had met a long time together. If this had occurred at a very early meeting, the group worker could not have let the group process work quite as independently; it might have resulted in Jim's removal from the group. But at this point the group members carried through in an adult way. Jim had to learn the consequences of snubbing and hurting others, in a situation he obviously wanted and needed. The non-intervention of the group worker in the meeting recorded was by no means "inactive." It was a conscious and attentive holding back. Later, the group worker purposefully made the members conscious of what had happened.

3. Verbal Communication

We saw in the previous discussion the importance of guided group interaction as a helping tool in social group work. Relationships among human beings—their feelings and their thoughts—are expressed in many different ways. One of the major ways of expression is words. Just as in individual interviews, the group worker also uses this form of communication purposefully and skillfully. Encouragement of interaction in discussion groups is a significant quality of social group work. A discussion group where the person in charge questions one member after the other and where each responds in turn is not group work. The group worker always tries to increase the interaction and mutual help among the members.

Here is an excerpt from a meeting of parents of mentally retarded children who met regularly with a group worker to help them think through possible plans for the children. The excerpt presents a second meeting with this group:

Example

We started out talking of the feelings of disappointment that we have in the children. Mr. Lowry brought up the fact that he had felt disappointed and there was a general feeling of denial

in the air. Mr. Jones, upon encouragement from the worker, commented that he was concerned about the things that his child
was being cheated of, mentioning the educational and peer relationship problems. There was a defensive feeling when W.
suggested that everybody had feelings of disappointment and
noted the naturalness of these feelings. Mrs. Sims brought up
her feelings of disappointment that Susan could not be "the oldest sister" and be a leader to the other kids. She stated some of
her desires. Mrs. Jewel suggested that perhaps the fact that her
oldest child was the satisfactory child made it more reasonable
for her to accept John. The group did not really tolerate her
denial. Mr. Vetter picked up and stated that he felt that it was
something different from feelings, and described his fear of the
future. Mrs. Jewel could understand that better. She said she,
too, was very much afraid of what would happen if anything
happened to her or her sister, for who would be interested in her
son?

From the beginning the group worker had created a climate that
allowed the parents to speak freely about their children and their own
reaction to them. This is not easy—and we see the forms of denial, of
trying to present the problems as comparatively small. Yet when they
talk to one another they begin identifying with one another and become freer with others, and especially more honest with themselves. A
mother of a very disturbed youngster said after such a meeting, "It
helps me so much to hear what someone else thinks and lives through.
It is a comfort to see that I am not the only one who has these problems. It is even more important that I begin to think, 'Well, this is
perhaps the same with me—or with Herb,' and I learn."

Group work allows for the "anonymity of insight." A person may
gain insight without necessarily having to admit it or to pronounce it.
At times this saves the person's self-esteem and allows him the privacy
of discovery of his innermost drives, without having to admit them to
someone else. Sometimes free and open sharing of feelings is most
important and necessary, at other times, the knowledge is beneficial
to the individual alone. When I hear of great pressure exerted on
group members to say whatever they feel I can't help but think of the
beautiful passage in Steinbeck's Grapes of Wrath:

. . . Uncle John's eyes were tired and sad. "I been secret all my days," he said. "I done things I never tol' about."

Ma turned from the fire. "Don' go tellin', John," she said. "Tell 'em to God. Don' go burdenin' other people with your sins. That ain't decent."

"They're a-eatin' on me," said John.

"Well, don' tell 'em. Go down the river an' stick your head under an' whisper 'em in the stream."

Pa nodded his head slowly at Ma's words. "She's right," he said. "It gives a fella relief to tell, but it jus' spreads out his sin."[10]

"Talking out" may mean relief to the troubled person, but it may also increase his disturbance or guilt feelings.

Because of the high value group work places on participation, group discussion is used for many purposes other than those of the therapeutic or social action variety. The capacities to listen to different points of view, to work through conflict, to argue rationally and to allow for rationality in those with whom one does not agree, are necessary for a living democracy and are not inborn.

Example

A group of teenagers in a settlement house complained violently about the restrictions imposed on them by the city curfew law. It was too stringent and completely unreasonable. John said, "We just won't obey it." Pat said, "I am scared to be picked up, but I'll come along." Ernest stabbed viciously at the table; Jim said that this was the way it always was, "You can't do a thing. They just do this to spite us."

The group worker wondered whether they knew how it happened that this ordinance had been passed. No, they did not. He explained, often interrupted by the angry youngsters. He then asked them again to give all the reasons they had against the curfew law. Jim said, "Why? We just talk about it." The group worker said that people can do something about ordinances or laws, if they care enough, find good enough reasons and join together to present them to the ones who make those laws. Slowly a less emotional discussion started.

The meeting ended with a resolution to work further on this.

10 John Steinbeck, *Grapes of Wrath*, copyright 1939 by John Steinbeck. Reprinted with permission of The Viking Press, Inc.

In the course of the next weeks a project started, with the youngsters taking responsibility for writing out their reasons against the curfew law, discussing this with others and their parents and bringing the pro's and con's to the group meeting. They visited their alderman with the group worker, and were surprised to find him interested. He suggested that they should attend a meeting at the city council to see how business was conducted. The youngsters were especially pleased when the mayor invited them after the meeting to visit him in his office.

They drafted a new suggestion for a different curfew law—a far cry from their original rejection of everything the law stood for.

We see here how help is given with learning of action in a democracy and how, at the same time, this means an inner growing-up process, which is frequently left uncompleted even in adults (one need only observe actions in parliaments or the United Nations). The group worker's responsibility and skill lay in the creation of an atmosphere free enough to allow the youngsters to express their spontaneous resentment, then in helping them with rational approaches to the problems and allowing an outlet for their disagreement in the form of responsible action as opposed to simple rebellion.

It is part of the skill in group discussion leading to bring in everybody, and yet not force anyone to participate in a way that makes him conspicuous or very uncomfortable. And it is also necessary to know when *not* to use group discussions, when a simple statement of facts, for instance, is far more appropriate. Discussion leading is of such importance in the use of the group work method that it is often taught as a separate course in the education of group workers.[11]

4. Non-verbal Communication

Verbal interaction is only one way in which human beings relate to each other. Group work, because of its origin in informal education

---

[11]   See Gisela Konopka, "A Brief Note on the Differential Use of Group Discussion," *The Social Service Review*, Vol. XXXII, No. 3, Sept. 1958, pp. 287-289.

and recreation, has always been especially attuned to the many other media through which help with interrelations can be given. The "use of program" was looked upon disdainfully at one time by those who considered activities superficial, but it is increasingly recognized as a significant helping tool.

Play for children is their most important expression; it is their occupation, not something "aside." In play they express feelings, thoughts, anger and love, fear and the conquering of fear. In play they begin to feel their strength and learn the despair of defeat. Adults need "play" in forms different from those of children, but it is necessary to both. The word "re-creation" is a very beautiful one. It includes the idea of creative work, of re-creating capacities. A student once said, "I think my mother never played." When he was asked what she did in the evenings when the family relaxed, he replied, "She was always doing embroidery." Then he realized that this was her play—not an active one but a quiet enjoyment of the lovely colorful strands of yarn. This was her recreation.

Activities, doing things together (or alone, when one needs this), allow for much expression, for identification with people whom one admires and needs, for a feeling of accomplishment, for "telling" without words. Peter taught me that, when as a young—or at least a new group worker—I tried to bring him to tell me about his worries. Peter was 11 years old and had already been in an institution for delinquents and was on parole. He was drawing and I tried to talk with him. He looked up, "Oh, Gisa, I am not much of a talker." But he continued to draw intensely. And I learned that, by glancing on that paper, I could learn more about Peter than he could ever tell anyone, since he really "was not much of a talker." The wild lines, the red and the deep black, the burning airplanes crashing down and the little boy running from a huge whirring propeller—in his drawing Peter had "said" all there was to say about his inner turmoil. When Peter leaned back against me when we sat in a circle on the floor, throwing a ball around, I knew he was yearning for a mother—but he never could say it in words.

Work with delinquents has shown frequently that they can not be reached by interviews. Yet sometimes hours spent without a word with an adult—cutting wood or fishing, for example—have made the first identification with a probation officer possible. Many youngsters are not as verbal as university students and are not as introspective.

Changes in their feelings and attitudes come more from *experiencing* than through talking out and interpretation. The purposeful and skilled use of program is, in my opinion, the most hopeful tool in working with the large number of young delinquents who act out. Since most delinquent acts are committed in small groups, it is important to keep the youngsters together to allow them the feeling of security they gain from each other while helping them with a change of values.

A young probation officer in Germany reported about his group work with 17 and 18 year olds under his supervision:

Example

These were boys difficult to reach. They had been small children during the hungry war years and were reared by parents who had not stood up for human values—many of them had quickly changed from Nazism to a sullen neutrality. The boys were quite cynical and had a "chip on the shoulder." They trusted no adult and complained that they were not trusted. To them, words were only shields hiding other meanings—this applied to themselves as well as to others. The probation officer was just another hated and rather despised adult.

The probation officer had started weekly group meetings with the boys. He had suggested a bicycle tour of about ten days in the summer. During those meetings they prepared for the tour, fixed up the bicycles, studied maps of where to go. The trip appealed to the boys, since they had not enough money to go by themselves and they had to report anyhow to the probation officer. It was a "convenience." The probation officer knew that he took a risk. He knew that bicycling meant riding on narrow paths, one after another. Any boy could disappear easily. Nevertheless, he made up his mind not to ride as the last, so as not to give the boys the impression that they were being watched.

Already during the first days of the trip he felt a different atmosphere in the group. Somehow the informal contact, the removal from the "office," seemed to change the relationship. The boys were less sullen. There was joking. Evenings in youth hostels brought them together on an equal footing with youngsters from universities, some of whom were foreign students, something they had not experienced previously.

On the fifth day they took quarters overnight in a barn of a convent. When the probation officer woke up, the boys had disappeared. He was frightened and deeply disappointed. Then he looked out of the window and saw:

In the farmyard stood the convent's truck. His boys were helping the sisters load the sacks of grain on the truck. They went back and forth with the heavy sacks on their backs following with obvious pleasure the directions of the sisters.

"I was ashamed of myself," the probation officer reported. "The boys' chip on the shoulder was not so irrational. I who had worked with them for quite a period of time, too, had doubted them."

The sisters prepared a wonderful breakfast for the boys. The probation officer had never seen the boys so glowing, so satisfied. He never let on about his doubts; he asked only why they had not awakened him too. One of the boys said a bit sheepishly, "We just liked to do this all by ourselves." And another one added, "You have enough work with us!" There were no more words, but a bond, a special positive one, had started between the boys and their probation officer.

I found that in European countries the group work method is frequently used in probation and parole work. It may have to do with a general recognition of the fact that many people are not very verbal and have a strong need to overcome remnants of an authoritarian culture. The group lends itself especially to this. An Italian social worker suggested that fear of group work in her country is related to remnants of fascism, that the social worker wants to be totally in "control" of the situation and is afraid of the strength that comes from group associations. She considered group work a method, indispensable in overcoming the old authoritarian patterns.

In the United States the use of the group work method in correctional services, especially outside the institution, is still comparatively new, but is spreading.

The use of non-verbal material is also important in working with adults. Family Life education has been predominantly directed to middle class parents who can communicate, and its importance must not be underestimated. Yet too often persons with less verbal capacity miss this help. Group work's tool of "program" allows for entrance into families who need help with rearing children, but who cannot easily participate in groups which use the discussion method exclusively.

Example

A settlement house in a low-income area in a highly industrial city offered a day camp for 1st grade children. The mothers of the children were invited to come one evening a week to make games or toys for the children. The purpose was threefold: to make these things, since little money was available for the program; to help the mothers learn more about the needs of their children, and to help the mothers raise their own self-confidence in dealing with their children—something that they seemed to lack.

While the hands were occupied, the talk was lively and unself-conscious. The following is an excerpt from one of the meetings; it shows the interplay between "doing" and "thinking," "feeling," "learning":

Mrs. Shaw worked on making a jigsaw puzzle. She exclaimed, half-angrily, half laughingly, "Now look! My lines look as crooked as if Sheila had made them." Sheila was her 6-year-old daughter, the fifth of seven children. She was excessively shy and always had a beaten look. She seemed to wake up only when stories were told. One day she had surprised everyone by spinning her own story in front of the whole group, showing much imagination and actual command of language. This had happened when the children had sat quietly around the group worker who sat with Sheila huddled on her lap.

Mrs. Shaw continued, while erasing and redrawing her lines: "That kid drives me crazy. She is so clumsy; she can't do a thing!"

Mrs. Aaron, next to her, said, "Oh, I was just such a kid! My mother always gave me so many whippings, I didn't dare to try anything. But today I'm a pretty good cook, and when Sam (her husband) was out of a job, I got myself some work in the factory and I was no worse than the other girls."

Mrs. Shaw said, "I just get so mad at her!" And then, with a little laugh, "But just look at my lines! They're no better than Sheila's."

The group worker told Mrs. Shaw about Sheila's lovely story-
telling. Mrs. Shaw looked surprised.

We see here a mother's beginning to see her daughter in a less negative light. It started with her realization that she, too, could not do
everything right. She then received some more understanding through
another woman who identified with Sheila and could show that she
had become quite an adequate adult. The group worker added an
observation of Sheila's strength. There was no "interpretation," no
drawing of attention to what Mrs. Shaw experienced—this would have
been inappropriate in helping Mrs. Shaw. Yet she *felt* a change in her
understanding of Sheila, as seen in her comparing herself again with
Sheila.

The group worker continued to work with both Sheila and her
mother through the rest of that summer. Sheila gradually lost her
beaten dog air. Her warm relationship to the group worker, the experience of doing some things well, the relationship with other children
who did not make many demands on her, and especially her mother's
new attitude all contributed to this change.

Appropriate use of program involves knowledge of the specific psychological impact of materials or games, and much imagination. No
group worker can be adequate in the use of all kinds of activities. He
either uses resources outside the group or involves group members as
helpers. He uses his self-awareness so as not to impose his own interests, but to consider the needs of the group members. He also is aware
of cultural differences in the use of program. The members of a
Golden Age Club, for example, told a group worker that they would
like to discontinue the meetings where they sang with a young enthusiastic volunteer. The group worker was surprised since this club
had asked especially for someone who could lead them in singing. He
learned, however, that the young man had listened rather disdainfully
to the kind of songs the group wanted to sing and then had proceeded
to teach them Bach cantatas.

The psychological impact of many materials still needs research.
Group workers have learned by experience and from educators, especially from preschool and kindergarten teachers, and more recently
from occupational therapists. There are materials such as wood, paints,
clay, and so forth, that lend themselves particularly to more solitary
activities in a group—necessary sometimes at the initial meetings of

groups. Some materials allow for more working out of feelings than others. Wood is stubborn, resistant, and needs an orderly state of mind if one wants to accomplish something. Yet scrapwood that can be wasted may be helpful to children who have to work out anger. They can hammer, cut or nail at will. Clay is soft and yielding, and can be shaped and reshaped—wonderful for the very insecure person since it permits hesitation, dreaming. Yet clay can be used differently; a very aggressive boy wedged the clay with vengeance, threw it hard to get out the air bubbles, and almost boxed with it. Weaving demands calm and helps the withdrawn youngster to accomplish something. It surely was a misplaced activity in an institution for delinquent girls where the girls—full of conflicts, drives, suffering, and resentment—were supposed to weave lovely smooth cloth out of fine yarn. And some materials can lead to surprises! Elmer, tiny, undernourished and "tough," with a string of thefts behind him, reached constantly for the lively colored felt and sewed (!) with strong bright colored yarn, obviously working out all his yearning to get out of his drab surroundings and allowing himself to be the soft, playful child hid behind the tough exterior.

There are also the materials and activities that allow for more interaction: the cook-out, the making a fire, story telling, the cardboard boxes to be made into a puppet theatre, dramatics. The latter is almost indispensable in good group work for a variety of purposes: Dramatics allow for expression of feelings. Many people cannot express themselves openly. They can do it though, when allowed to play a part in a play.

Example

Ella was always polite, always doing everything asked of her. She was a "prim little old lady" and the girls in her camp cabin misused her by letting her do the disagreeable work, but gave her little recognition in return. The group worker discussed with the camp counselor how important it was to let Ella come out of her shell—she was a very unhappy girl.

The occasion came when the cabin members suggested they put on a play for a camp fire. They wanted to write it themselves. It should be about parents and kids and school and camping. Sylvia tried to "cast" the girls, assigning Ella the role of an older sister. The counselor, sensitive to the opportunity for Ella, suggested that no casting be done in the beginning. Each girl should just speak up spontaneously whenever she felt she wanted to enter. Thus they could work out the story. They began this in the evening with the lights out.

Out of the dark came Ella's voice, angry, obstreperous, resistant. She took on the role of the youngster who did not want to go to camp, who talked back to her parents, who finally went, but who instigated all kinds of practical jokes against the girls in her tent. She played out all her resentment. The girls were amazed and impressed.

Ella's behavior outside the play did not change overnight. Yet during rehearsals she became more and more alive. The girls began to treat her less like a doormat.

The final presentation of the play brought huge applause. A sparkling Ella danced around the fire and, for the rest of the camp season, she was a pleasant, and no longer a submissive camper.

Ethel Waters, the great actress, wrote beautifully about what the acting out of a dramatic part meant to her emotionally and how it changed her behavior toward others:

> I could not convince them that the role gave me the sort of release I'd long needed. Being Hagar softened me, and I was able to make more allowance for the shortcomings of others. Before that I'd always been cursing outside and crying inside. Playing in *Mamba's Daughters* enabled me to rid myself of the terrible inward pressure, the flood of tears I'd been storing up ever since my childhood.[12]

For some people even the personal presentation of a role in a drama is too threatening, too revealing. Yet they yearn to have the feeling of release Ethel Waters talks about. Puppets are a good medium for them because they present a mask. Ella found her courage first in the dark; others need the little dolls to hide them.

Moreno has developed dramatics into a treatment medium for mentally sick people.[13] The use of this technique requires special train-

---

[12] From: *His Eye Is on the Sparrow* by Ethel Waters. Copyright 1950, 1951 by Ethel Waters and Charles Samuels. Reprinted by permission of Doubleday and Company, Inc.

[13] See Jacob L. Moreno, *Psychodrama*, Beacon, N.Y.: Beacon House, 1946-1959.

ing and is not usually part of the equipment of the social group worker. Moreno's method is helpful to certain patients and under certain conditions, but—as is true of all techniques—it must not be used without diagnostic thinking. The social group worker uses dramatics like any other tool in relation to his understanding of the individual and his situation. Jack Simos describes such diagnostic thinking in his stimulating book *Social Growth Through Play Production*.[14] In the following excerpt he presents the impact of participation in dramatics on one boy in a treatment institution. The boy is named by the character he portrayed in the play.

Example

Moody was a rather wiry, dark-complexioned, black-haired boy, who had been at the institution for about four years, although during this time, on one occasion, he had been tried in a foster home where his demanding attitude and his fidgety restlessness could not be tolerated, and from which he was, therefore, returned to the institution. He was sixteen years old and the only full orphan residing at the treatment center, his adoptive parents having been killed in an accident when he was eight years old. Although electroencephelograms did not yield positive evidence, there was suspicion of brain damage deduced from his behavior and from psychological testing. At any rate, he had been dealt with as such. His overall IQ was 85 and he functioned on a dull, normal level. He had suffered temper tantrums and outbursts of rage which were so severe that he frothed at the mouth. He was so completely out of control that it required three adults, on one occasion, to contain him.

. . . He was a boy who suffered failure after failure; in his four years at the institution he could not point to one successful achievement. Yet he was selected not only for the play but for the prominent part of Moody. . . .

. . . Because he was so fidgety and easily distracted, he was often a disciplinary problem during rehearsals but not to the extent anticipated.

The trauma of the first run-through, . . . was too much for

---

14 Jack Simos, *Social Growth Through Play Production*, New York: Association Press, 1957.

him, however. He was so frustrated at missing some lines that he almost had a temper tantrum but managed to control himself, at least to the extent of running outside to let off steam. After calming himself, he returned and objectively studied the script to determine where he had slipped.

His portrayal was the most colorful and imaginative achievement in the group. . . . But he had no real difficulty with lines and thoroughly understood their meanings and the whole play. The one exception was a scene which called for resignation but which he insisted on interpreting as defiance. He could not seem to humble himself even in a play.

Needless to say, he received a great deal of praise for his performance and was looked upon with a new respect. His feeling of accomplishment could be literally observed in his bearing. His shoulders straightened: he carried himself more erect, and his whole demeanor took on a new look of confidence.

He also developed a greater self-control. Although he subsequently became involved in a few incidents where he overturned chairs and destroyed property, these never attained the degree of violence and uncontrollable rage which had characterized his temper tantrums heretofore.

In a psychological retesting shortly after his performance in the play it was discovered that his IQ was 101.[15]

The group worker had observed Moody's dramatic way of expressing himself (this was omitted in the excerpt quoted) and saw his possibility as an actor. Dramatics allowed Moody to express some of his own feelings (to see, for instance, that he could not portray resignation) but it also made demands of self-control on him through a medium he wanted, not through the hated adult authority alone. It also gave him the feeling of success, of being appreciated by others—a feeling so desperately needed by every human being and usually increasingly denied to those who need it most. And, as we find so frequently, the removal of emotional blocks allowed intelligence to function more freely.

Dramatic activities are an especially valuable program tool in group work, because they combine uniquely the opportunity for diagnostic

[15] *Ibid.*, pp. 99-102.

study, release of feelings, demand for a certain inner discipline, use of imagination, reliving of painful or joyful experiences, verbal and non-verbal expression and feelings of accomplishment and appreciation by others.

Children's play and games have many characteristics of dramatics. The doll family play of little girls or the fierce-pretended soaring into space of little boys fulfill similar needs. In an experiment with regressive shock therapy with highly disturbed psychotic patients, the social group worker and occupational therapist together made use of this knowledge. They considered normal play activities of the age group to which the patients were regressed and offered outlets for them in a more adult form. In case the patient should remember later, he should not feel embarrassed by having acted on a childish level. For example, adult women at a certain stage of regression were offered play with dolls, which they accepted with eagerness, and were told that they could sew and dress them for the children on the children's ward. They did use the dolls like children, but they were thus protected against any future embarrassment. They felt free to use the toys only when they were in a group. In the evaluation of the experiment it was acknowledged that patients seemed to make better progress when shock treatment was accompanied by this social experience. The results were not conclusive, however, and need further study.

Experiencing is one of the key words in social group work. Experiencing of relationships with a helping person, with equals, with things, with one's own feelings, thoughts, emotions, skills and interests. Group association always involves experiencing and learning. The group work skill enhances or corrects this experiencing through the conscious use of the media we have discussed. In the previous examples we saw their being used to help individuals in their normal growth problems, to help mentally or emotionally disturbed children or adults or those who have become delinquent. We saw the application of group work skill to social action. Because of this quality of realistic experiencing of oneself in relation to others, social group work is also well suited to help with the difficult problem of race relations and other inter-group tensions.

Legislation makes justice possible. Yet beyond this, *change of attitudes,* inner change of feelings toward other religions or races are necessary. Discrimination harms the one discriminated against as well as the one who discriminates. The group work approach allows for experiencing of differences and similarities and the working through of feelings about them. Once, belief in the ameliorative power of the group process was so great that it was assumed people would appreciate each other if they only met. This is true sometimes, but not always. It may also intensify each person's prejudices. Group work adds to the mere encounter of people the help and skill of a person, who uses all his understanding, his acceptance, his knowledge of how to work through conflicts and his appreciation of non-verbal media. Neighborhood and settlement houses, YM and YWCA's and other youth serving agencies have been in the forefront in using social group work to break through distrust between racial and religious groups.[16]

To illustrate the helping process of social group work through the use of program, relationship and verbal interaction, case material of group work is reproduced here as it was presented at the Annual Meeting of the American Orthopsychiatric Association in 1947:

Example

We usually think of the preschool child as least affected by racial or cultural tensions. Yet the four- and five-year-old early learns the attitudes of his environment. A small preschool group consisted of: Bert, a Jewish boy, age 4; George, a Negro boy, 4; Chris, 3½, and Jim, 4, two white boys of Irish-English parentage. Greatest anxiety in this group was seen in Bert, who was referred because of extreme aggressiveness with other children. He was removed from nursery school because he could not adjust to regulations. Bert was the youngest of three siblings with strict parents who had little understanding of and patience for the needs of a young child. They lived in one of the most dilapidated districts of the city with little playground space. In the neighborhood lived mostly people of Jewish and Italian background and Negroes. In the home were also the grandparents, orthodox Jews. It is clear that many other factors were involved to produce disturbance in Bert than his cultural background alone. In play inter-

---

[16] See Galen M. Fisher, *Citadel of Democracy*, Berkeley, Calif.: Howell-North Press, 1955; Dorothy I. Height, *Step by Step with Interracial Groups*, New York: Publication Services, National Board, Y.W.C.A. 1955; Eleanor L. Ryder, "Some Principles of Intergroup Relations as Applied to Group Work," *Social Work with Groups*, 1960, New York: N.A.S.W. 1960, pp. 52-61; Jack Weiner, "Reducing Racial and Religious Discrimination," *Social Work with Groups*, 1960, as cited, pp. 62-73.

views he showed much anxiety toward adults and a great need to release active energies. In the group he showed reluctance at first in playing with George, the colored child. Apparently helped by George's outgoing and warm-hearted behavior he soon teamed up with him. His conflict about being Jewish came into the open around Christmas time. The children listened intently to the *Night Before Christmas* when Bert suddenly pointed to Santa Claus saying, "Bad Santa Claus, I don't like him," and slapped the book shut.

Two weeks later, without any provocation, he suddenly shouted profanities, among them, "Dirty Jew, dirty Jew." Each time he said this he looked provokingly at the worker. Through the caseworker's contact with the mother we knew that Bert had only recently received a severe beating because he had said "Dirty Jew" at home. It was clear that the child was struggling with his own status in being Jewish.

It was planned to use the Christmas party the following week to show him that being Jewish was as good as belonging to any other religion. Bert was delighted with the Christmas tree. His mother had said that he felt deprived in not having one at home. He and his sister had rigged up an umbrella with cotton and twigs pretending this to be a Christmas tree, and hid it so the grandparents would not see it. At the Clinic he touched the twigs and the ornaments of the tree, exclaiming over them. When the children sang, the worker asked Bert whether they did not light candles at home too, and whether he did not want to sing his song for all of them. He hesitated, but when the worker herself started the Chanukkah Song, a very surprised and happy look came over his face. He sang while the other three boys admired the unusual language. Encouraged by the admiration of his little friends and the first recognition of his being Jewish by children who were not, he asked whether he might hold a candle. With the Christmas tree in the background, ice cream cone in one hand, and the candle in the other, Bert proudly said the Hebrew benediction. The importance of the event became clear when an excited and happy Bert ran downstairs at the end of the party and told his mother, "I lit the Christmas tree and I lit a candle and I sang a Chanukkah Song and she (pointing to the worker) knows it, too." Through this experience

Bert got a feeling of acceptance from the adult and from the other children who admired and enjoyed his performance. He was able to accept himself as a Jew among non-Jews.

The second group consists of four adolescent girls. Betty, age 13, was referred by Juvenile Court because of loitering, staying out nights, and conflict with her parents. She was a lively girl of Hungarian parentage, and Hungarian was spoken in the home. There were many family conflicts.

Harriet, age 16, an attractive, serious girl, who had been a recluse for three years, showed compulsive symptoms. Her movements were extremely slow. Psychiatric interviews helped to find the causal basis of the problems and some interpretations given by the psychiatrist helped her considerably. She expressed the desire to join a group at the Clinic to "get used to people." Harriet's father was dead and she lived with her mother and sister. Both parents had come from Germany.

Edith, 14, a tall and attractive colored girl, had been referred by Juvenile Court because of conflict with her parents. At the age of 11 she had given birth to a child. Edith was an ambitious girl who was intent on making good in school. She had insisted that she be allowed some social outlet and therefore was invited to join the group.

Dinah, a 15-year-old colored girl, was referred for severe psychosomatic symptoms, intense conflict with her mother, and strong sibling rivalry with two younger, more attractive sisters. Dinah's family lived in a housing project.

Expressions of tension in the racial and cultural area were innumerable. Betty, as member of a comparatively recent immigrant family, showed her insecurity when the girls talked about learning languages. She said, "I know another language, I know Hung . . . , I mean Latin, the way they sing in church." She was not able at this point to admit her Hungarian background. Two meetings later the girls played records. One of them was the Hungarian Rhapsody. Harriet said she loved classical music, that she thought this record beautiful. The worker said, "It is the Hungarian Rhapsody, it has the fire of Hungarian music." Betty looked pleased and said that she knew a little Hungarian, even spoke some words when the girls encouraged her to do so. Her language background had not only become acceptable but had even given her some status in the group. At this point Harriet mentioned that she knew a few German words, thus revealing her own background. Harriet's difficulty, closely related to her fear of contact with people, was in contact with the colored girls. She was much too gentle and polite to express these feelings in the presence of the girls, but at home she mentioned that it worried her when a colored girl hung her coat over her own coat. Because of the many contacts under various conditions offered by the group, Harriet found, much to her surprise, that she and Edith, one of the colored girls, had many interests in common. Both loved history, cooking and singing, and both heartily disliked arithmetic. Harriet exclaimed, "Why, I never thought we could like exactly the same things." Edith felt free to talk about her being a Negro. After feeling the acceptance of the worker, she could even ask about her worries over discrimination of the schools.

Dinah had a harder time. She was very conscious of her dark color and repeated that she liked Edith's light brown color and how pretty Harriet was. It helped a great deal when Edith and Harriet started commenting on some of Dinah's pretty dresses. At this time the worker brought a magazine to the group. While looking it over Dinah pointed to a blouse similar to her own and asked whether it was all right for her to wear a blouse with such a low-cut neckline. The worker answered (and she could do so genuinely) that this was especially suitable because she had such lovely smooth skin. The surprised look said more than words. From then on, Dinah took more care of her appearance, apparently accepting herself with more ease, and also began to discuss discrimination. The girls discussed the lynching of a Negro and compared it with Fascism in Germany. Dinah said, "I would never want to live there." Edith replied, "But we are not always treated right here either." The worker encouraged their conversation. Harriet agreed that things should be changed in race relationships.

Proof of Harriet's change in this respect was seen in the way she herself piled coats and jackets together without regard to whom they belonged. At the time of Harriet's referral to a neighborhood group the worker discussed with her whether it made any difference to her to be in a group with colored girls. Harriet said that she hardly knew the difference anymore, and added, "I was afraid of all girls a year ago, now I sometimes wonder why —and so I was even more afraid of them—but now I am no longer afraid, and it makes no difference."

In a group of 12-year-old boys there was apparent conflict between Aaron and Ralph. Aaron, a severely disturbed, 12-year-old Jewish boy, had a great need to point out his being Jewish, apparently testing whether others would accept him. Ralph, referred because of difficulties in school, was a very light colored boy, who appeared almost white. The father had deserted the home, and Ralph lived with an indulgent mother in poor economic circumstances.

In one of the meetings Ralph constantly taunted Aaron, who had said that he could not eat cookies because of the Passover holiday. Ralph said he would not like being Jewish, and when asked what he would like to be he quickly said, "Italian—because there are so many of them." Later he called Aaron "Moses." Aaron retaliated by saying that Jesus had not lived. Ralph turned to the worker and asked, "Did Jesus live?" And then, "Did Moses live?" Aaron insisted that his mother had told him Jesus never lived. Ralph said with great pride that Jesus had died on the cross. Seeing Aaron's unhappy face, the worker added that Moses died on a mountain seeing the Promised Land. Aaron added happily, "Yes, it was the Mount Sinai." A few minutes later Ralph asked Joe whether there were colored boys in his school. Joe said casually, "Only a few, but I like them." Ralph nodded his head "Yes?" Worker asked whether the color of people made any difference. Ralph, full of relief, said loudly, "It sure doesn't." Then he asked Aaron if he might use the jig-saw and when Aaron gave permission, he said, "Thank you, Aaron, thank you so much."

We see how these two boys, each insecure as members of two minority groups, attack the other minority group because of their own insecurity. Ralph showed his conflict with his own group when he expressed the wish to be Italian, this being a majority group in his neighborhood. The group situation allowed these two boys not only to express their feelings, but to do it without being hampered by an adult or forced into a serious fight as is often observed in unprotected situations. Aware of the conflicts of both boys, the worker was not interfering in their fight, nor was she so passive that they were left helpless and frustrated. Some time later Ralph brought a dark colored boy to the group introducing him as his friend, thus indicating his own accept-ance of his race.

The above records bring forth the apprehension of the child belonging to the discriminated group. We will now illustrate the fears of a group of six- and seven-year-old girls belonging to the majority group. Dolly was referred because of moodiness. Her brother's removal to an institution by court order had left her fearful. The two children, of English parentage, had lived with their mother (the father was dead) in a housing project. We knew of recurring quarrels with colored children in the neigh-borhood.

Dolly first refused to sit beside a colored girl; she said she was afraid of her. A similar reaction was seen in her 11-year-old brother. When he first came to the group and saw the colored boy, he recoiled saying, "Oh God, is he in our group?" In the course of only a few meetings this boy had learned through the close contact with a gentle colored boy that there was nothing to fear and soon the two were seen walking home together.

The sister showed the same initial fear. This time the colored child she met was not as gentle as the one her brother had met and she had to face the reality of this girl's aggression. She tried to avoid conflicts. The worker encouraged her to fight back. When Dolly learned that the colored girl could be both ag-gressive and amiable, and that she could play and fight with her as with anybody else, she seemed to relax.

Dolly had a hard time working through prejudices fostered in her home and neighborhood. It was the freedom she felt in contact with the worker and the knowledge of complete accept-ance by her that made it possible for her to work through some of the prejudices in quite a mature way. The following incident was recorded at a time when mothers often brought their chil-dren to the group and stayed for the first few minutes. Dolly said in a loud voice to the worker, "You know, my cousin does not like you because you are Jewish." Her mother, embarrassed, said "Hush, hush, don't say that." The worker smiled at Dolly and said that they could talk about this later, that she need not be worried. She was worried though, and in a serious way screwed up her face and said, "But I like you, and she just doesn't like you because you are Jewish." Since many mothers were around and very embarrassed, the worker put her arm around Dolly and said that they certainly would talk it over later in the day. At the swimming pool Dolly cornered the worker again and said, "I do like you, I told her, I did not care, I like you better than I like her." The worker said she liked Dolly too, and that people have to know each other to learn to like each other. Later in the day, Dolly asked, "Are you really Jewish?" and then anxiously, "Do Jews believe in God?" When she was reassured, she seemed to feel better.

Some weeks later the girls looked through the book, *One God.* Dolly proudly said, "I know now that Jews do not believe in Jesus, but they believe in God and that is good too." She wanted to take the book home to show her family. It was around this time that Dolly, who had previously refused to sit beside Eva, a colored girl, said, "I want to be friends with Eva." She had learned to overcome her fear of the unknown through acceptance from the worker and contact with people of other groups. In a less frank and accepting environment this child would never have dared utter her thoughts and therefore would never have worked through her feelings regarding Jews and Negroes. She had learned to individualize people as people and not as races.[17]

This country is moving toward integration through the use of law and the courageous action of citizens. To make integration more than a reluctant existence side by side, to learn to appreciate people of a different race, group work skills become increasingly important.

5. Purposeful Choice and Creation of Environment

Concern with a healthy environment, human and other, is a general social work obligation. The conscious use or creation of environment will be discussed here only where it falls into its more narrow concept as a part of the group work process.

The office, with walls that allow for privacy and furniture which

---

[17] Gisela Konopka, "Group Therapy in Overcoming Racial and Cultural Tensions," *The American Journal of Orthopsychiatry,* XVII, No. 4, Oct. 1947, pp. 694-699.

lets the client feel that he is considered a person with dignity, was found to be helpful to the casework process. The long, hard benches for relief recipients, the questioning in large rooms where everyone could overhear everybody else's problems, the brown, cheerless walls, were symbols of a welfare approach lacking the basic philosophy of modern casework and group work. There is no question that excellent practice can be done in a most desolate environment, but then it is done *in spite* of it.

Since a sense of intimacy and individualization is inherent in the group work approach, the group needs for its meetings a place to allow for closeness and mutual attention.

Example

The group worker met her group of ten-year-old boys after school in the gym of the nearby neighborhood house. They needed a physical outlet after sitting still at school. They ran and jumped and shouted.

After about half an hour of this, the group worker called them together to move into a small clubroom where they could make plans for their next meetings. The boys were delighted. "Will this be our very own, every week?" Roger asked.

Roger seemed to express the feelings of the others too. Physical surroundings are consciously planned.

Example

A group worker planned to meet with an out-patient group of adult epileptics who needed help with social relations. They were not able to hold onto jobs because several of them had been kept at home for a large part of their lives and did not know how to meet strangers. Only one in this group had ever dated. It was important to have the group meetings in the hospital to symbolize their being part of treatment. The meeting room should not be an office, but a comfortable living room so that the patients could get used to a social, informal situation. The nurses offered their nicely furnished dayroom for use of the group. Before the meeting the group worker arranged the chairs so that people could see each other, but not in a rigid circle. A few chairs were left at the side with small tables full of magazines next to them. This would allow the shyer members to withdraw when they needed to, without being too obvious.

She also arranged for refreshments. Food and coffee per se were not so important but it was important to have something for their hands to do; hands can feel like awkward lumps when one is in a new social situation, and the group worker realized this.

For a committee meeting of a community planning group the room can be arranged quite differently—often a round table is an appropriate setup for such a group while it can be a retardation to a group that consists of shy members whose purpose is to discuss emotional problems.

It has been frequently advocated that classrooms be used during after-school hours for recreational and informal educational purposes. This is appropriate for certain kinds of groups, yet others should not be placed in this environment. Acting-out youngsters, for instance, with school problems cannot "feel" that the club has another purpose than school, and will be provoked into destructiveness if they meet in school rooms.

Turner describes an experiment with "unclubbable boys," in London (in the U.S.A. they would be called gangs). These boys met with their club leader on a river barge. The program gave outlets for adventure, spirit, achievement and "manly" labor. The environment itself had meaningful impact; the old barge was like a home but, with the open river surrounding it, was not too confining. It was, on the one hand, a house which had to be kept in order and which provided for pride in a form of ownership, and, on the other, it was a moving vehicle which carried the boys from one place to another and demanded their skill in handling it.[18]

Every social worker knows the impact of housing on people. Slums threaten more than the physical health of people. The famous German caricaturist of the 1920's, Heinrich Zille, used as a caption under one of his biting sketches, "You can kill a man with an ax, but also with housing." Lack of privacy, ugliness, and dreariness weigh as

[18] See M. Lloyd Turner, *Ship Without Sails*, London: University of London Press, 1953.

heavily on the soul as on the body. The concern for decent housing belongs to many professions. There is one specific form of "housing"— or environment—which is of direct concern to the social worker, and especially to the social group worker: this is the environment in institutions where children and adults who have been removed from the general, regular stream of community life live for twenty-four hours every day. Institutions are group–living agencies with the total impact of such, only intensified by the fact that the individual cannot leave at will. This applies equally to mental hospitals, treatment centers for children, delinquency institutions, and prisons. Even today many of these places are dull, ugly boxes built for mass living, without privacy. Instead of rebuilding healthy human beings they seem like slums, or worse, and contribute to the "mangling of the soul," as Fritz Redl once called it. I have seen mentally disturbed children kept in a large cage where they could only feel inhuman and like criminals. I have seen in a modern mental hospital a children's unit which consisted exclusively of wards with hospital beds, which provided no playroom, no comfortable chairs, no place to keep a piece of private belongings; toys—essential for the normal child to grow on and so much more essential for the sick one—simply were not available.

I have seen dayrooms, totally devoid of furnishings, in institutions for mentally retarded pre-school children; I have seen the children locked in them, with nothing available to stimulate whatever spark of interest or creativity they might have had, with nothing but emptiness that would destroy it further. I have seen children do nothing all day long but crawl around on the floor, like little animals.

I have visited an institution for the blind with cheerless, grey walls and long lines of beds, without a single sign of beauty. The excuse was, "The children can't see anyhow." My reply was, "Can't they feel? Can't they feel the smoothness of a beautifully shaped piece of wood, the strength of a stone sculpture, the manifold forms of ceramics, the textures of materials for bedspreads, tablecloths, curtains? What about staff working with them. Don't they react differently to color in the rooms instead of the deadly 'institutional grey or brown?' "

I have visited training schools where the youngsters ate on long tables from ugly metal dishes. The noise made it impossible to hold any kind of conversation—something a youngster should learn to make mealtimes more enjoyable—and the ugliness of the eating utensils gave the boys a feeling of being inferior, of being "prisoners," and they acted accordingly.

I have seen modern prisons built with tiled walls to make cleaning easy, but they gave the feeling of coldness, of being a bathroom instead of a living unit. I could go on . . .

There are small things in the living environment that count heavily when one is separated from home and feels inferior: no mirrors in hospitals for mentally sick women; steel mirrors in detention homes for girls (safety is supposed to make this necessary, yet in a place where regular mirrors were installed, not a single girl slashed it in years); drab clothes that do not belong to a specific person; naked light bulbs. Once I visited a children's unit in a mental hospital and had breakfast with the children. The room was attractive, and so were the trays brought in for breakfast. I happened to sit at a table with four withdrawn, mute, teenage girls. Nobody touched the food. On each girl's tray was a whole orange. I began to peel one, divided it and gave it to the girl next to me who ate it with pleasure. Then I felt a finger poking me. One of the girls silently pointed at her orange. I peeled all three of them and the girls ate. The kitchen help came to take away the trays from all the tables. I looked around—almost all of them were half full. The fresh orange was a fine idea, but nobody had considered that these slow patients did not know how to get it ready to eat. Nobody considered their slowness in general. The schedule was made according to hospital routine.

These attributes of the environment are the business of the social worker. Not every institution can start to build new units although this becomes increasingly necessary. But intense and imaginative attention to environment can vastly improve existing facilities and make a therapeutic group life possible. One of the large, old institutions for delinquent girls changed the environment by arranging for separate apartments in the different stories of the old house, dividing the large sleeping quarters into smaller units, building a private closet for each girl, and adding dressers.

New institutions have often accepted the basic concept of an institution as a group-living community which must allow for individualism. Large mass institutions—for years not allowed in the Scandinavian countries—are beginning to disappear. Planners are now giving attention to beauty as well as to utility in designing new buildings.

This does not require precious or expensive materials. The physical environment must differ according to the specific purpose of the particular institution and the particular population that it accommodates; a treatment center for emotionally disturbed children should not look like a prison for adult offenders. Planning for both must be directed toward the kind of guidance that is necessary to help the human being find himself and to restore his capacity to live with others. A primitive forestry camp can provide as helpful an environment to a prisoner—assuming it does not exploit him—as the most highly civilized, cheerful and comfortable cottage of a modern hospital to a mental patient.

Example

In one correctional institution morale was low and every attempt at rehabilitation seemed to fall flat. Then the new superintendent began to change the physical environment. The men had always taken their meals at long benches facing the wall or the back of the men in front of them. He arranged a normal table situation, and replaced the tin food utensils by plastic ware. Food was brought in on hot steam tables where once it had been served half-cold. He made other changes. Sheets were changed once a week instead of once a month—this meant an increase in the number of laundry workers, which meant, in turn, fewer idle hands. In the past, when the men were out of their cells, they usually stood around in the corridors or sat on the floors. The superintendent had the prison workshop make chairs which were placed in the corridors so that the men, if they wished, could sit like other human beings. In the past, the men had had to speak to their visitors through wire screening so heavy that they could hardly see to whom they were talking. The superintendent had these torn out and replaced the security of the wire by a human guard. And he added a homey touch: prison-gardeners were commissioned to see that a vase of fresh flowers was placed in the room during visiting hours, thus creating a more pleasant atmosphere. These changes came about slowly and began to open up possibilities for real treatment. The men no longer talked to each other only in secret, but began to enter into open discussions. They talked about and appreciated the changes, and began to take an interest in themselves. This made it possible to establish a prison council and to begin involving the men in concern with their own fate as a community.[19] And this opened the door to the use of other therapeutic and educational methods.

Changes in environment are like the use of tranquilizing and other drugs in psychiatry. They do not "cure" the patient; they only make it more possible to work with him. A healthy and suitable environment is prerequisite to a healthy group life and individual satisfaction.

Summary

The helping process of social group work is carried out through:
1. the purposeful, warm, understanding, professional relationship between group worker and group members;
2. the relationship among group members (the guided group process);
3. verbal communication;
4. non-verbal communication, and
5. purposeful choice and creation of environment.

None of these media can be used dogmatically and indiscriminately. Their use must vary according to the group worker's understanding of the individuals and the group, according to a particular agency's purpose, and according to the needs and purposes of the group and its individual members. They are used by the group worker—*a person*—hence they must be used with care, for they can take on the qualities of his personality. The social group work process has the aspects of an art based on science.

BIBLIOGRAPHY

Coyle, Grace L., *Group Work With American Youth*, New York: Harper & Row, Publishers, 1948.
————, "Definition of the Group Worker," in Harleigh B. Trecker, Editor, *Group Work—Foundations and Frontiers*, New York: Whiteside, Inc., 1955.

---

[19]   Maxwell Jones has enlarged on this in his book, *Therapeutic Community*, published in London in 1952 by Tavistock Publications.

Guzie, Frances P., "Emerging Patterns in the Use of Program in Social Group Work," *Group Work Papers 1957*, New York: N.A.S.W., 1958, pp. 38-49.

Konopka, Gisela, "The Application of Social Work Principles to International Relations," *The Social Welfare Forum, 1953*, New York: Columbia University Press, 1953, pp. 279-289.

———, "The Method of Social Group Work," in Friedlander, Walter A., Editor, *Concepts and Methods of Social Work*, Englewood Cliffs, N.J.: Prentice-Hall, Inc., 1958, pp. 116-200.

———, "A Healthy Group Life—Social Group Work's Contribution to Mental Health," *Mental Hygiene*, Vol. 45, No. 3, July 1961.

———, "Discipline in Youth Groups," *The American Journal of Catholic Youth Work*, Vol. I, No. 1, Winter 1960, pp. 21-28.

———, "Social Group Work: A Social Work Method," *Social Work*, Vol. 5, No. 4, Oct. 1960, pp. 53-61.

———, *Group Work in the Institution*, New York: William Morrow and Co., 1954.

Northen, Helen, "Interrelated Functions of the Social Group Worker," *Social Work*, Vol. 2, No. 2, Apr. 1957.

Perlman, Bernice, "Group Work with Psychotic Veterans," *American Journal of Orthopsychiatry*, Vol. XIX, No. 1, Jan. 1949, pp. 69-78.

Phillips, Helen U., *Essentials of Social Group Work Skill*, New York: Association Press, 1957.

Redl, Fritz and David Wineman, *Children Who Hate—Controls from Within*, Glencoe, Ill.: The Free Press, 1951.

Schwartz, William, "The Social Worker in the Group," *New Perspectives on Services to Groups: Theory, Organization, Practice*, New York: N.A.S.W., pp. 7-29 (with discussion by Ruth E. Smalley, pp. 30-34).

———, "Group Work and the Social Scene," in Alfred J. Kahn, *Issues in American Social Work*, New York: Columbia University Press, 1959, pp. 110-137.

Simos, Jack, *Social Growth Through Play Production*, New York: Association Press, 1957.

Trecker, Harleigh B., *Social Group Work: Principles and Practices*, revised edition, New York: Whiteside, Inc., 1955.

Weiner, Jack, "Reducing Racial and Religious Discrimination," *Social Work with Groups 1960*, New York: N.A.S.W., 1960, pp. 62-73.

Wilson, Gertrude and Gladys Ryland, *Social Group Work Practice: The Creative Use of the Social Process*, Boston: Houghton Mifflin Co., 1949.

Wittenberg, Rudolph M., *So You Want to Help People*, New York: Association Press, 1947.

CHAPTER EIGHT

Principles of
Social Group Work
in Practice

*Man is born a pre-destined idealist for
he is born to act. . . . To act is to
affirm the worth of an end and to persist
in affirming the worth of an end is to
make an idea.*[1]

"There is nothing we can do with him," was the general at-
tude of the neighborhood, adults and children alike, in regard to John.
"He is born mean." Parents forbade their children to associate with
him. On the playground children called him tauntingly, "the killer." At
the age of nine he indeed had an impressive record of misdeeds: he stole
with skill; he tripped smaller children. Yet he himself was one of the
thinnest, smallest nine-year-olds that one could imagine. He flew into
a rage at the slightest provocation and had hit a girl so hard with a
piece of wood that she had had to be hospitalized with a broken arm.

[1] Harry C. Schriver, Editor and Annotator, *Justice Oliver Wendell Holmes,
His Book Notices and Uncollected Letters and Papers,* New York: Central
Book Co., 1936, p. 143.

He was one of the few children who managed to escape from the juvenile detention home. He seemed to be of average or better intelligence, but testing was almost impossible because of his hostile sullenness in the testing situation—to him, adults were the ultimate enemies. His school achievement was very low and he could not read. His mother was unhappy about his behavior, but was also convinced that he was "born that way, just like his father who deserted us." She was an unhappy woman, incapable of giving warmth to her children. John was the second of three children. All of them showed difficult behavior, but his was the most destructive.

Give up? Accept the fact that this nine-year-old is destined for a "life of crime"? Here were difficult forces to overcome—in the child, in his human environment. The basic attitude of the social group worker is one of optimism. He is the "idealist" of whom Holmes speaks so beautifully. It is not an idealism which disregards reality with its limitations, but one that makes action possible. It is a stubborn belief in the capacity of the human being to grow and change if given help. This optimism is part of a general trait of American culture. But it is not the kind that Jacques Maritain rightfully designated as an illusion:

> In some respects the American conception of life appears as a continuation of the eighteenth-century optimistic views on Man and Nature.
> . . . belief in the goodness of Nature, the natural goodness of Men, in the Rousseauist sense.[2]

It is an action-idealism with consideration of all the facts without sentimentality, but with the conviction that often the feeling of genuine hope conveyed to individuals or groups can help them to move out of situations that would otherwise seem to drag them deeper into difficulties. A philosopher, Leonard Nelson, a follower of Kant and Freud and a creative thinker in his own right, wrote a philosophical treatise on this in which he developed clearly and logically the necessary and *possible* "alliance of Idealism with Realism."[3] In this, he separated the realistic idealist from the purely sentimental enthusiast or the pessimist who uses a pretended realism to avoid action:

[2] Jacques Maritain, *Reflections on America*, New York: Charles Scribner's Sons, 1958, p. 131.
[3] Leonard Nelson, *Politics and Education*, London: George Allen & Unwin Ltd., first published in 1928, translated by W. Lansdell, p. 186.

The Idealist is neither a dreamer nor a doubter, but he looks at the world as it is, with the eyes of the Realist, and from such realism his energy and his courage spring. . . .
Realism teaches the Idealist to know the means which are necessary for the attainment of his aim. It teaches him that pious wishes have no power to move things in the world of space, and that we must get our hands busy if we want to make this world better.[4]

With such attitude of thoughtful weighing of facts (realism) and hope for possible change (idealism) the group worker approaches a child like John, a group concerned with a slum clearance project, or a bleak mental hospital ward. This basic attitude has not only the result that the social group worker himself becomes active, but usually it activates the individual or group too. This latter phenomenon is seen increasingly in all educational and healing arts.

John, for instance, was not seen as a "hopeless case," but rather as someone in need of the efforts of several members of a child guidance team. (Such a team consists of a psychiatrist, a psychologist, a case worker, and a group worker.) It was agreed that the first approach could be made only through group work, because of his deep suspicion and hostility toward adults. He needed to be a little boy among other children in a group which was small enough so that he could feel important. The group worker had to be prepared for much hostile behavior and to protect the others from him but, at the same time, without rejecting him. John needed to experience some tangible success in something, either in things he did with his hands or in the simple— and for him, not so simple—experience of having spent an hour with other children without insults and fights. He needed to be "left alone" inside a group without being neglected. He had always known only the role of the outcast or the one who got attention because of misbehavior. He needed to feel that an adult believed in his capacity to change without making him say so in words, without his promising to be "good," without his being asked to make a return in exchange for the attention, affection—only cautiously shown—or quiet, helpful restraint extended to him.

These were things John needed; they explain why he started first in a group conducted by a social group worker. At first he tried to live up to his reputation as "the killer." But how could one keep this up,

[4] *Op. cit.*, p. 171.

even a "hardened" nine-year-old, when limitations always included a conveying that he could act differently, when he saw that those other kids "had their problems" too and that the group worker met them with the same kind of respect. Then there were activities that were fun, things John would have liked to do, but from which he persistently had been excluded—like doing woodwork. In the beginning he did rip apart pieces of lumber or made sharp swords, but he was not the only one to do this; others did it too. What would the group worker do? She admired his skill when he stopped just cutting things apart; she commented on the sharpness of the edge, "Well done, John. What would you like to do with it?" "Kill someone." "Whom?" "You." "Really?" And John suddenly felt something he would have liked to have pushed far away from him. He turned quickly. Tears welled up—tears! Such a silly thing! Sure he hated her; she made him cry, did she not? But he had never cried before. He felt anger and yet. . . . He did not understand.

The group worker realized John's struggle with himself, the first softness beginning in him, even if John himself could not admit it, and she wisely neither forced an answer nor "explained."

Layers of hate cannot be torn away, they must come off slowly, lifted with infinite care, like those the archaeologist lifts off a precious piece of art he has found covered and encrusted with the dirt of centuries.

The group worker purposely let John alone in this precious minute and turned to another child, thus not making him feel that she had abandoned him. John was relieved; he was neither the center of attention nor was he forced to express hate or to apologize. He could watch what other children did: Jim, who also had made a sharp sword, cut paper with it and seemed to enjoy this; Simon used his to make patterns in the sandbox—"like a baby," thought John. Without realizing it, he moved closer and closer to the sandbox. Suddenly his sword touched the soft sand, swirled it around, stabbed it. For twenty minutes John was blissfully a baby, an aggressive one, playing with sand. The group worker made no comment. She knew that a most important process had started: John had allowed himself to be the baby he never had been and yet had yearned to be. Part of the baby was aggression, but part of it was also the need for love.

John had many more experiences: flare-ups, relapses into open anger, sudden feelings of tenderness. There were even beginning discussions with other boys. It happened usually when they were eating and when Owen started talking about school—Owen was the "talker" in the group. They all hated school, and mostly reading. It was John who blurted out one day that it was awful, that he hated all the other kids, because they could read street signs and he could not. The group worker asked, "Would you like Mr. Dennis (the psychologist) help you learn to read? You know, I think you can catch on pretty fast. Remember when we did the woodburning the other day? You knew the letters we used right away." "She really likes me," thought John— or better, *felt* it. "She really believes I can do things."

Weeks had passed and since those first meetings, John had begun to trust and believe in his counselor—he had certainly tested her, over and over, by kicking others, and even by kicking her, but now there was a new conflict within him: he wanted her all for himself; the other kids should not be there. "Can't *you* teach me?" said John.

The group worker understood. When the layers of hate begin to fall away the skin under them is tender. The child had returned to an earlier stage—that of an infant—and the adult he has learned to trust should be all his own, his mother. The sharing that was so helpful in the beginning because it allowed distance from the adult now had become irksome. Now the child was ready for a more intensive one-to-one relationship, but, at the same time, he had to learn to accept the sharing of beloved people—of mothers, fathers, teacher.

John still needed the group, but he also had to be helped to accept relationship with another adult. The group worker could not simply refuse John. To him that would mean that he was again rebuffed, as he had been so often in his early life. And yet she had to help him transfer his good relationship to others too.

The group worker explained to John that she was not as capable as Mr. Dennis of helping him with his reading but that she would gladly sit in at the first session if this would make him feel a bit more comfortable. She also told him more about Mr. Dennis and his way of doing things. John was not yet ready for this step: he did not want to go—but, at least, he was not hurt.

The words TIME and PATIENCE must be written in capitalized letters in social group work.

A few weeks later Owen told John that he was a "dope" for not having gone to get help with reading. He, Owen, had now gone through the primer, and "Boy, it is much easier now!" No one in authority could have called John a "dope," even at that time, without arousing old resentment. A few months earlier, no child could have called him that. But now he was so much more a boy among boys! "Dope yourself," he shouted at Owen, but he did not hit him. The group worker knew she too could be more direct now. "Why not try it, John?" No answer yet. . . .

It was around Easter, and the boys had gone with the group worker into town to buy "surprises" for their party. In the department store John passed a counter with furry toy rabbits; he returned to it again and again. The group worker wondered what he wanted. "Could I have one of those?" This was said shyly and a bit ashamedly. "Surely, if they are not too expensive." Again the miracle to John; here was an adult who did not think it unusual that a ten-year-old wanted a toy rabbit. In the bus John held the paper bag with the rabbit. From time to time his hands reached into it and he stroked it. Once he caught the group worker looking at him. He stiffened. Would she laugh? But she did not; she just nodded agreement.

The group worker realized that this was a very crucial moment for John. For the first time he had allowed himself, consciously, to be a little boy with a need for tenderness. It was important that no one make fun of him at home, especially not his mother. Here was a moment where the judgment of the social worker had to be fast, clear, and—if necessary—unconventional. Usually the case worker had interviews with the mother; the group worker had only a few contacts. This time, however, she decided to stop with John at his home to enlist his mother's support. She asked John on the way whether he wanted to show his mother the rabbit. He said he would like to, but wondered whether she would make fun of him.

At home all three talked together about the trip. John kept the rabbit hidden in the paper bag. Mother finally inquired what he had there, and John shyly produced the toy. The group worker turned quietly toward mother, "It is lovely, is it not. It means much to John." She had not taken from John the responsibility of showing his purchase to his mother, but she supported him and, at the same time, enlisted mother's help, making her feel that *her* actions were important to John. Mother, who had learned much about herself and John in her interviews with the case workers, smiled and admired the beauty of the rabbit. And John went to bed with the rabbit cuddled in his arm.

The next week at the Easter party, Jim brought young, fluffy chickens to the group. He held them tightly—so tightly he almost suffocated them. The group worker showed him how the little chicken suffered by this, even if he wanted only to prove his love. John, for the first time, found words for feelings: "Loving is soft, isn't it?" The group worker's arms went around both boys, then Owen and Gary joined them. They talked about their fears, of needing big people to protect them, of former hates, of anger.

A warm bond had given them courage to let down the hard barriers against each other and the adult.

They asked to make Easter cards for their mothers (it was not the group worker's suggestion; it came from them).

They began to retransfer their love to the person who was the real power in their lives. They could do it only because they had worked it through and out on the group worker. They also could like each other, not only vying with each other for the love of the adult. They became ten-year-olds, but only after they had been allowed to be very little boys without having to be ashamed of it.

They asked for spelling lessons. John asked Owen (and the group worker chalked down a silent "progress," because he asked another boy and not her) whether Owen *really* thought Mr. Dennis could teach him reading, whether he was mean, whether he liked "kids." And John began reading lessons. . . .

It was some weeks later that John brought a neighborhood friend to the group. He "showed off" in the healthy and delightful way in which any ten-year-old introduces his friends and "his" club. The friend was duly impressed by the things they made, by the boys, by the whole place.

John had taken another step—he had gained status with a neighbor.

We have followed this one child through his experiences with group work treatment to show the use of the different media in social group work, the integration of the underlying attitude of respect and optimism with the reality of understanding the child in his changing feelings and relationships on the part of the group worker, the diagnostic decisions made in relation to the existing needs of the individual child and other group members, and the use of relationship, of transference, of group interaction, of verbal and non-verbal program activities—all this to help the child recover a sense of worthwhile self. Thus he gradually became able to relate to others in a giving way, whereas, initially, his relationship to others was mainly destructive. We see from this illustration how closely intellectual understanding of individual and group dynamics is intertwined with sensitive empathy and infinite patience, and how they both help the child to grow by making demands which are not overwhelming.

We see the general sequence of the group work process as moving from "getting to know each other" (and in the hostile person this includes much trying out of the person he considers responsible or in authority) to keep affection (and sometimes dependency and jealousy of the sharing with other members) to the working through of one's problems or handicaps on a verbal or non-verbal level to renewed trying out (but on a level different from in the beginning) to a moving out to healthy and normal relationships with adults and children and the need for and the beginning to actively reach out for achievement.

Although in this example I purposely chose to focus on one child to present the helping process, it also showed the interaction of several children, the way they influence one another, and the way the skilled social group worker uses group process either to relieve an individual from too much attention or to help him gain it.

It also illustrates the slow development and importance of group bond, and its freeing force when the individual group member feels true acceptance. In many forms of therapy the freeing of one's inhibitions to express hostility is stressed. This is frequently needed *in many people*, especially when people are too frightened (or too constricted) to show negative feelings. In our present culture though, negative feelings are expressed with more ease than in earlier times, while warmth and love are often carefully and successfully hidden—either because they seem like something to be ashamed of or because those feelings have been rebuffed so much that the individual has put on so many protective layers that he himself is no longer aware of them. To develop a group climate which allows for the expression genuine positive feelings while allowing also for the working through of conflict, anxiety, and other negatives is one of the skills of social group work.

Let us return to theory.

The previous chapters have evolved the following scheme of the group work method:

Social group work is a method of social work which helps individuals to enhance their social functioning through purposeful group experiences and to cope more effectively with their personal, group or community problems.

Premise 1. Social work as a profession is concerned with enhancement of person's social functioning.

Premise 2. There is significant correlation between social functioning and group experience.

Premise 3. People need help—at times, professional help—to enhance social functioning.

Premise 1 is a matter of agreement, tradition, social sanction and definition.

Premise 2 is proved by clinical and laboratory research.

Premise 3 is proved mainly by observation and clinical experience.

There are many ways, lay and professional, to enhance social functioning. Social group work is one of them. Its specific effectiveness lies in the psychological make-up of human beings: two basic needs—*the need to belong* and *the need to have self-respect*—are dependent on fulfillment of positive group experiences. A third need is located in the totality of human society, namely, *the need to cooperate with each other.* For the individual it means taking responsibility for one another, and this includes—and requires—group interaction.

The problems which social group work addresses itself to, range from healthy developmental social needs of individuals to severe disturbances in them, and includes problems of group relationships.

The *point of entry* is generally a request for help, sometimes openly expressed, sometimes not.

Group work skills are *procedural* and *interactional.*[5]

Procedural skills mean the use of the scientific method: the process of collecting facts, of assessing them, and of establishing objectives for individuals and groups. They are based (1) on knowledge (*dynamics of individual and group process*) and (2) on the individual capacities of the group worker (listening, observing, empathy). Ruby Pernell describes them as:

[5] These terms are taken from Ruby B. Pernell, "Identifying and Teaching the Skill Components of Social Group Work," a paper presented at the Annual Meeting of the Council on Social Work Education, St. Louis, 1962.

the steps in a methodological, knowledgeable procedure of giving help: the identification of the Professional Purpose, Study, Diagnosis, Selection of goals, Treatment and Reporting.[6]

The interactional skills are the means through which the group worker becomes effective. They are based: on his own and on his profession's ethical convictions and on his sensitive use of self (art). Pernell summarized the interactional skills as:

> Those behavior responses appropriate to individual and group need, within the purposes of the social group work service. These we identify according to the scheme . . . as Accepting, Relating, Enabling and Supporting, Limiting, Guiding, Alleviating and Interpreting.[7]

The scheme Pernell referred to was evolved by Etta Saloshin in her doctoral dissertation as one instrument for the analysis of the activities of the group worker. This classification scheme is reproduced here:[8]

I. *Accepting* (by worker of person, feelings, ideas, or behavior)

II. *Relating*
   A. Member or group to worker
   B. Member or group to member
   C. Member to group

III. *Enabling and Supporting*
   A. Individuals or group to *accept* self or others
   B. Individuals or group to
      1. *express* themselves
      2. *accomplish* (or have feeling of accomplishment)
   C. Individuals or groups to *involve* themselves in:
      1. activity (program)
      2. decision making
      3. assuming and carrying responsibilities

6 Ruby B. Pernell, "Identifying and Teaching the Skill Components of Social Group Work," paper presented at the Annual Meeting of the Council on Social Work Education, St. Louis, 1962; mimeographed, Graduate School of Social Work, University of Pittsburgh, No. 4366, p. 5.

7 *Loc. cit.*

8 Henriette Etta Saloshin, "Development of an Instrument for the Analysis of the Social Group Work Method in Therapeutic Settings." Ph.D. thesis, March 1954, University of Minnesota, Minneapolis.

   D. Individuals and group to *gain insight, understanding and security*

 IV. *Limiting* behavior

   A. Harmful to others or self

   B. Destructive to property and material, or to relationships

 V. *Guiding* of discussions, activities and group movement.

 VI. *Alleviating*

   A. Tension

   B. Conflict

   C. Fear and anxiety, or guilt

 VII. *Interpreting*

   A. Function of group-worker-agency

   B. Individual's or group's behavior or feelings

 VIII. *Observing and Evaluating* (diagnostic appraisal)

   A. Individual behavior

   B. Individual's effect on group

   C. Group behavior

   D. Worker's effect on individual or group (own practice)

 IX. *Planning and Preparing* (by worker)

   A. Group formation and composition

   B. Program

   C. Treatment or service

Out of knowledge, philosophy and skill evolve basic principles for the practice of group work. The word "principles" is used here in a dual sense: as "the essence" of the group work method, determining and describing its nature and as a rule of conduct, as "guidelines" for the social group worker.

There have been several attempts to delineate such "essentials" or principles. My own first attempt was worked out in 1955 and was used also in the Curriculum Study. It consisted of the following ten points:

1. The function of the social group worker is a helping or enabling function: this means that his goal is to help the members

of the group and the group as a whole to move toward greater independence and capacity for self-help.

2. In determining his way of helping, the group worker uses the scientific method: fact-finding (observation), analyzing, diagnosis in relation to the individual, the group and the social environment.

3. The group work method includes the worker forming purposeful relationships to group members and the group: this includes a conscious focusing on the needs of the members, on the purpose of the group as expressed by the members, as expected by the sponsoring agency and as implied in the members' behavior. It is differentiated from a casual unfocused relationship.

4. One of the main tools in achieving such a relationship is the conscious use of self. This includes self-knowledge and discipline in relationships without the loss of warmth and spontaneity.

5. There should be acceptance of people without accepting all their behavior: this involves the capacity for "empathy" as well as the incorporation of societal demands. It is the part of the method that is most closely intertwined with a high flexibility and abundance of warmth in the social group worker as well as identification with values and knowledge.

6. Starting where the group is: the capacity to let groups develop from their own point of departure without immediately imposing exacting demands.

7. The constructive use of limitations: limitations must be used judiciously in relation to individual and group needs and agency function. The forms will vary greatly. The group worker will use mainly himself, program materials, interaction of the group and awakening of self-criticism in the group members.

8. Individualization: it is one of the specifics of the group work method that the individual is not lost in the whole, but that he is helped to feel as a unique person who can contribute to the whole.

9. Use of the interacting process: the capacity to help balance the group, to allow for conflict when necessary and to prevent it when harmful; the help given to the isolate not only through individual attention by the group worker alone but also by relating him to other members.

10. The understanding and conscious use of non-verbal as well

as verbal material: I especially put non-verbal material first, since the group worker deals to a large extent with this, especially in work with children. His capacity to use program materials, which do not demand verbal expression and yet are helpful, should be very wide.[9]

This statement is not completely satisfactory, because it includes too great a variety of concepts, and does not strictly present principles. The following is a new attempt:

1. *Recognition and subsequent action in relation to the unique difference of each individual* (Individualization in the group).
The group worker must never see the group as an anonymous mass. His responsibility is to understand each individual and to help each individual in regard to his own specific needs as well as in regard to the needs of the total group and the society in which it exists. This principle includes skill in diagnosis and the complicated skill of focusing on individuals *in* the group.

2. *Recognition and subsequent action in relation to the wide variety of groups as groups* (Individualization of groups).
The group worker realizes that a group is more than the sum of its individuals. It is an organic whole with specific characteristics of its own, expressed in its form of bond, its particular interaction between members, its subgroupings, its form or lack of leadership, etc. Its characteristics are related to the group's goal and composition. This principle includes the skill in diagnosing a group and in acting according to this diagnosis as well as the understanding of the individual as expressed in principle 1.

3. *Genuine acceptance of each individual with his unique strength and weakness.*
The group worker does not only *understand* the individual. He acts toward him in a way prescribed by his profession of social work. Acceptance includes the profession's value orientation, the respect for each individual. He does not necessarily *approve* of each individual's actions or qualities, in fact he does use some

[9] Gisela Konopka, "The Generic and Specific in Group Work Practice in the Psychiatric Setting," *Group Work in the Psychiatric Setting*, New York: Whiteside and Morrow, 1956, pp. 21-22. See also Marjorie Murphy, *The Social Group Work Method in Social Work Education, op. cit.* pp. 125-126.

value system to assess them as "strength" or as "weakness." He accepts the individual in his totality.

4. *Establishment of a purposeful helping relationship between group worker and group members.*

Group work practice is based on the assumption that change in an individual can occur only through interaction with others. To accomplish change in a beneficial direction, people need help, and in certain instances, professional help.

5. *Encouragement and enabling of helpful and cooperative relationships between group members.*

This principle is based on the same assumption as principle 4. It is recognized in group work that relationships between "equals"—between the members of the group—have as much importance as individual relationship to the group worker. These relationships can move in a negative or positive direction. (The determination whether the change is "negative" or "positive," "healthy" or "sick," "good" or "bad" includes an assessment of the individuals, the group and the use of the professional value system). It is the group worker's role to work toward relationships between members which become beneficial to them.

6. *Appropriate modification of the group process.*

The group process is expressed in interrelations between group members, the formation of subgroups, the establishment of bond, the development of leadership, the creation of isolates, etc. The group worker must see these constellations, assess them diagnostically and know when to work with them, strengthen them, or help to change them.

7. *Encouragement of each member to participate according to the stage of his capacity, enabling him to become more capable.*

"Participation" is a key word in the use of the group work method. It means that each member must be helped to involve himself to become "part" of the group effort. This capacity to participate varies from individual to individual. The group worker must accept the stage of the individual's capacity to participate (this is often expressed as "starting where the member is"), help him participate on his own level without feeling pushed or embarrassed and guide him into a healthier or more capable stage.

8. *Enabling members to involve themselves in the process of problem solving.*

The group worker does not solve problems *for* the group. He must not play the omnipotent person who always knows what is best for individual members or for the group as a whole. He helps members to become part of problem solving and to find their own solutions in interaction with others and the group worker. 9. *Enabling group members to experience increasingly satisfactory forms of working through of conflicts.*

This principle relates to forms of conflict solving in group interaction and in the individual. The group as a whole may be enabled by the group worker to move from "slugging out" a difference of opinion to solving conflicts by talking them out, learning to compromise or to use different democratic methods. The individual, for example, may be helped to stop running away when a conflict situation arises and to face the situation and gather the strength to work it through. Significant for the group work method is the fact that this can be *experienced*—as well as talked through—in the presence of a helping person, the social group worker.

10. *Provision of opportunities for new and differing experiences in relationships and accomplishments.*

Here again the key word is "experience." It is characteristic of the group work method that it lends itself to living through of problem situations with the help of the group worker, instead of reflecting on them. Working through of new relationships is part of daily human life. Group workers work with this problem when special help is needed, as, for instance, when people move from rural to urban communities; when racial groups meet which have never met before or have met only in the relationship between master and servant, not as equals nor as friends or neighbors; when a child moves from the latency period into adolescence and must find new ways to act towards the opposite sex; when a youth group has only seen authority as an enemy and now is challenged to revise attitudes and feelings by meeting adults who work with it.

"Accomplishment" is assumed to be one of the major ingredients of general mental health. It is often denied to people. It is the group worker's responsibility to allow for this vital experience by providing opportunities for accomplishment to individual members as well as the whole group.

11. *Judicious use of limitations related to the diagnostic assessment of each individual and the total situation.*

The principle of acceptance, as enunciated under principle 3, is frequently misunderstood as meaning total permissiveness. This is not considered helpful, since it would include permission to harm each other or to harm oneself, physically or emotionally. Limitations are therefore an important part of the intelligent and purposeful work with individuals and the group. This principle includes diagnostic thinking and skillful use of all the media available to the group worker, such as relationships, use of the group process, program, and so forth.

12. *Purposeful and differential use of program according to diagnostic evaluation of individual members, group purpose, and appropriate social goals.*

By *program* is meant any activity which the group does in the presence of the group worker during the course of group meetings. These activities must not be planned according to the particular needs or interests of the group worker himself, but only with reference to the group members. This principle includes diagnosis of individual and group needs and their assessment in relation to group and agency purpose as well as to professional values and ethics of human relationships.

13. *Ongoing evaluation of individual and group progress.*

Periodic evaluations or assessments are part of the group work method; they help to keep the group worker's efforts purposeful and flexible. They are also frequently (not always) shared with the members of the group and help them to move toward individual or group goals.

14. *Warm, human, and disciplined use of self on the part of the group worker.*

This principle is part of all previously named principles, but especially of principle 4. It is presented separately to underline the importance of the quality of the group worker's approach to individuals and groups. This principle demands of the group worker a discipline which prevents him from using the group for his own personal satisfaction (this does not exclude his satisfaction in doing a good, professional job), yet it also requires him to be a real person, not just a cold, impersonal or shadowy observer.

In terms of characteristics of the group worker, these principles presuppose practitioners with (1) a high capacity for empathy; (2) flexibility; (3) keen perception and intelligence to analyze and assess not only individuals, but highly complex situations; (4) capacity to relate warmly to people; (5) creativity or imagination.

Since the group worker's self is the major tool of the group work method, and since the method does not include "neutrality" or a "shadow" relationship, but a disciplined, warm use of this self, the principles come to life only if used by a person who has and who increases the above potential qualities in himself.

In addition to this it must be stressed that these principles implicitly include the values of respect for every human being and of responsibility for each other. Without them, as mentioned earlier, the method becomes an empty technique.

The last part of this chapter will present and analyze record material. Each record will illustrate a wide variety of principles followed in the reality of group work practice. The incidents are taken from practice in different settings.

The reader is reminded again of the fact that social group work is an art based on science and, therefore, the personality of the group worker enters into its practice. These recordings were made by the social group worker immediately following the meetings.

The first two examples present first meetings of a group worker with members of the group, the *beginning* of the group work process.

Example 1

This example demonstrates the *beginning* of the group work process in a *natural* group. This is a friendship group of five 13-14 year-old boys who hang around the neighborhood. They had come by themselves to the community center and had asked for a place to meet. They were told that they were very welcome and that it was the custom to assign a social group worker to each club. They had accepted this. The only thing known about them was that all five were low school achievers and that they were known to annoy merchants in the neighborhood by hanging around in their establishments, but they were not openly delinquent.

The group met at 7 P.M. at the Center. Present were five boys: John, Herb, Mort, Sam and Chuck. The group had no definite program in mind for this evening. Instead, they wanted to just "go riding" in the station wagon. The group worker agreed to this.

Adolescent need for adventure. Car as a status symbol, but out of reach at that age.

Group worker accepts these needs as legitimate; car also offers an intimate "meeting room." Allows members to start where they are.

During the evening, the boys displayed quite uncontrolled and impulsive behavior. They opened the car door, threatened to jump out, and, at one point, fooled around with the football and dropped it out of the window, losing it. At the first disagreement, they began their impulsive and testing-out behavior. The group worker stopped the car and they all got out, picked up dried cattails and began throwing them, primarily at the group worker and at the station wagon.

Judicious use of limitations. (Limitation is achieved here simply by changing the situation).

Group worker joined in with them and allowed them first to take out many of their feelings on him, while returning some of their "fire," making it a real give-and-take situation, keeping it on a friendly basis. Later he was able to help them choose sides and make a kind of game out of it. This worked fairly well and the group was able to get back in the wagon after spending much of their energy and to drive back to the city.

Group worker accepts members' needs to "test" a new adult—confronts them with a non-punishing, but not "passive" adult.

Creates outlet for hostility through games (creative use of program).

Their acting-out behavior again started as they arrived in the

Interesting example of "role" behavior of a total group. Outside of

neighborhood. They rejected at first all attempts of the group worker to set limits on them. They had planned to ride to a drive-in; after talking it over with the group worker, they all agreed that they would behave themselves at the drive-in, otherwise, as one of them put it, "They won't give us anything to eat."

This they were able to do and they returned to the neighborhood about 9:30 with the group worker dropping the boys off at their homes.

As he did so, John said to him that he hoped the group worker wasn't mad at the group. He said, "We were just trying to find out what kind of a guy you are." They discussed this for a while and the group members were able to see much of their behavior directed at "testing" of the group worker. They assured him that they would not create this many problems at future meetings. They planned to meet every week.

the neighborhood, the boys allow themselves to "mellow" and shed the "tough" shell. In their neighborhood they must again live up to the role they think will give them status.

Group worker chooses an opportunity to know the boys individually.

A sign of beginning relationship, and some help for insight.

Comment

We see here a beginning relationship between group worker and members, but still a very tenuous one. The group was an entity before the group worker entered. He was the "stranger in the group." The testing process is a natural one in the beginning, but was obviously intensified here by the fact that the group had not asked for a group worker and had only accepted agency policy.

The group worker began to get some knowledge about the group as a whole, but very little as yet about each individual in it. However, he acted according to the principles of acceptance, judicious use of limitations, individualization of the group, and use of program based on an assessment of the needs of the members as he saw them.

Example 2

This example demonstrates the *beginning* of group process in a *formed* group. This is a group of 15-16 year-old girls in an institution for delinquents. The purpose of the group is to help the girls to discuss freely their problems, to work through some of their feelings about their placement and about themselves. The group worker is originally from India, but has no difficulty with the English language. This extract is taken from the recording made by the group worker after her first meeting with the girls.

Norma and Jean offered the group worker a chair, and sat down close to her. Norma is a pretty girl, with a cheerful expression and a friendly smile. She seemed easily excited and very demonstrative of her feelings. She tried to learn the spelling of the group worker's name. The group worker said that she had made name tags for herself and the girls which would help "us to learn each other's names quicker."

Technique of individualizing and helping girls to learn a "social custom."

When the group worker took out the tags and the pins from her bag, Norma said that she had come fully prepared to meet them. She seemed very happy with her name tag and pinned it on quickly.

Being prepared indicates that the group worker cares.

She complimented the group worker on her attire, heaved a

Beginning indentification, because of a shared value.

sigh, and said she wished she had a similar dress.

Jean offered to show the group worker their dorm. The group worker told her that she had taken a tour on her first visit, but that she thought it would be more interesting today, since she now knew some of the girls.

Group worker understands the girls' need to show "their" place, to give. She accepts this with warmth.

Both Norma and Jean led the way through the dormitory and gave explanations of the living arrangements. The group worker complimented them on their dorm. Norma and Jean pointed out their own beds and the little stuffed animals which decorated the room.

When they returned to the meeting room they were joined by Ida and Sue. Ida gave the group worker a weak smile in reply to her greeting and sat down next to Norma. Sue stood smiling slightly on the edge of the group; she seemed to be appraising the group worker. She finally sat down next to her.

Sue was an attractive girl, seemingly sophisticated, but when she began to speak, she kept fumbling for words and had difficulty in expressing herself. The worker introduced herself, asked their names, and gave each of them a name tag. Sue liked this idea, and tried to pronounce the group worker's name. Ida remained quiet. The group was joined by Peg and Ann,

Group worker observes carefully, noting appearance and speech, in order to get to know each girl.

who came in running and said a gay hello to the group worker and the others. They went through the same introduction procedure.

Liz walked in very slowly and took a seat at the far end of the table, facing the group worker. After the introduction, she reminded the group worker that she had been the girl who was lying in bed sick when the worker was shown around the dormitory some days earlier.

Ella, Jane and Mae came in next. They seemed more hesitant than the others.

The girls asked the group worker various questions about herself, ranging from her age and family to the significance of the red mark on her forehead and the political situation in India. Peg and Sue were especially interested in comparing rates and types of juvenile delinquency in India and the U.S.A., the system of dating, the age of marriage and the restrictions imposed on young people by their family and the school.

The group worker's foreign origin allows adolescent girls some vicarious enjoyment of adventure. It is significant that they move immediately into an area that relates to their own problems.

The worker realized that this was a beginning of discussing their own feelings about all this, but she did not pursue this lead at this time because the girls showed great impatience in raising their questions.

Norma tended to be more patient than the others; Ida was rather quiet; Mae said nothing,

In a later meeting the group worker should move here into the helping role with the girls.

The first meeting allows the girls to completely determine the content. The group worker listens, observes, and notices.

even when encouraged by the group worker. Yet all of them seemed to be listening. Ann wanted to know where India was, and tried to find a map. When she could not find it, the girls laughed at her. The group worker assured Ann that she would bring one and show it to her at the next meeting.

Group worker is sensitive to possible group rejection. She does not reprimand the group, but counteracts the apparent group rejection by showing her interest in Ann.

Peg asked the group worker what she thought about their laundry; Ann said it was hard work. Peg insisted on hearing the group worker's opinion.

The group worker said that it seemed to give them a good experience in working on a job, since this is probably the first such experience for many of them.

The group worker consciously offers the girls a new value: work experience. She does this cautiously, realizing the difference between this and the girls' values. She hopes to open new thinking—not to close the door by preaching.

She added that she was glad that Peg had brought up this topic, because it was time for them to discuss what they were here for. She asked whether any of them knew the purpose of these meetings; three hands went up and the girls started speaking at the same time. The group worker waited a moment. Then Sue said that all the girls had got into trouble and were confused, and now they had an opportunity to discuss their problems with a group worker to get help with them.

Beginning of working with the girls and establishing the purpose of their meetings.

Peg said that she was told that

discussion in a group helps everyone and that they should feel free to air their grievances about their stay in the home and anything else that bothered them.

Liz said that most of them were new and did not understand everything about the home, and so this group meeting would help them. The others nodded.

The girls express the focus of the group meetings.

The group worker said that all these explanations were correct and that she hoped the girls would bring up any problem which affected the individual which they thought could be discussed in the group. She said the girls would be helping each other and themselves.

She also discussed the confidentiality of these discussions. Peg stressed that this was important, but stated that she doubted if anyone would really keep to this and not discuss things with their friends. It seemed she had a particular person in mind, but everybody nodded.

Group worker brings in need for confidentiality. It requires agreement among the group members to adhere voluntarily to this.

Ann asked whether someone was perhaps listening through the key hole. Everybody laughed, but Ann said it was important, and asked the group worker if she could check.

The group worker said she certainly could. Seriously, Ann opened the door, looked left and right, and then said it was all right. This time, she laughed with the others.

Taking problems of a member seriously is the base for a helping relationship.

Peg asked rather angrily why people referred to this home as an *institution*, since it was supposed to be a "home" for girls. The group worker wondered what she understood by "institution." Peg said that it is a place where one is taken against one's wishes because of some wrong-doing.

Members now feel free to open up and discuss specific problems.

The group worker asked if anyone else thought so too, or wanted to add something.

Help with interaction helps members to use group process, not only member-group worker relationship.
Worker gives information; also, indirectly, reassurance.

Since no one volunteered, the group worker said "institution" only means a building which has been set up to carry on some specific purpose, such as a school which educates or this particular home which aims at helping girls who get into difficulties with the law.

Norma said that apparently, then, there is nothing wrong with this word. Peg said it may not seem so now, but it used to make her very mad when people said that she was in an institution. The group worker said that this was understandable since, like Peg, many other people associate the term "institution" with a place of punishment. She stressed again that the meaning was much broader and included places such as schools and hospitals.

Acceptance of individual member's feelings.

There was some expression of anger against personnel in the institution, and then the girls returned to the discussion of what

More "opening up" by the girls. Expression of resentment, anxiety.

this "institution" meant to them.

Peg said that they get no choice of institutions; there is only one other place that is worse. Liz agreed with her.

Peg said that she would do much better in her own home. Sue commented that they are here because they did not do well in their own homes. Peg persisted. Ella asked Peg why she had been removed from her own home. Peg said that she had run away and stayed away for almost four months and was brought back. "For four months! What did you do while you were away!", Ella exclaimed. Peg smiled, but was unwilling to answer.

Interaction between the girls shows individual differences; also, Peg is slowly compelled to move toward a fresh look at her own part in being in the institution.

The group worker said that no one was compelled to answer if she did not want to. Peg then admitted that things were not so bad at the home, but she wished they were allowed to go out.

Group worker establishes the right of members to withhold information. This reassurance relaxes Peg and allows her to drop some of her defenses.

The group worker admitted it was hard when one could not go out at will, but pointed out that the home had certain rules which could not be changed.

Group worker conveys understanding, but also interprets agency policy.

Since they cannot change the rules, it might be helpful to discuss how one can best live with them.

Group worker tries to stimulate new ways of dealing with problems. This is too early and it is not picked up.

Norma said that there were girls who bossed the newcomers and assigned them all the unpleasant jobs. The group worker

Group worker tries to help Norma by making specific suggestions. She may have reacted too quickly here and cut off an opportunity for Norma, and others, to discuss more

encouraged her to speak about this to her housemother who would help to assign jobs more equitably.

Ann suggested that a record be written of everything they would be discussing at these meetings; she volunteered to do this. Norma added that the recorder should also write how much help they got from this.

The group worker said it was all right to record this, but asked them where they would be keeping these records, since they were confidential. They could not think of a suitable place. The group worker suggested that they consult with their housemother who could assign them some place.

Norma said that they are a group and should have a name. She wanted it to be an Indian name because the group worker was Indian; she asked the group worker to give it one.

The group worker suggested that they think of a name in English and then she would give them the Indian translation. This was not yet picked up by the others, although they listened attentively.

The group worker reminded them that it was time to end the meeting. The girls suggested that they see the group worker individually in-between the meetings;

fully the problem of their status as newcomers in a group of peers.

Group worker accepts and limits in the girls' interest—an important way to establish trust.

Norma increasingly shows high identification with the group worker.

The group worker refuses to act for the group and so involves the girls without withholding herself.

Group worker limits (use of given time for group meeting), but accepts the girls' needs for additional contacts; these are also necessary for the intensive treatment purpose of this group.

she agreed to this and wrote down their names.

They commented on the fact that she spelled their names correctly.

They tried to prolong the meeting by asking for pictures of Indian costumes, and so forth. The group worker finally stood up and said it was time to leave. The girls returned their name tags, saying they would like the group worker to take care of them.

Norma preferred to keep hers, saying she would wear it around the home.

Norma shows intense identification.

Comment

This first meeting shows some of the same characteristics as all first ones; namely, the getting acquainted with one another and some "trying out" of the worker, but in a form different from that used by the aggressive boys in Example No. 1. Here the girls "try out" the group worker to see how far she will go in joining them in criticism of the institution and thus become "one of them." The group worker constantly counteracts this by her understanding and acceptance; at the same time she maintains her professional helping role.

The relationship develops comparatively fast because of the girls' great hunger for attention, typical of all institutionalized people; the attraction of the group worker's foreign background; the group worker's personal warmth and her real group work skill. The process is also accelerated because the girls were well prepared for this experience by their housemothers.

In this first meeting, the group worker has begun to individualize the girls; establish the purpose of the group in the framework of the agency; define her own helping role, and create an atmosphere of free interaction.

Several important topics were opened up, but the group worker skillfully avoided pursuing any of them at this first meeting so as to provide all group members with an opportunity for each to express her own interests.

Several of the principles listed on pages 165-170 can be identified in this illustration. Because of the fact that this was a first meeting, the group worker was called upon to interact almost continually with first one individual and then another, although she also interacted with the group as a whole. When relationships are more established, she can—and must—use the interacting process more intensely. *The encouragement and enabling of helpful and cooperative relationships between group members* is an important task before her. She must find every opportunity to let the *members* be the helping persons and she must discipline herself not to be always directly in this role.

Example 3

This example demonstrates the clarification of *group purpose* in a group which has met for a longer time. It is an excerpt from a discussion group of teen-agers who are in foster families and who have difficulties getting along with other teen-agers. The group work service is provided by a family service agency.

Worker turned to Mary Lou and said, "Since you were in the group last year, I wonder if you would be willing to tell us about it—what you thought the meetings were for and some of the things you did." She laughed and said, "You want *me* to say?", somewhat pleased to be called upon and yet a bit flustered. She explained how, at the first meeting, no one knew the other, but soon discovered all the members were being seen by the same caseworker and, although each person was different and each person's problems seemed to be different, you learned to make friends and felt free to talk about your problems. You did not always like all

To work meaningfully with group members, purpose of meetings must be clear to them. Since this group has met for sometime, the group worker calls on a member to explain the purpose so as to (1) establish the importance of member participation and hasten the interaction process and (2) give special status and encouragement to a particular member.

the members, but you learned to tolerate each other. She went at length to explain some of the activities and made particular mention of the times she contributed the refreshments. She said they realized that what the group was, was what they made of it and June, their group worker from last year, would say things that would help them pin-point the discussion. The group was as good as they made it by their contributions. Sometimes they got bored with just talking, so they went bowling or out for pizza. It took awhile to really understand what the group was for, but they enjoyed it and she felt that she got a lot out of it.

Comment

The group member has explained well the specific helpfulness of the group and the role of the members and the group worker. Among teen-agers, this explanation by a peer carries greater weight than would interpretation by an adult.

Example 4

This example demonstrates primarily the *helpful, conscious, differential use of program according to diagnostic evaluation of individual members, group purpose and appropriate values.*

This is a group composed of four 9–11 year-old boys on a children's psychiatric ward. The group meets for one hour twice a week in a large playroom. The group had been meeting weekly for approximately three months; during all this time, the boys continued to demonstrate their need to release aggression. They manifested this by grabbing anything in the room and throwing it at one another. Bob, one of the members, and the youngest, was especially aggressive, but also unable to participate with others. Underlying his aggression was actual fear of the other boys. He also had attached himself closely to the group worker and had difficulties in sharing him with the others.

To help Bob become more involved in group activity and also to meet the needs of all the boys for aggressive play, the group worker chose to bring to the group an attractive plastic ball which would not hurt anyone who might get hit with it.

Before introducing the ball to the entire group, he brought it to Bob's room where the group worker and Bob played a game of catch. This was done to give Bob the satisfaction of having seen the ball first and to not have to share immediately the beloved worker with others.

A day later, the group worker brought the ball again, but this time he played with Bob while he was in the ward with several other children. Bob was able to accept this experience in sharing the worker because the others were less involved with the group worker than he was.

Three days later, the group worker brought the ball to the group meeting and Bob asked to play with it. Group worker said that he certainly could, and that everyone would be playing with it today.

The other boys responded eagerly when they saw the ball.

Next step in helping Bob to learn how to share a toy and a friend.

Jack suggested a game of catch. All the boys formed a circle except Bob who withdrew into the corner and stood behind a table, working with some clay.

Group worker said that the boys would like to have Bob in their group too, and that he knew he was eager to play with the ball.

Group worker understands Bob's ambivalence and lets him know that he is wanted as part of the group.

In the game, George started to throw the ball in different ways; playing ball is one of George's best skills, and he is slightly more mature in his interests and skills than the other boys.

Group worker then suggested that maybe each one could think of different ways of throwing the ball; he developed a type of "follow the leader" out of this. When one person threw the ball a certain way, each of the others had to follow suit until it reached the person who had begun the game. Then the next person had a turn at inventing a new way of throwing it.

Skillful inclusion of a leader so that everybody can participate.

Throughout the whole meeting, the ball was the center of attention and the boys used it in many ways. George finally organized a ball game and everyone took turns batting the ball with a stick.

Bob maintained his position in the corner and continued to work on the clay, but every time the ball rolled over toward him, he

The group worker does not demand that the boy participate, recognizing his deep fear and jealousy, but again encourages him and gives him attention.

grabbed it and held onto it. The group worker again recognized that he wanted to play with the ball and again invited him to join the others. He also reminded him that the other boys needed the ball for their game.

Several times Bob gave up the ball readily, but once he stubbornly held onto it and said he would not give it back, although he made no attempt to play with it.

The other boys came over to him and tried to get the ball away from him. The group worker intervened to prevent its being taken away from him by force.

The group worker protects Bob because he knows of his fear of others. He also recognizes that Bob several times has successfully overcome his impulses (he returned the ball)—quite an accomplishment. He does not want to add more frustration.

While this was happening, George "accidentally" smashed what Bob had been making out of clay. Bob immediately flew into a rage and ran out of the room crying and screaming. He huddled with the ball in a corner of the hall outside the room. All the boys ran after him and continued to try to grab the ball away.

Worker stood between him and the others and said that George was very upset because he had spent a lot of time working on the clay, and that he was holding the ball because he knew the boys wanted it.

Group worker limits and explains Bob's behavior to him and to the others, thus letting him feel he is understood and helping the others to experience compassion.

Suddenly Jack ran back into the room and returned in a few minutes with an exact replica of what Bob had made out of clay. Group

Emotionally disturbed children need to feel secure and wanted to be able to give. Jack's gesture shows that he feels this way. Since

worker said this was very nice of
Jack to do this for Bob; Bob remained unappeased. At this
point, George and Jack had to
leave for another activity. Sam
and Bob lingered on.

*George cannot yet accept this, the
group worker moves in for him. He
knows that Jack needs this
recognition.*

Worker suggested that the two
of them might want to play catch
for a few minutes while he was
cleaning up the room. Bob did
this eagerly, and both boys enjoyed the game for a short time.

*Without the preceding support,
Bob would not have been able to
move out to a peer.*

Comment

This example shows how much must be understood about individual dynamics if the group worker is to move purposefully. Bob
needs help with his feelings of sibling rivalry. It is known that people
move from one developmental stage to a next one only when they
gain satisfaction and see it either as desirable or not too threatening.
An infant is better willing to accept the cup instead of a mother's
breast if it had full satisfaction in the early stage and the weaning is
not done abruptly. The group worker uses this knowledge by introducing the sharing of the ball (and the beloved adult) gradually.

Movement toward a more healthy attitude is achieved (Bob finally
can play with another boy) by careful planning of program media, by
insight, and by minimum use of verbalization. This is more appropriate in this case because of the age and sickness of this child.

Example 5

This example demonstrates mainly *the provision of opportunities
for experiencing new forms of relationships, self, and ways of
problem solving.*

This group consists of seven adolescent boys who were referred to a neighborhood house because of social adjustment
problems in school: underachievement, emotional immaturity,
shyness, withdrawal, feelings of inferiority, and insecurity. This
is about the ninth meeting of the group. The excerpt describes
a situation which occurred when the group worker was driving
the boys in the station wagon. Unstructured discussion was tak-

ing place at this time. The boys exchanged stories and told jokes. The group worker recorded:

Jack then said, "Did you hear about the lion who swallowed a 'niggah'?" The boy said, "No." "Yeh," Jack replied. "He swallowed a chocolate man." The boys laughed. I did not laugh and waited for the laughter to subside. The boys became aware of my seriousness and looked questioningly at me.

By not doing something (by not joining in their laughter), the group worker draws attention of the boys to himself.

I asked Jack what might not be "good" about that story. He looked puzzled. I asked the boys what the word, "niggah," meant. They said, after a moment's hesitation, "Negro." I asked them if they felt that there was any difference in the meaning of the two words. They said nothing. I said that the word, "niggah," is a derogatory term and hurts people. I illustrated this by mentioning other undesirable terms that could be applied to other groups such as our parents, friends, religious groups, and ethnic groups.

Group worker works toward a change in values and relationships with another race by drawing attention to the use of derogatory terms and helping the youngsters to think instead of preaching to them.

We discussed this during the remainder of the trip.

Somewhat later in the afternoon, we happened to see Mrs. Jones with her daughter; they are Negroes. I stopped to talk to them and introduced the group members to them. After introductions, Mrs. Jones and I talked a bit about our work at the Urban League; the boys raised questions

Meeting a person of another race alone does not change attitudes. "Value changing" occurs through experiencing emotions. Here the helping agent was encounter with members of a different race and the boys' identification with the group worker.

about it. They seemed to be genuinely interested. Obviously many
of the boys had never before met
a Negro.

Comment

The new experience was not planned by the social group worker.
He used the opportunity when it arose, being aware of the fact that
the insulting behavior of the youngsters was apparently more related
to ignorance than to deep-seated prejudice. He did not preach to
them, but helped them become aware of the feelings of others by
using comparisons that were familiar to them and that they could
understand better. He also understood the phenomenon of "identification" and used the good relationship he had with the boys by letting
them feel that he himself would not act or speak the same way that
they did. At the same time that he disapproved of their behavior he
tried to understand them and not to "shame" them. He understood
that, in this case, the adolescent would only rebel and would not be
free to accept new ways of interacting with others.

To demonstrate the helping process of social group work in time
sequence, the records of seven meetings of one formed group are
presented in the following pages.

It is a formed group in a treatment institution for emotionally
disturbed children and adolescents. Some children in this institution go to public school; others, do not, because they are incapable
of accepting the pressure of a public school.

This group consists of six children who can tolerate only limited
hours of tutoring and therefore who are not in school. Criteria for
their selection for group work treatment were:

1. Each one had been in the institution for some time, but had
   been incapable of accepting responsibility for his or her behavior; they blamed "the outside," "the other one," as disturbed or disturbing.
2. Each had difficulties in getting along with children and adults
   alike, although behavior patterns varied greatly.
3. Three of the six children selected were incapable of involving
   themselves in individual treatment.

The purpose of the group was:

1. to help them to speak more freely about their resentments, hopes, and interests;
2. to give them the special attention of an understanding adult;
3. to allow them support by the group or withdrawal if content of discussion became too threatening (this was expected to help the three most withdrawn members to feel more comfortable and to free them;)
4. to experience some new forms of behavior;
5. to gain some insight into themselves; and
6. to help them to relate more closely to each other in an environment less demanding than that of the daily living group.

Those selected were Elaine, 14 years; Susie, 16 years; Anne, 12 years; Pat, 13 years; Jim, 13 years, and Ed, 13 years.

Elaine had been in eighteen different foster homes before she was referred to the treatment center. She had been abandoned as a small child. Several times she had returned to her own home where she was used by the parents to steal for them. Elaine was unable to make relationships in foster families; she was aggressive and cruel to siblings. She made sexual advances to the males in the foster families. She was finally placed in a mental hospital and referred from there to the treatment center. She was an intelligent, physically attractive girl who dominated the living group.

Susie's parents were divorced and there had been serious conflict in the family for several years. She had a younger sister in a foster home; she herself could not accept a foster home and showed withdrawn or hostile, almost paranoid, behavior. She had some seizures which resembled epileptic seizures. At age 15, she was hospitalized in an acute state of psychosis and received some electric shock treatment. She was a girl of average intelligence, but incapable of involving herself in individual therapy.

Anne's parents were divorced. One younger brother lived with the mother. Anne originally was no behavior problem. She had been a good student. She suddenly refused to attend school and became a complete recluse. So far it had been impossible to determine any specific cause for these changes. She was referred to a mental hospital in a state of complete muteness. From there she came to the children's treatment center.

Pat's parents were divorced. She was an only child. She had been referred to the hospital a year before referral to the children's treatment center in a state of acute psychosis and with severe tics. The school reported that her behavior had been difficult for a long time previous to this, that she was stealing, lying, and constantly touching other people.

At the time of the group meetings, Pat was well in touch with reality, but still needed to touch people. She seemed to be of average intelligence.

Jim was referred mainly because of severe temper tantrums and highly aggressive behavior. The family was generally intact. His mother seemed to have special difficulties in accepting a very active boy. The father was engrossed in his work. He was a handsome boy and seemed to be of average intelligence.

Ed's parents were unknown. He had been abandoned as a small infant and grew up in several foster homes and children's institutions. He acted out aggressively and was referred to a mental hospital. His comparatively low intelligence and cold indifference made treatment difficult.

Record 1

The Assistant Director, Miss Andrews, had called the six children together for a ten-minute meeting and explained that they would meet regularly with Miss Smith, the social group worker. The children had come in, full of hostility and resistance. Every single one made remarks that showed they were coming against their will. *Susie* wondered whether she had "done something." *Pat*, who had greeted Miss Smith with great affection earlier in the morning, was apparently puzzled by the hostility of the others and did not know what to do. This meant that she was relatively quiet. She got up early because she could not sit still, not even for ten minutes. *Anne* was the one who tried to calm the others. *Jim, Ed,* and *Elaine* were most outspoken in their resistance, saying that they were mad at the counselors and therefore would not come to anything that was suggested by them: "If they don't cooperate with us, why should we cooperate with them?" Miss Smith explained that she had suggested these meetings so that they would have more attention and could talk about some of the reasons why they wanted to get out of there; she also suggested that they could do some other things if they did not want to talk.

Elaine insisted that they talk too much with too many people already; *Jim* said that he sees his own doctor, although he could not remember his name; *Ed* complained that nobody listens anyhow. Miss Smith mentioned that she thought they were already starting quite a good meeting and it would be interesting to hear why they were so angry.

Elaine complained about not getting any decent clothes, and *Ed* began to talk about how wonderful the jail was and how one could tear up bed clothes which one could not do here.

The explosion was violent, yet with the exception of *Pat*, they all stayed and did not walk out

Group worker accepts hostility and explains purpose of the meetings.

Group worker accepts the children's feelings and lets them know that they have in their own way started to fulfill the purpose of the meetings.

until Miss Andrews and Miss Smith closed the meeting.

After the meeting, *Pat* came up to Miss Smith and said she would like to come, but she would be just "crazy" if she did not have cigarettes during the meeting.

Comment

Children in institutions usually have a long series of experiences of being pushed from one person to another. All six of these children have had demands made on them to relate to adults who then rejected them. They feel resentful and protective of themselves. In a highly authoritarian environment these children would come to such meetings without objection but with their guard up. The atmosphere of this institution is such that it allows them to express their resentment and distrust. The group worker knows that it will take time to overcome this.

Record 2

The children were present on time. They were much friendlier than the first time, and grouped around Miss Smith readily.

Miss Smith had prepared cookies and had brought some pictures for them to choose from and to use in any way they wanted to.

The offering of food is not a "bribe." It gives oral satisfaction to these very immature children; it helps to create an informal atmosphere; it is a symbol of the group worker's giving interest.

Ed and *Jim* were the first ones to arrive; they were very polite in taking only one cookie, commenting on them and saying that Miss Smith was a good baker. This was quite different from their earlier hostile attitude towards Miss Smith.

The pictures were chosen to allow for individual withdrawal if a group member had a need for it.

Elaine, Susie, and *Anne* came

in next. At this point the kids stuffed themselves with cookies because competition started. Miss Smith had to reserve some for *Pat* who had not yet come in: otherwise they would not have left any for her. This little incident is quite symptomatic of Pat's position in the group.

Miss Smith asked the youngsters whether they could give her three minutes in which she would again mention why the group was meeting, after which it would be *their* meeting. She said that she understood their anger since they meet too many people and probably could not feel free to talk openly with everybody. She suggested in this meeting that they could either do things or they could talk with one another about their problems; she told them she would not *press* them to reveal themselves.

Explanation of group purpose while accepting the children's feelings. Also some interpretation as to the reasons for their hostility.

Elaine burst out with the fact that it was true that one needed to talk to people, but then, also, something must happen. She complained loudly and violently about having been on restriction since June just because she ran away at that time. She described, angrily, being in isolation at a mental hospital and not being permitted to go shopping now. She also complained that other youngsters who also had run away

Beginning of opening up.

had not been put on restriction at
all.

Jim contradicted this in a very
calm manner, saying that these
kids had been on restriction too,
but for a much shorter time. *Ed*
constantly was supporting *Elaine*.

It was evident that *Elaine* and
Ed played into each other's emotions and increased each other's
hostility. *Elaine* complained
about Dr. Abel, the psychiatrist,
and his discussing with another
girl whether she had been involved
in a sex episode involving several
boys and girls. She violently denied that she had any part in it.
Jim smiled and said that he could
vouch for the fact that *Elaine* had
no part in it, "but don't ask me
how I know." *Susie* could vouch
for the fact that *Elaine* was not
involved but she, too, would not
want to be asked how she knew;
she asked that the others stop
talking about it.

Ed's hostility during the meeting was directed mostly against
Miss Andrews, a counselor—
Joanne—and his father. He insisted that Joanne slapped people
around, but did not dare do it to
him anymore as he had "once
kicked her back. Now when she
cannot vent her anger on me, she
goes to the girls and slaps them
around." (He obviously had
learned about projection.) He
talked about going to conventions

*Group worker observes group
interaction and member roles. Jim
brings in reality and is able to
contradict Elaine.*

*Children are still guarded, but
begin talking about their concerns.*

Group worker observes and listens.

with his father. When Miss
Smith asked what kind of conventions they were, he said they
were related to appliances; that
his father had four huge business
concerns; that he sits like "stupid
old Carter (the director) with
his feet up on the desk and does
nothing."

*Ed's view of all persons in
authority is much related to his
feelings about his father. Group
worker purposely encourages his
talking about his father to allow
him to vent feelings.*

Later in the meeting, just before *Ed* left, he refused to help
Miss Smith pick up something,
saying he hated women and
would have nothing to do with
them. He showed great resentment toward anybody presenting
either parent figure.

Anne was very quiet during
the meeting. She was most interested in the pictures Miss Smith
had brought. She checked the
printing on the back of the pictures and asked Miss Smith to
translate, since the writing was in
French.

*It is significant that this "mute"
girl makes her first contact through
focus on a language.*

Susie chose a striking picture of
Christ from those Miss Smith had
brought and then asked her about
a poem on the card that was also
written in a foreign language;
Miss Smith translated it. It was
interesting that during the short
time that Miss Smith translated
poetry the children were quiet
and listened. They made no remark related to the content, but
they seemed to react to the sound
of words. *Elaine* said that *Susie*
also wrote poetry. The poetry she

quoted consisted of hostile ditties, especially about Miss Andrews.

Miss Smith wondered whether they would like to start a newspaper since some of them seemed to like to write and talk about things. She suggested that *Elaine* should write about how it felt to be on restriction, that that would be a good way of letting people know about it. *Elaine* did not react positively but, interestingly enough, *Ed* picked this up. He made a formal motion that *Elaine* should write this in her spare time since she was so much in her room. *Elaine* said she had a typewriter and if anybody wanted to write something, she would type it. Miss Smith did not get the impression that these were actual plans, but felt that they were quick reactions to a suggestion that seemed to stimulate them in some way.

All this discussion was interrupted constantly by a great deal of jumping up, asking for cigarettes, and unrelated talking.

Miss Smith had asked the counselor whether it was permissible to smoke in that room; apparently this was all right. Miss Smith thought it interesting that *Jim* reacted very reasonably and positively when she said that as long as they wanted to smoke he should also bring ash trays and see that they were used. He ac-

Group worker channels aggression into some positive activity.

The stage of restlessness in which these children are, is accepted. The group worker's calm helps to allow for beginning interaction—as seen above.

It is important that the person who comes into an institution from the "outside" accept the rules so that consistency is safeguarded. If the rules are considered wrong, then this must be taken up with the administration, not the children.

cepted this without any resistance.

At one point during the meeting one of the youngsters suddenly discovered that the group was meeting in Mr. Carter's office. *Susie*, who up till then had been stonily silent, smiled ironically and said, "Oh! Mr. Carter!" Then she took a handful of pieces of paper that she had rolled up nervously and threw them on the floor. This hostile gesture was a signal for more hostile behavior on the part of the other children. Miss Smith could feel contagion start. The next minute *Elaine* also threw paper on the floor, *Pat* poised her cigarette to dump the ashes, and the two boys lifted their bottles to pour out the pop. Before this, Miss Smith had sat quietly next to *Susie*; now she got up in an unhurried way, walked over to *Pat* with whom she had the best relationship, turned to her but talked to everyone, saying, "We have the privilege of meeting in a pretty nice office. Would it not be better not to get it too messed up?" Would this approach work? Miss Smith was gratified to see that neither the ashes nor the pop went to the floor. *Pat* used the ash tray; the boys drank the pop, as if this had been their intention all the time. No further comment was made.

They began to talk about the

Group worker observes "language of behavior." Susie's first open reaction is a hostile one, directed toward absent authority. It is non-verbal.

Group worker anticipates destructive action before it is accomplished. She shifts her own position (gets up), but not abruptly. Aggressive action by the group worker would arouse more hostility. Non-intervention would be seen by the youngsters as permission to be destructive. The group worker keeps calm and friendly—a contrast to the hostile atmosphere—she relates to the total group through one of the members who can accept her. She uses reasoning and enlists the help of the group, without "preaching." She allows for "face-saving." Hostile people feel often relieved when prevented from "acting out," but do not want to admit this.

fact that there was a staff meeting going on and asked who was being staffed. Miss Smith replied, "Andy." *Ed* said that Andy had told them that he would go to public school and, if this were so, he—*Ed*—would *never* go to school. Here *Elaine* was helpful by saying that he wouldn't be in the same school as Andy, so he would not have to worry. The youngsters expressed hostility toward Andy, but *Elaine* defended him.

Again the "group process" is allowed to work. The children help each other.

There was much shouting against counselors—wanting to slap their faces and to kill them. At one point Miss Smith said, "Well, smash their faces, all right, but what good will it do?" This was surely the wrong thing to say. *Ed* quickly said that Miss Smith had given them permission to attack the counselors.

Hostile children pick up quickly any semblance of adult sanction to be destructive. There is a great difference between the principle of acceptance and permissiveness. The latter may be harmful if the individual feels delivered to his impulses or feels encouraged to harm others.

Jim got up and said he wanted to leave; he was given permission to do so. There was some talk about what they wanted to do next time they met. *Elaine* clamored for movies; Miss Smith suggested that this was something they could do outside of the group meetings, but if they wanted to take a walk in good weather, she would find out if this was possible. After a little while, *Elaine, Susie* and *Ed* left. (At one point, *Ed* asked Miss Smith if she had really been in an internment

Group worker limits the meetings to their purpose, allowing for different forms of fulfilling it. Movies present purely spectator activities and are not conducive to interaction; walks may stimulate discussions.

camp. This was not followed up, but apparently had much meaning to him.)

Miss Smith stayed a little longer with *Anne* and *Pat*. At this time, *Anne* became more active. She was very reasonable, showed Miss Smith the pictures in which she was interested, and tried to read some of the headings that were written in English. There was, at first, a rather positive interaction between the two girls and Miss Smith. Yet when *Pat* reached for some of the pictures that *Anne* held, *Anne* did not want to give them to her. *Anne* immediately got up to leave and said she could not stand *Pat*.

Miss Smith stayed with *Pat* another fifteen minutes. *Pat* spoke about the girls' not liking her. Miss Smith wondered why; she said she just didn't know, that *she* did like *them*. Miss Smith suggested that it could be that they felt pushed by her; she nodded her head and said this could be. She said she had come to the center originally for temper tantrums, but she felt she was much better now. She had been in a hospital and had hated it, "especially those dopey psychiatrists and dopey nurses."

Pat said she was glad we had these group meetings. She also liked several of the counselors.

Group worker works with one of the subgroups—the two girls who have little ability to express themselves.

The "silent" girl can express hostility only in the intimacy of the small subgroup (pair).

It is part of group work to allow the group members individual contacts with the group worker. Such contacts help the group worker to get to know members in a different situation (child/adult) and allows the group members to receive some individual attention from the group worker.

Pat's need to be liked by her contemporaries forces her into conforming to their expression of

When *Pat* was alone with Miss Smith she could speak about positive feelings which she did not reveal under group pressure. She was physically affectionate, but seemed to react rather reasonably to a friendly hug. She then could let go. For example, she tried to climb on Miss Smith's lap and put her arms around her. Miss Smith was friendly but did not let *Pat* sit on her lap; *Pat* was able to accept this without feeling hurt or pushed.

hostility. The individual contact allows her here to be herself— hopefully strengthening her ego.

One of Pat's problems is her constant need for physical contact. The group worker must help her to limit this without rebuffing her. This is only help on a more superficial level. It is hoped that satisfactions in the group and some insight gained may lessen Pat's infantile needs.

Miss Smith went to the girls' dormitory with *Pat*, and offered to help her clean up her dresser. The rather amusing answer was "Oh, no! Let's not do that! I must know where everything is!"

After leaving *Pat*, Miss Smith took *Ed* a sweater he had left at the meeting; he was very gracious and thanked her for having thought of him.

The group worker shows her interest and concern by doing the "little things" mothers do for children.

Record 3

This morning a new boy, John, had come for a trial visit to the center. John was a 12-year-old, tall, and a very hyperactive boy. He had been afraid to stay inside the house. Miss Smith had followed the crying boy when he ran outside, and had walked around with him.

When she returned, she saw *Ed* sitting at the window; he had observed them. *Ed* said, "That kid is a pretty big baby, isn't he? What's the matter with him?"

Miss Smith asked, "Ed, have you ever been afraid of something?"

Group worker enlists a boy's understanding of another boy— and also allows him to feel that one must not be ashamed of fear.

Ed looked very thoughtful and said, "Yes, sometimes."

Miss Smith went on, "Well, that is what is happening here; he is afraid that he will be locked up. He has had such an experience once."

Ed got up from his chair and said, very seriously, "I can talk to him. I am a kid like he is. He understands *me*."

He went back to his room and got his jacket. He persuaded John to sit in his parents' car with him. The boy finally agreed to this, and *Ed* talked to him quietly. He explained to him that no door was locked; that the food was good; that people were not mean, and that he should not be afraid. *Ed* succeeded in calming this very upset newcomer.

Ed is helpful to the new boy; it also helps Ed to see his own situation in a more positive light.

Record of Group Meeting

Elaine and *Anne* came in first. *Elaine* looked unusually pretty in a new blue and white sweater. The counselor told Miss Smith that *Elaine* wanted to talk to her alone. *Elaine* said quietly that she thought the girls would like to use this group meeting to talk over a lot of things, but that it does not work because of the presence of the boys. She wished Miss Smith would let the boys go; she thought they were too agitated and loud. Also, "when boys and girls are together, one cannot talk freely."

Miss Smith explained to her that the staff had thought this might be an opportunity for boys and girls to learn to *talk* to one another; she added that she knew that the boys, too, needed help, yet perhaps their meeting together was really not so good. She suggested that all of them talk it through during the group meeting.

Elaine was not sure that she wanted this. (Later, during the meeting, she gave permission to bring up her concern.)

Pat was away shopping and was not in the group today.

Susie, Ed and *Jim* arrived together. *Susie* brought a record player and a stack of records, but they were not used during the meeting. *Ed* was very quiet and still glowing with the satisfaction he had derived from his contact with the new boy. He started out by saying that he thought he had helped him. Miss Smith agreed and thanked him for what he had done. This was interesting to the other youngsters, and *Ed*, calmly and thoughtfully, told about the

The request of a youngster is taken seriously by the group worker. She gives the reason for the agency's decision, but allows for revision. She suggests involvement of the group in the discussion because this is a serious problem concerning all of them.

Confidentiality is kept. The subject is brought up only when Elaine gives permission to do so.

incident. He added that he thought this was a "pretty good kid who can make it."

Miss Smith suggested that John could "make it" only if other kids would help him. He was scared of others because he thought they might tease him. *Jim* wondered why the boy should be afraid of teasing. Miss Smith threw out the question whether there was anything kids get teased about? There was some talk about bringing teasing upon oneself. *Ed* said that this big boy surely would be good at ball playing and then nobody would tease him.

Miss Smith said he was good at it, but that he was self-conscious about his being so tall at his age. *Jim* identified with this by saying that he, too, was tall when he was 12 years old, but it had only bothered him for a little while and now he thought it was fine because he could play good basketball.

They then had a little and relatively calm discussion on the way they could help each other. *Ed* was the leader in this, pointing out how important it was and how he thought they all could get out much faster if they would help one another more.

Miss Smith brought up the question of *Elaine*'s having said she felt badly about not being allowed to go out, and there, too,

Group worker helps youngsters think through their own relations with others.

Beginning insight (see purpose of the group meetings).

Group work builds on the beginning insight and helps the children recognize that feelings about oneself have impact on one's actions.

Group worker helps to focus on a member of the group who needs special help.

206 PRINCIPLES OF SOCIAL GROUP WORK IN PRACTICE

they could help themselves and each other. *Elaine* was very quiet and calm during all of this meeting; she said that she tried to become more reasonable, but it wasn't always easy. *Ed* complimented *Elaine* on being "a recreational worker" and helping others to arrange parties and dances. *Elaine* mentioned that this was her intent, that she liked to cheer up people, that she had even done this when she was locked in with adults on the ward of a mental hospital; she added that this wasn't always easy because sometimes people were too mean and made it too hard for her. At this time she again expressed sharp hostility against Dr. Abel. As had happened the last time, she insisted that he called her a liar and always "just sits there."

Elaine projects again on others.

Miss Smith raised the question of whether it wasn't enjoyable to have somebody's attention. *Elaine* felt that they needed attention badly, but she did not like to be stared at; Mr. Olds (the caseworker) did not do it that way. She recently had tried to stare down Mr. Olds and he didn't like it either!

Group worker tries to let Elaine express some positive feelings about psychiatric interviews, since she is aware of her ambivalence.

Some people need as much help with expression of warm feelings as with those of hostility.

Miss Smith had again brought cookies. There was less grabbing this time and far more concern for others who wanted some. She had also brought some old Christmas cards. *Anne, Elaine,* and *Susie* were especially interested in these. There was some squabbling between *Anne* and *Elaine* when *Elaine* accused *Anne* of never participating in anything and of not even wanting to dance. *Anne's* response was "Oh, pooh!" *Elaine* and *Ed* told *Anne* that this was what she was doing all the time: her only response was, "Oh, pooh!" *Anne* just shook her head.

Anne had seen that Miss Smith had also brought paper and charcoal; she asked to draw. This immediately stimulated the others, with the exception of *Jim.* They all took paper, including Miss Smith, and sat down to draw. *Jim* was restless, as usual, and jumped up to get cigarettes; he then asked for a typewriter and typed for a major part of the meeting while the others were drawing.

It is important to children that adults do things with them.

During the drawing period, some discussion was carried on with *Elaine's* trying to be serious and *Ed's* defeating it. With *Elaine's* permission, Miss Smith introduced the idea of *Elaine's* feeling that the boys should not participate because they did not involve themselves. She was a bit amused when *Ed* objected to this on the grounds that the boys needed the meetings too, and argued that there was no reason

Group worker remembers the promise made to Elaine to discuss her concern. It is brought up when Elaine feels frustrated.

why the girls alone should have that privilege. (What a contrast to the first meeting!) For a short time, he did listen to what *Elaine* was trying to say, but then he would digress and suggest that all the children band against the counselors and that way achieve what they wanted to.

At one point, *Jim* pulled out the paper from the typewriter and brought it over to Miss Smith asking her to read it aloud.

It was just practice typing—no words. Miss Smith read it, however, pronouncing the funny sounds that this kind of jumble makes. The youngsters, including *Jim*, howled with good-natured laughter and, for a little moment, *Jim* was, in this way, the center of attention. He then asked for paper to draw.

Group worker joins the spirit of fun. The relaxing "pause" is very necessary in meetings which have much emotional content. Also, Jim is thus drawn out of his isolation.

This spontaneous drawing brought out the fact that *Anne* could draw very well; she drew mostly faces. *Elaine* drew lovely, calm landscapes; *Jim*, a Mexican. Miss Smith commented on *Elaine*'s calm, and she replied, "This is the way I feel right now." *Susie* drew caricatures of several staff members, with a delightful sense of specifics: "He always bends over the desk" or "He always puts his feet on the table." Her drawings were caricatures, but they were not hostile. She showed pride in them and wanted

Children express feelings without using words.

the staff members to see them. Miss Smith suggested they all draw what they wanted to be. *Susie* drew a girl on a horse; *Elaine*, a tree; *Anne*, a walnut; *Jim*, a stiff man with a big, round stomach and a pipe in his mouth.

With the exception of *Jim* and *Anne*, they were verbal about their drawings and could explain what it was they wanted to be.

Miss Smith mentioned laughingly that she had always wanted to be a duck; *Elaine* immediately drew one, but said that she would not like it because ducks "get hunted," a very significant remark. *Jim*, always the least verbal, drew a picture and said that it was "a ship passing another ship." Miss Smith felt that this remark was symbolic of the way *Jim* relates to other people.

When all the drawing paper was used up, the youngsters became quite restless. They tried to play with the tape recorder; Miss Smith promised to find out whether they could use one the next time. They left, except for *Ed*. The meeting had lasted over an hour—a longer time than had been spent the previous time.

Ed stayed, working at the typewriter. He showed a surprising amount of determination to learn; he wrote his name over and over, repeating it every time he made a mistake. He told Miss

This is helpful to the group worker to understand the children better. It also frees the children to express their hopes.

Anne's drawing of the walnut was highly significant—a closed object one must force open to find its content.

Smith that he wanted to learn. He then went on to talk about the new boy, saying that he thought he was just "in a state of shock with fear." Miss Smith asked him how he knew so much about people; he replied, "I was a long time in a mental hospital —I *know* how it feels."

Group worker gives Ed recognition for his thoughtfulness and understanding.

Record 4

Miss Smith came in early and met the girls at the breakfast table. Their greeting was warm.

Relationship has changed considerably since the first meeting.

Susie and *Pat* came into the meeting room a little ahead of *Elaine* and *Anne,* and used the tape recorder. A counselor came in to say that *Ed* and *Jim* had preferred not to come. Miss Smith learned later that they had gone hunting with the other boys. This seemed right for them.

The girls sat close together on the sofa. *Elaine* expressed her delight that they were without the boys and could finally talk things over. Miss Smith suggested that *Elaine* start with whatever she had on her mind. Very seriously, she said that she was annoyed with the way the girls' quarters looked. "Nobody here but Kay and I care whether the place looks decent or not. I wish we could do something about this." They talked a little about this; Miss Smith tried to help the other girls to express themselves.

Pat said she just didn't know how to fix up things. *Susie* said it was boring to put things together and she would just fall asleep on the bed. *Elaine* retorted that she slept too much anyway. *Anne* did not involve herself. *Elaine* once again expressed her frustration. Miss Smith wondered whether they wanted her to go with them and help them to clean up and, perhaps, go on from there. *Elaine* objected to this, saying that the kids would never learn how to do things for themselves because they get too much help now. Miss Smith asked when they thought was the best time to clean up. *Susie* said, "At midnight." Miss Smith wondered if they cleaned up at midnight, when would she sleep; *Susie* replied, quite seriously, that she liked to sleep during the day and to be up at night, but, she added, she would try to clean up a little during the day.

The discussion shows beginning sense of responsibility, with Elaine's carrying the lead. The group worker gives support, but does not pressure those girls who are not ready to take on such responsibility.

Miss Smith had brought along some beautiful Hallowe'en cookies; the girls admired them and ate them quite fast. She also had brought some little gifts for them which she had purchased on a trip to Canada. There was little reaction to them; the only overt reaction was that each one tried to exchange the one she had received for another one.

Deprived children always have a fear of being "cheated." The reaction to the gifts shows this deep distrust in spite of a beginning trusting relationship with the group worker.

They spotted the recorder and

were very eager to begin working with it.

Miss Smith played back the recordings that *Susie* and *Pat* had made while they were alone in the room before the meeting began. *Pat* had talked most of the time and was unintelligible. *Susie* had expressed hostility toward Mr. Carter. Miss Smith had the impression, however, that the hostility was only in words, that underlying it were feelings bordering on adoration. *Susie* constantly begged Miss Smith not to erase the dictation so that Mr. Carter could hear it later.

Again the incapacity of expressing positive feelings.

When the girls gathered around the microphone they saw, through the glass window, the staff meeting being held across the hall. This stimulated many remarks about staff members.

Miss Smith suggested that they record what they wanted to say and then talk it over. *Elaine* was immediately enthusiastic about this idea and dictated with much feeling and clarity. The other girls were very quiet and considerate of her. When she played it back, they squealed with delight, especially whenever she said something against a member of the staff.

Group worker at this point structures the meeting to allow for a more focused expression.

Miss Smith tried to encourage *Anne* to dictate. Her extremely constricted personality was again seen in the way she used—or was

Children who cannot speak freely to others, frequently open up when they can talk to something impersonal, as a microphone; or

unable to use—this medium. She wanted to recite the Gettysburg Address; she could say only a few words. She changed into playing a "Knock, Knock" game on the tape recorder—then stopped abruptly.

Susie was asked to dictate. This time she spoke with real emotional expression. *Pat* followed. Her comments were more shallow than those of *Susie* and *Elaine*.

When Elaine reached for the recorder again, Miss Smith asked her to wait a bit. The girls clustered closely around Miss Smith; she had her arm around Susie. She told the girls that this group session had much meaning because they talked about things that really concerned them. She wondered whether it was all right for their recording to be transcribed so that they could discuss at the next meeting the problems they had raised. The girls gave this permission with great sincerity. *Susie* insisted, though, that she wanted to call Mr. Carter to *hear it.*

Elaine then began to dictate about an upset in the girls' group that had happened just the day before; *Susie* followed her.

(A transcript of the recording follows this extract.)

When the girls listened to what they had dictated, they

when they can speak through a disguise, e.g., puppets. This is the reason why the group worker uses this medium.

Group worker sees progress in the way children use the group. She makes them aware of this to motivate further involvement.

She considers the recording valuable enough to be preserved and on which to build a base for more discussion.

Transcript must have girls' permission (ethics of the profession) since confidentiality has been guaranteed.

showed the usual delight of all people who hear their own voices and their surprise at how they sounded. They laughed hysterically any time names of staff members in authority were mentioned (e.g., Dr. Abel, Mr. Dill, Mr. Carter, or Miss Andrews). They squealed and shouted.

This meeting had taken almost one and one-half hours. *Ed* joined the group for a few minutes toward the close of the meeting.

Length of stay is significant since attention span of the children is low. To stay longer means that they were highly motivated.

Girls' Recording

Elaine. I think this place is very annoying. It is very dirty, and you are getting sworn at by little brats just about every day. I think Carter runs this place rather poorly because he shows favoritism to people. Olds—he lies, oh, how he lies! He tells Ollie (another girl) one thing and then will go and tell me another thing, and Ollie and I will come down and tell each other what he said, and back and forth. He will tell Ollie something about me. One day he called Ollie "a damn girl" because she went to see her foster parents, and I told Ollie about it and she went up and asked him about it and he said, "No," that he did not say that. But Ollie and I have a plan that some day he is going to say something and we

Elaine actually was in a phase of deep attachment to her case worker. Her attack on him was caused by jealousy. It was very helpful to her to be able to say these things; it was her way of saying, "Please love me— only me."

are going to go up and catch him in his lies. Ha, ha!

Pat. I think Evans is a dirty, low-down bastard. I am very angry at him. I am thinking of putting a hole in his bucket and filling it up and slugging him in the teeth. Heavens, tamergatroid! And I'll throw a mop in his face or a bucket of water. Like me and Susie almost put soap in his face, but instead he made us throw it out the window. And that darn, low-down boosterhead, Olds. As far as he is concerned he can go jump in a lake. I think he did, didn't he? Well, I'm going downstairs after our meeting and I'm going to go pop Evans in the mouth or make a hole in his buckets, or throw some soap or something on him. Or maybe I'll dump cleanser in his hair. Maybe he would be happy to be gray-haired then.

Miss Smith. Please don't.

Pat. Why?

Miss Smith. You might hurt him.

Pat. Heavens, tamergatroid! I'd be glad to. Mr. Carter, the bald-headed monkey, as far as I'm concerned, he can drink lots of coffee and drop dead. And Andrews! Oh heavens, tamergatroid! I can't stand her, but *sometimes Abel is all right.*

Elaine. Dear Mr. Olds: I would like to know why Joyce is not

The same phenomenon: the incapacity to express love and the hurt of not feeling loved back. Evans was a janitor of whom Pat was very fond.

Group worker relates here to Pat's outer expression of hostility, not to underlying dynamics. Pat, at this time, is not capable of insight—she needs reality limitation so as not to drive herself into serious aggressive action.

Pat must react negatively, but the last part of the sentence shows a start toward allowing herself to be more positive.

being on restriction and she has gone out for about the last past week, and one night she stayed out over night and came home in the morning, and she had the counselors scared out of their little panties. And she's gone and she said she'd be back at one certain time and then she doesn't come back at that time. Well, what I want to know is why I'm still on restrictions for something I did a half a year and two weeks ago. I think it is very, very cruel and mean. Oh, and there's another thing: I called my boy friend last night, no matter what my restrictions are, and he said that he mailed a letter to me and if I do not get that letter today, I'm going to search this whole house.

Miss Smith told me to say something that we could discuss in the group so I'm going to. I'd like to know why on earth—Pat and me, well—we sort of started a little riot the other night and Donna (a counselor) took Pat and kicked her and she's got great big black and blue marks all over her legs where Donna had kicked her. I swear someday I'll catch up with Donna and kick the . . . out of her. And Ollie—you should see her eye! Ollie didn't do that much. Ollie went out because Susie and Joyce were screaming, and Ollie ran out and wanted to

This account shows Elaine's need to reject any responsibility for her actions. To her, the world is a hostile place with people out to hurt her and others. The group worker knows that her account is thoroughly distorted, yet she does not interrupt, to let this unhappy and distrustful

see what was wrong. Ollie was going back into the dorm and Andrews grabbed Ollie's arm to turn her back and when Ollie tried to get free, Andrews took her by the neck and threw her down on the floor and then Ollie was hit in the eye about two times. What I would like to know is why on earth the counselors are so mean. They always say that we're so sick and all that.

So the other night I didn't lead. Well, I led the kids into some of that riot—but not all of it—and I followed along in some of it. And then when I wanted to go in and I wanted to talk to Joyce and try to calm her down, they said that I couldn't and I said, "Well, why? You always said that I'm a leader and that. . . . Why can't I prove it now?" And Bertha (a counselor) had the nerve and the gall to speak up and say, "You did prove it to-night, and boy! Did you prove it!" And I don't think that's very fair because they're always accusing me of being the leader. So then, when I do want to show that I can be a leader for the right things, they won't let me do it. And Ollie was crying because she had been hurt so much in her eye and all and she was in the bathroom crying. And just about then Susie was tied in with some people; she wasn't talking, but at

girl have an opportunity to have "her say."

In listening to her carefully, the group worker learns to understand Elaine: her feelings of rejection, of being mistreated; her sense of being misunderstood; her yearning to be a "good" leader; her jealousy of the "sibling," Ollie; her infantile cry for adults to love her—regardless of how she acts.

What Elaine needs most at this moment is someone who listens. The group worker and the group members give her this needed satisfaction.

least she would have had someone to talk to. Joyce was the
same way. She could have talked
to someone if she wanted to. And
Ollie—she didn't want to talk to
anybody; she wanted to be left
alone. And *I* wanted to take my
problem out, and Mr. Olds came
and right away he asked for *Ollie!*
And I ran around for about two
hours and waited, and he said I
was acting most adult and I
didn't need anybody to talk to.
But that wasn't true because I
wanted to talk my problem out,
too, but nobody would listen. I
don't think that's fair. . . . Sin-
cerely yours, Elaine.

Miss Smith. I think this is very
good that everyone puts down
what he thinks about this and
then, next time, we can really
talk it over.

Group worker opens the way for others to express their feelings too— while suggesting that much of this needs thinking through.

Susie. Last night at the riot,
when I was screaming to get
loose, Joyce came out and one of
the men counselors came out and
dragged her into another room.
Then when I tried to get through
to her to get one of the men
counselors off of her, he smashed
my fingers, and I don't see why
the counselors have to be so cruel
all the time. They should get Ella
off of the counselors; she's one of
the cruelest ones. Ella and Joe,
and a few others, should be taken
off and put on with some kids
that can stand them.

Susie is highly stimulated by Elaine's account; here is a beginning of group contagion which could be dangerous. The tape recorder and group worker's intervention (see report of meeting on the preceding pages) provided the necessary limits.

Record 5

Mr. Olds told Miss Smith that there had been another upset in the girls' dormitory; he was not sure what had brought it about.

Susie, Elaine, Anne and *Ed* came first. They spotted the recorder immediately and *Ed* and *Elaine* tried to do some recording. Miss Smith had this time purposely not brought along any program material; she had wanted to see how the children could handle a meeting without such. She suggested that they not use the recorder today since it was not working too well. She had brought along only the transcript of what had been recorded at the last meeting; she proposed that they discuss it.

Susie, Elaine and, strangely enough, *Anne*, were very outspoken and positive and wanted to talk about it and to read what had been recorded. *Ed* could not involve himself; this was understandable since he had not been present the last time. He began to dictate in spite of the poor quality of the recorder. *Pat* came a little later and seated herself apart from the others in the group.

When *Ed* stopped dictating and joined the girls, *Elaine* left and began some dictation. She

The recording machine in the room proves to be too attractive. The children are not yet ready to

talked about the "riot" in the girls' dormitory. She told how the girls had not wanted to disturb others at night; they therefore had pulled the television set into their bedroom and had turned it on very quietly. The counselors objected. Joe (a counselor) had come in and removed the television set. That had made them angry, and they then had turned on their radios louder than usual. Again the counselors interfered, and the fight started.

move into an orderly discussion. The presence of an "outsider" (Ed) also prevents their going into the content of the previous meeting.

All the children listened in while *Elaine* dictated this. Miss Smith asked at what time they had turned on the television set. *Elaine* said it was 10:30 P.M. Surprisingly enough, *Anne*, who was much more alive at this meeting than usual, spoke up loudly and with great emphasis. She agreed that there had been nothing wrong with the girls' use of the television set. She did not like to be kept awake and would have objected if it had been disturbing. The girls had it on so softly that she had slept through the whole thing until the counselors began to interfere.

Group worker tries to help the girls understand the reasons for the counselors' demands.

Anne begins to feel more comfortable in speaking up. Her support of the girls allows the discussion to become less hostile.

Miss Smith wondered what late television meant in getting up the next morning when they had to go to school. *Ed* said that none of the girls went to school, but *Elaine* said—truthfully—that wasn't so, that there were several who had to go. They said they had promised that they would get up on time.

Elaine suddenly began to discuss the matter of orderliness in the girls' room. *Elaine* said that, in general, it is getting much better, and that the most disorderly people are *Pat* and *Anne*. *Pat* could not take this criticism; she got up, went outside for a moment, and seemed quite unhappy. *Anne*, surprisingly, once more involved herself. She said that she did not want any help with cleanup; that it annoyed her that other girls were always around. Someday she would change—but because *she* wanted it, not because of *Elaine*'s pressure.

It is not clear how transition to this subject started. It may be that Elaine, by admitting that there may be a reason for the counselors' behavior, had become uncomfortable. She needed now to turn her hostility on someone else—this time Pat and Anne. The group worker missed here an opportunity to help Elaine come to grips with her problems.

Record 6 (Summary Recording)

Jim came, but stayed separated from the group. He played for quite awhile with the recorder; he disturbed the others so much that they objected to it. He was willing to stop when they told him so; however, at that moment, he also lost interest in the group meeting, and left.

The rest of the youngsters stayed together for about three-quarters of an hour. They expressed hostility against several of the counselors. This time hostility was not expressed in shouting, but in a strong plea for Miss Smith to believe them when they said that some counselors treated them badly. Only *Ed* screamed that he would smash them or use a switchblade or a Luger on them. Miss Smith listened, but then asked the children to give her three minutes and listen to her. She told them how, a few years ago, they had sat together—counselors and children—and had thought through the purpose of this place; that the staff members knew that they were youngsters who had been hurt in the past and that only friendship and understanding would help them— this was the intent of their work, but sometimes it was hard for the counselors to give this friendship if the children would not allow it. Did they think that something like this played a part in their relationships with the counselors right now? They did calm down, and insisted that not *all* the counselors were so cruel.

Group worker takes the youngsters seriously. She does not argue against them; she explains the purpose and philosophy of the institution. She is direct in discussing relationships between the children and the counselors.

Ed screamed that Mr. Carter was stuck up. Miss Smith said that she had never found this; *Ed* suddenly became quiet and said, "No, he really is not, but he, too, doesn't listen enough."

Group worker contradicts here because she feels that her relationship with Ed is now strong enough to allow this. Ed admits that he exaggerated in his anger—a small, but important step forward for a boy who previously would not accept any limitation by an adult.

They ended the meeting with *Elaine*'s asking Miss Smith whether they could dictate some suggestions as to how the children could get along better; Miss Smith promised that the follow-

Elaine, too, begins to think in terms of "getting along" instead of only fighting the adults.

ing week they would have a functioning tape recorder.

Miss Smith spent some time with Ollie and *Elaine* in the dormitory where they discussed *Elaine*'s earlier recording. *Elaine* had asked Miss Smith to give it to Ollie. In the course of this contact, Miss Smith suggested that *Elaine* might want to do her dictation at the next meeting in the form of a letter to a new girl coming to the center. *Elaine* accepted this suggestion eagerly.

Group worker realizes that Elaine is the leader in her dormitory group. She intensifies her efforts to establish a relationship with her which will help her to identify more positively with adults and use her leadership more constructively.

Group worker does this to give Elaine's efforts a concrete direction and to draw her away from the role of the complainer. To write a letter to a specific (even if fictitious) person allows for expression of feelings, but imposes a discipline to explain them to someone else and to think more carefully.

Record 7

This meeting consisted almost entirely of a tape recording, mostly done by *Elaine*. The other children listened calmly and with great interest; Miss Smith knitted.

The recording is reproduced because it shows the change toward taking more responsibility for their own actions and the development of a more positive attitude toward treatment and the center.

Elaine. A lot of kids say that this place is icky, but if you have been at the old center . . . or at the kids' unit in the mental hospital, this place is really, really nice. For one thing, we get a dollar allowance every week and about all we have to do is just make our beds, and a lot of the kids in homes have to wash dishes, take care of brothers and sisters, and all, and they don't even get a dollar. I think we are pretty lucky to get that.

If you are going to be coming down into—if you are a girl you would be coming down into the girls' dormitory. I have got one gripe against that. The little girls' dorm is messy all the time except for Anne—she keeps her place pretty clean. But over in the big girls' dorm there is one pig called Joyce; she's constantly in a mess, never clean. But if you go up with the boys—if you are a boy you go up to be with the boys —well, I don't know what that's like because I am a girl.

Change in attitude toward one of the group members.

The counselors and Dr. Abel and Carter and the nurse—well, all of the people except the two secretaries and us kids have, ah, have, ah, have what is called a staff meeting every Thursday on one of the kids. Well, I have been on restrictions for quite awhile, and they will have meetings on me to decide, you know, just how much restriction they are going to take off for awhile.

If you are a girl, I mean, and you have smoking privs and you can afford cigarettes and you don't smoke like a steam engine, you, you are allowed, well, a whole cigarette every time you smoke. But there is one girl down in our dorm—name is Pat—and she smokes like a steam engine and she is allowed only a half a cigarette at a time, because otherwise she just about has a nicotine fit if she doesn't have cigarettes all day.

Identification with institution's limitation.

We have some real, real nice—well, everyone of the counselors is nice except, well, for one that I don't like; her name is Ella—but everybody's got their own opinion of everybody else. Well, if you're one that doesn't like to be ritzy and all, and doesn't like to follow manners, well, I don't think you're going to like Ella either.

Elaine accepts the possibility that Ella is not all bad—that her feelings about her may be subjective.

This isn't like being in a home because you don't have a mother and father and all, but the counselors—if you are feeling low or something like that—the counselors will come and try to comfort you and try to talk to you, and if you ask and you catch him at the right time you can, Mr. Olds will sometimes talk to you if you are feeling low or something like that.

Elaine expresses her feelings of deprivation at not having a family.

Elaine accepts the comforting role of the counselors and the case worker.

One girl got to go out yesterday. She socked Miss Andrews in the nose and then she got to go out. Miss Andrews took her out and if you have ever been to the drugstore, you know that they have got those lalapalooza (a big dish of ice cream and fruits)

things or whatever you call them;
well, Miss Andrews took her out
for one of those. I am just wondering what on earth would happen to me if I punched Andrews
in the nose! I would probably be
sent to the girls' training school!

Feelings of injustice are still strong.

You are allowed to, well . . .
some of the kids go out to public
school and then some stay here
and go for anywhere from 45 minutes to half an hour with the
school teacher named Miss Farrow. Eh!

Pat. I sometimes am very messy
but sometimes when I feel all
right, I, ah, my name is Pat. I am
13 and I am a child here, too,
and, ah, I keep my place clean
sometimes, but when I don't feel
so well and am kind of tired
'cause I get new medication, now
I try to keep it clean. 'Cause I
went out last night I was quite
busy deciding what to wear and
that, and Elaine was nice enough
to let me wear her heels and that.
We went all through this one
cafeteria restaurant.

*Pat reacts to Elaine's dictation
as a standard setting device.*

Elaine. Well, there is something I forgot to tell you. Ah, it
has to do with our money problems on allowances and like that.
Well, we have this thing that is
called a girls' club and we have a
fund for that and each girl, you
know, gets a quarter to put in
every week and we go—we can
use it for anything; we can go

swimming, to movies, roller skating. We haven't gone roller skating yet, but we have gone swimming many, many times, and we have gone to two shows since I have been here; their names were *Exodus* and *The Guns of Navarone.*

Susie. My name is Susie and if you're a boy and you go into the boys' group—Oh! Let's see! I am trying to figure out! Some of us don't like two of the counselors up there. Joe, for instance. I don't think you would like him too much.

Miss Smith. My name is Nanette Smith. I must say that every week I look forward to coming to this place because I like the kids, but especially the group I work with. If you want to know what this group is here for, well, it's a group where we sometimes talk about things that make us angry; sometimes we talk about things that we enjoy, and today you have heard some of those.

The girls pressed Miss Smith to dictate too.

There are many other people on this staff, but they are not right here in this meeting. If you want to, perhaps the girls can introduce them to you. We could start with the director and then tell you something about the other people besides the counselors. What do you think of that?

Elaine. This is Elaine again.

Miss Smith, the one who just got through talking, is very, very nice. She, ah, you won't be able to hear this tape because it's going to be typed out, but if you could listen at all you would hear that Miss Smith has an accent, and that is because I think she is part French, but the way I figure it, no matter if you got an accent, no matter what color you are or anything like that, I like you; no matter what, *what* you are.

Well, I guess I will do what Miss Smith suggested. Well, I will start off with the director, I guess. The director's name is Doctor . . . Mister—excuse me! Mr. Carter. He is English and he is very, very nice and understanding. And then, well, he is the director and he helps and sees that you come or not and puts his opinion in. Well, that's about all I can think of to say about him.

And then there is Miss Andrews. She is a very, very nice woman, and I tell you she really puts up with a lot. You got to hand it to these people. They have got a lot of patience, except there is a couple that doesn't have a lot of patience, but that can't be helped. We kind of bring it on ourselves sometimes, and Miss Andrews—excuse me just a minute—Miss Andrews is the program director here.

And then there is Mr. Olds.

Elaine increasingly expresses positive feelings.

This spontaneous admission is very important.

Excuse! I like Mr. Olds very, very much. He is pretty understanding and he is the social worker here.

This is the first time Elaine allows herself to say that she likes Mr. Olds.

And then there is Dr. Abel, ah . . . he is the psychiatrist here; he is one of the psychiatrists here, and he is fair in my opinion—but you may think different of him.

And then there is Mr. Crankston—*Dr.* Crankston; he is, I think, a psychiatrist too. I am not sure but I think he is. He's fair, too, in my opinion.

And then there is another doctor here: His name is Dr. Merton. He is a psychiatrist too. I see him and I think he is just a wonderful man. Thanks to him I am going to be going some place for Thanksgiving, and I am real thankful to him for that. At first I just . . . Oh, excuse me! I was going into my private affairs . . . I will stop there.

Oh! I have got to warn you about something! If you see Dr. Merton and you want to play chess with him, he is a very, very good chess player. And then, oh look at his beautiful, beautiful blue eyes! I tell you they are just beautiful!

And now, oh, there are two secretaries. One is, excuse me just a minute, well, excuse me, I had to consult Miss Smith on something else and she didn't know it either, but there is one fairly young secretary up here. She is very, very cute and her name is Jeannette (I don't know what her last name is). And then there is another secretary; her name is Carol. She is very, very nice, too.

Miss Smith. This is Miss Smith again: I think we should tell you something about why this place is here anyhow—maybe Elaine can do that. I also think there is one other girl in this room, Anne, who hasn't said anything, but I don't know whether she will. But maybe Elaine can tell you why we have this children's center.

Elaine. Hello! This is Elaine again! Well, I guess I will do as Miss Smith says and tell you why this place is here. Well, it's here for children that are real mixed up and that have gone through a lot of hardships through their life; they are here to get well and to be able to go out and get along in the world, get along with people. Most of the kids that have been here have been . . . have come in real, real violent and all, and have gone out real, real nice; they have just reformed—you wouldn't know them. This place is here—it may seem at times just a mean, horrid place for punishment, but it's here for only your own good—to help you. The people here do want to help you very much, although, at times, I will admit even myself that I get to

Group worker tries to pull in Anne, but does not press her. Anne refused to speak.

Elaine explains purpose of the agency well, and yet is free to give her feelings—of thinking of it also as "mean."

thinking that it's pretty horrid, but then I get over that.

Oh! There is something I have to, ah . . . we have O.T. The girls have it Tuesdays and Fridays; the boys—I don't know when they have it. Our O.T. director is Miss Jones.

And then, as I mentioned awhile back, we have a school teacher here and her name is Miss Farrow. And then we have a janitor and his name is Evans. I guess that's all. He has another part to his name, but I don't know where that comes in.

And then we have a handyman —he repairs things—and his name is Mr. Keller. And then we have a laundry woman, and her name is Stella Tree.

Well, I guess that's about all I have to say here. Well, I wish you the best of luck. Your little friend, Elaine.

Comment

The seven meetings presented here show movement in the social group work process. This is a *formed* group, formed by the agency with a therapeutic aim. The group members start out with expression of hostility toward and distrust of the group worker. She represents to them a symbol of all adults who are enemies. Individually and as a total group, the group members are not willing to open up with her or to accept any value presented by her. This attitude is pervasive, but, in this particular group, does not constitute a bond among the members. They are each separated from the other as if living on an island. In the course of the meetings, there is general movement towards a beginning trust of the group worker and of one another. It is achieved predominantly by the group worker's complete acceptance of each individual and an honest working through of problems with them. *Insight* is achieved only to a small extent, but behavior change occurs through some insight, group members' criticizing or helping each other, and *experiencing* the satisfaction of less hostile behavior. *Group bond* is beginning to develop as seen in the greater concern for each other, the voluntary attendance at group meetings, and the acceptance of one member—Elaine—to act as a spokesman for the group.

There are beginning signs of the emergence of two meaningful, self-contained sub-groups—boys and girls.[10]

Group worker/children relationship has moved into a sense of trust, given by the children. Beyond that, the relationship to the group worker is quite varied according to the needs of the different individuals.

As a group, the children have moved toward the fulfillment of some of the goals set for this group: they begin to speak more freely about their feelings; they accept the special attention of an understanding adult; they relate somewhat more closely to one another, but not as a total group—only in sub-groups.

To evaluate movement, we must also look at each individual and see whether the group has achieved some of the purposes set for it.

Elaine shows an almost dramatic movement from sharp pervasive aggressivness toward everything and everybody to a recognition of her own part in this situation and a beginning trust in others, such as the group worker and the counselors. She emerges as a leader in the group, with drives toward more positive actions as well as verbal improvement. Her movement is somewhat too fast so that the skilled group worker will recognize it as a tenuous one and expect relapses.

Elaine's relationship to the worker is one of cautious acceptance. There is not a close identification. The relationship is still a superficial one. In view of her developmental history, one would not expect any other form in which she can relate to a woman. She had never had any close parental relationship and must have felt maternal rejection

10   The reader should know that the group actually separated into a boys' and a girls' group at the request of the members when the group became increasingly meaningful to them. Disturbed adolescents seem to prefer not to meet in a heterosexual group. They struggle so hard with their feelings of sex-identification that they are more comfortable if they are not too stimulated by the presence of youngsters of the other sex in a small, intimate group. At the same time, they need some less intensive contacts with the opposite sex to try out and experience their capacity to handle those relationships.

especially strong. The group can offer to her only a motivation toward search for a closer relationship. If she is thus motivated, she may be ready for individual treatment, a deepening of insight, and a strengthening of human ties.

Susie's main progress lies in the change from silent and sullen hostility to a capacity to speak up freely and to express ambivalence in relation to people, indicating that she has some positive feelings too. While she starts out with showing practically no capacity to handle frustration, she begins to accept criticism of herself by the other girls (when they say she is not very orderly, for instance). She also shows the capacity to wait for her turn in recording. She begins to express herself not so much in direct verbalization as in drawings, which express her feelings and her perception, and in poetry, which she is beginning to share with this group. Susie has gone through an acute psychotic stage. Although her movement looks on the surface less dramatic than Elaine's, it actually indicates just as great a step forward toward health.

Her relationship to the group worker is a "neutral" one. She shows no warmth toward her, but also does not include her in her hostile attacks on others. In fact, it seems as if this is the one person whom she excepts from her violent emotions. The opportunity to work through her feelings in the presence of someone with whom she does not have to get deeply involved means much to Susie—in fact, it makes it possible for her to become expressive.

Anne has made less movement than the other two up to this time. She had been completely mute when she entered a mental hospital and had only begun to relate when she started in the group. She frequently withdraws during group meetings into individual activities separated from the group. This is purposely supported by the group worker who tries to convey to her the idea that she is not being pushed and can move at her own pace. *Anne's* history contains no clue as to any explanation of her illness. The group worker works on the assumption that *Anne* suffered some traumatic experience in her early life and that she will need great feelings of safety before this experience can return to consciousness and be worked through. The group worker's attitude relaxes *Anne* and allows her to make beginning steps toward more interactional skills. *Anne* starts by asking for a translation of a foreign language, showing her struggle with verbal communication. She expresses herself in drawing—significantly by drawing faces which include the mouth, the verbal organ of the person. She

draws herself as a walnut, indicating her awareness of herself as being "closed up" and perhaps her unconscious wish to have someone
break her open. In the fifth meeting she interacts verbally with the
others and speaks up in support of them or in contradiction of them.
Yet, in the later recording session, she is still very inhibited and cannot
use this medium to express herself.[11]

Anne's relationship to the group worker is difficult to assess because
of her reluctance to express herself. One may infer positive feelings
because of her regular attendance at the group sessions (which was
voluntary). One has the impression that the group worker at this time
represents to *Anne* a safe haven from which she may venture out
when she feels like it, but which makes no frightening demands on
actual involvement.

Pat was farthest back in her development when she entered the
group. Her behavior was no longer out of touch with reality, but was
very infantile. Positive movement seen in the group meetings lies
less in *Pat* herself than in her position in the group. She started out
by being a rejected isolate in her living group as well as in the treatment group. During the group meetings her position changes into a
somewhat more tolerated member of the formed group. Since *Pat* has
been very aware of her poor relationships with her contemporaries and
has suffered under them, this change has great meaning to her. She
is not yet capable of basically changing her own behavior which
brings isolation upon her, but she shows a few signs of movement in
regard to this: she can accept some limitations; she discusses—up to
this point, only outside of the group—some of her problems with the
group worker, and she is able to record some of her shortcomings.

To *Pat*, the social group worker is obviously a mother figure. She
wants from her much attention and affection. Her feeling toward the

---

[11]   At a much later meeting, Anne started it off by saying that she would use
the tape recorder to "shout." The girls supported her. She first used it
cautiously—but used it! In fact, she cautioned the others by mentioning
frequently that "everything is recorded what we say." In the middle of the
session, she began to give an account of a childish stealing episode done
with her sister as an (instigator). This was the first time that anything like
this was expressed by her or her family. It is significant for the value of the
group work method that this occurred through the support of her "equals,"
with the added safety of the presence of an adult who had proved acceptance through patience with her and the "unacceptable" behavior of
others combined with the use of an "outside tool"—the tape recorder.

group worker is one of "hunger" for body contact, like the need of an infant. It has no great emotional depth, yet it is a vital necessity for her. The worker's acceptance of her need gives her some satisfaction and apparently the beginning strength to control it—at least in the presence of others. *Pat*, however, has a long way to go to achieve even simple maturity.

The development of the two boys, *Jim* and *Ed*, is not as significant as the development of the girls. They show definite signs of wishing to move out of the group constellation. This is seen in their spotty attendance. *Ed* is involved only on the surface, even when he is present. He can relate to his contemporaries and contradict them, but, in general, he has no interest in discussing problems or becoming a part of this particular group. It becomes evident that this is not a helpful group constellation for him.

Ed's relationship to the group worker is characterized by indifference. He neither displays hostility nor acceptance, nor the kind of "neutrality" (as Susie's) which is a positive and safe protection from which one can venture out.

Jim would probably be more involved with the group if other boys, besides Ed, were present. He has a need to express himself, to talk out anger, and to feel some sense of accomplishment. The group situation gives him that opportunity. In spite of his spotty attendance, he shows movement and some insight into his own feelings, as seen in the incident with the newcomer and in beginning identification with the group. He shows changes in feelings and behavior from angry hostility to feelings of responsibility for and liking of others. The group situation, however, which is dominated by the girls, is not the most conducive to his full development.

Jim's relationship with the group worker is meaningful. His feelings toward her are highly ambivalent. He is torn between beginning trust and a wish to be close to her and fear of involvement which would make demands on him.

In group meetings, with such disturbed children as the ones described, seven meetings represent only a very short time period. In view of this, the development toward the goals set is remarkable. It can be explained only by the power of the group process itself, and the skillful way in which the group worker used herself and the social group work method.

Summary

Group work practice is based on an optimism which assumes that the human being can be helped to grow and change. It is not a romantic optimism, but one that drives toward action—a realistic idealism.

Its three premises are (1) social work as a profession is concerned with the enhancement of people's social functioning, (2) there is significant correlation between social functioning and group experience, and (3) people need help—sometimes professional help to—enhance social functioning.

Out of knowledge, philosophy and skill evolve basic principles of social group work. They are:

1. Recognition and subsequent action in relation to the unique difference of each individual.

2. Recognition and subsequent action in relation to the wide variety of groups as groups.

3. Genuine acceptance of each individual with his unique strength and weakness.

4. Establishment of a purposeful relationship between group worker and group members.

5. Encouragement and enabling of helpful and cooperative relationships between members.

6. Appropriate modification of the group process.

7. Encouragement of each member to participate according to the stage of his capacity and enabling him to become more capable.

8. Enabling of members to involve themselves in the process of problem solving.

9. Enabling group members to experience increasingly satisfactory forms of working through of conflicts.

10. Provision of opportunities for new and differing experiences in relationships and accomplishments.

11. Judicious use of limitations related to the diagnostic assessment of each individual and the total situation.

12. Purposeful and differential use of program according to diagnostic evaluation of individual members, group purpose, and appropriate social goals.

13. Ongoing evaluation of individual and group process.

14. Warm, human and disciplined use of self on the part of the group worker.

In an analysis of practice we can observe these principles in action. We see the importance of *time* in the helping process and the complicated net of interrelationships which the group worker must understand and with which he must work. The goal, help with social functioning, is not reached quickly or in a straight line, but often through several backward and forward movements.

BIBLIOGRAPHY

Basic readings for this chapter are the same as for Chapter VII with the following addition:

Klein, Alan F., *Society, Democracy, and the Group*, New York: The Woman's Press, 1953.

CHAPTER NINE

The Social Group Worker's Role in Various Fields of Practice

We were pridefully serious about our jobs, but not about ourselves.[1]

In the preceding chapters, we discussed the development of social group work, the movements from which it grew, the values it incorporates, and its growing identification with the profession of social work which it, to some extent, helped to change and by which it was changed. We saw the group worker in action in his direct use of his method and his integration of knowledge, values, and skill.

We will present now the "job," the work social group workers do in different fields. Fields of practice change because of changing needs in society—or so we would like to believe: this would be the ideal way of determining service. Yet human beings are fallible; they are not

---

[1] Remark heard in a broadcast by Edward R. Murrow who was speaking about the early days of broadcasting from overseas.

239

always discerning enough to recognize needs; not always courageous enough to give up a traditional service which no longer has the importance it had in the past; not always strong enough to withstand forces which press them toward service in fields chosen by selfish interests, and sometimes they are gullible and follow fashionable fads. All this applies also to the social worker and to those fields in which group work serves. "Self-knowledge" and "critical appraisal" of one's work must apply to fields of practice and its agencies as much as to the individual practitioner. Yet agency planning is an unwieldy and complicated process because we deal with *institutions,* and one of their particular qualities is resistance to change. To remodel or create agency structures in the light of actual needs involves efforts of the professionals serving in them; of the lay boards in both private and public agencies, and of the constituency in membership organizations and intelligent, informed public opinion.

The field of "group work and recreation" is a traditional division of welfare councils all over the United States, and dates back to the early industrial revolution when group work and recreation were practically one. The teeming tenement districts were hiding pale children who never saw green trees or a ray of sunlight and who did not know the joy of play. Their mothers were working long days and weeks in the factories and were so deadly tired when they returned home that they could not give much attention to their children. There was a desperate need for playgrounds and camps. Women factory workers and household employees were shamefully exploited. Group work was needed to help them gain confidence through meeting together and to help them stand up for their rights, including the demand for leisure time and places where one could spend it with healthy satisfaction. Today the big cities still have slums and a need for action to obtain additional recreational facilities. Yet, in general, the working day has been reduced, recreation is a service recognized by the public, and opportunities for it are within the reach of most of the population. Social group workers serve, and should serve, in the field of recreation where needs are still unfulfilled and where individualized group services are required, as work with handicapped or upset children or with special adult committees concerned with social action. But they do not belong in this field *alone.* Their services are increasingly needed —and used—in other fields. In the light of this, is the traditional division of welfare councils between "Group Work and Recreation" and "Family and Children's Services" still tenable? Does it represent present needs? To this writer, this organization of private welfare services is an example of institutions' keeping forms alive which are no longer appropriate to the changing social scene.[2]

In the following pages a number of fields are presented in which social group work is either recognized as one of the methods by which its agencies give competent service or where, at this time, trends in this direction can be perceived.

We will follow a given outline: we will (1) present the purpose of the given field; (2) enlarge on the needs it serves; (3) describe the functions of the social group worker in relation to purpose and needs, and (4) discuss any possible adaptation the group work method needs if practiced in this field.

A. Settlements and Neighborhood Centers

Originally, settlements and neighborhood centers existed to serve the social needs of persons in a given geographical and deprived neighborhood. The services were not differentiated. The neighborhood worker learned about the problems of the people he worked with by living with them, visiting them, and talking with them. He worked on whatever problems presented themselves. Thus, settlement houses can be credited with the beginning of a great variety of social services which includes well-baby clinics, school social work, recreational services, services to released mental patients, services to immigrant and minority racial groups, and nursery schools. Settlement or neighborhood houses have kept this flexibility. In 1958, the "Arden House Conference" designed to reassess the purposes of neighborhood centers, described them thus:[3]

"1. To serve as one of the few agencies in contemporary society that is not 'wholly formalized, bureaucratized, channelized . . .' that offers a personal, face-to-face relationship in which a whole human being can be seen and talked to in something like his entire life situation.

---

[2] On this subject see also Robert D. Vinter, "New Evidence for Restructuring Group Services," in *New Perspectives on Services to Groups: Theory, Organization, Practice; Social Work with Groups 1961*, New York: N.A.S.W., 1961.

[3] See National Federation of Settlements, *Neighborhood Goals in a Rapidly Changing World*, A Report of the Action-Research Workshop held at Arden House, Harriman, N.Y., 1958.

"2. To help give people roots, a sense of identification with a place, other people, existing agencies of their society, and, if they stay long enough, with the ongoing good and traditions and obligations of that society.

"3. To experiment in using new knowledge and social techniques for dealing with human problems.

"4. To provide decentralized services to people who need help in areas close to their homes.

"5. To help promote cultural activities—'an active participant culture,' countering pressures toward passivity in American life, helping to develop ways of using our increasing leisure for creative activities.

"6. To provide important services in the planning and execution of programs for urban renewal."

These goals are directly related to the present situation of an urban society characterized by its high mobility, by mass living, and by shorter working hours. The settlement houses accept these as realities and plan services to support the positives of the situation and to counteract the negatives. Such goals demand the skills of a variety of professionals. The social group worker is a major one among them. His functions in a settlement house include the following:[4]

1. *Direct work with groups of children and adults.*

Such groups have either the purpose of increasing socialization, of restoration, or of social action, or a combination of them. Purely recreational groups are today generally conducted by public recreation departments. Yet settlements provide such service in neighborhoods where it is not available or to groups which present special problems (i.e., mothers on ADC grants who need special arrangements to be free of the care of their children for a short time but who are unable to afford baby-sitting services; groups of mentally retarded adults or children who are unable to join other children on playgrounds, and so forth).

Since integration in its widest sense is one of the basic goals of the settlement house movement, group workers work with groups of discriminated minorities (racial, nationality, religious) helping them to become more self-confident and enabling them and the majority group

---

4 It has to be understood that the functions described must not necessarily be carried out by one person alone. They indicate the role of the group worker, but the different functions can be divided among several people.

to experience working, talking, and living together. Group workers in settlement houses may work with homogeneous groups of Negroes or Caucasians, Indians or Mexicans, Puerto Ricans or Swedes, etc., always with the aim toward their becoming an integral and respected part of the community. The idea is "unity through diversity," of pluralism in its best sense. Such groups are made up of children, youngsters, or adults. Program may vary from play to learning a new language or to finding out about job opportunities; from teen-agers' discussion of social customs and how to come to terms with them to adults' trying to find new ways of action to make their demands be heard in this complicated and often discouraging society.

Group workers usually aim toward establishment of integrated groups consisting of different races, creeds, and nationalities, without pressing people toward this when they are not ready for it. They work toward meetings with others if groups are too resistant to or fearful of mixing with different people. The art of work toward racial integration deserves a total book by itself. Settlement houses, the Urban Leagues,[5] and some Y's have been in the forefront of this work among social agencies.

Other adult groups may wish to get together and ask for consultative assistance from the group worker to help with social action in regard to specific needs of the neighborhood—housing, poor public transportation service, and so forth. Such action groups may also be initiated by the staff of the neighborhood house if the staff recognizes needs which may not yet be recognized by the neighborhood residents, for example, providing training for youngsters who drop out of school. It is then the group worker's task to find neighborhood leadership and to work with it so that action includes the active involvement of citizens.

Groups also may be sought out by the group worker for service even if they are not asking for it and do not welcome it. This is a comparatively recent development. It is exemplified in work with young gangs and sometimes is called *street corner work* or *floating group work*. The service in this case grows out of a demand of society, not of the members themselves. They usually have become or threaten to become a serious danger to other people. Bond in these groups usually is strong because the group presents to the individuals in it the only

---

[5] Group workers are needed in and employed by the Urban Leagues in a combination of group work and community organization capacity.

security available and gives them a feeling of status which they cannot, or think they cannot, gain in school or neighborhood. The group as a whole provides for pleasure, for adventure, for successfully carried out unlawful activities, which the individual alone cannot accomplish. The goal of the neighborhood worker who goes out to work with these groups is to help them find satisfaction in lawful, non-destructive activities and to help establish or re-establish new confidence in adult society. In addition to this, there may emerge specific goals and tangible help in relation to each member's particular needs, such as return to school, help in finding a job, help in moving away from home if necessary, or talking with the parents to help the individual be better accepted by them. Work with gangs is probably one of the most difficult and most highly skilled forms of social group work. In this, the group worker has no "props," no office to meet in, no room with tools for activities. He has no power over the group: he cannot form it; he cannot choose the right combination of members; he cannot eliminate any member he considers too difficult or impossible to work with. His group members are not motivated to want to have a group worker with them, nor do they want any service from any kind of agency. He usually meets indifference and hostility because he represents a society they hate and despise. All the group worker has is the support of the settlement house which has assigned him to this work and his own conviction and skill.

Besides direct work with such a variety of groups, the social group worker in the neighborhood house, and in many other fields, takes on the responsibility of teaching others to do direct group work. Another function, then, is:

2. *Supervision of volunteers and of part-time staff to help them with their group work.*

Not all groups need the services of a professional group worker. Settlement houses have groups with a purely recreational purpose if public recreation agencies do not provide service in the neighborhood. Such groups can well be conducted by lay volunteers if they do not include individuals with serious problems or if their cultural composition is not too foreign to that of the volunteer. The service of the volunteer in neighborhood houses has a great value in itself since it contributes to the active involvement of the local neighborhood as well as the wider community. Work with volunteers or part-time staff, therefore, is more than a matter of overcoming a shortage of trained personnel: it requires teaching, consulting, and group work skill with a close view toward community organization.

3. *Neighborhood work.*

This brings the group worker in contact with the basic problems and needs of a neighborhood and usually beyond its limits. It demands that he become active in behalf of such needs. Social action— participation in the collection of facts for new or changed legislation —is part of his responsibility.

Every group worker's job responsibility in each field includes more than direct work with groups alone. The settlement or neighborhood field, because of its undifferentiated function and because of the fact that the social group worker is the major professional on its staff, allows for an especially high degree of variety and flexibility of the group worker's function. A sample of a job description is presented to illustrate this (Names of location, etc., are disguised):

> This position requires a social group work trained person who is able and interested in doing a varied Settlement job. It will provide opportunity for creative development of new services as well as the organization and refinement of existing services. Some of the possible assignments will be as follows:
>
> 1. School Referral Groups—group service to children and young people in the school setting, individuals with special problems and needs around relationships and school achievement.
>
> 2. West Neighborhood Services—working with a staff team and with other agencies to give neighborhood and family services in an isolated and deprived city area.
>
> 3. Group Leadership in Camp Setting—utilizing Neighborhood Camp for giving special service to selected groups, referral groups, family camp, etc.
>
> 4. Recruitment and supervision of leadership for leisure-time services (primarily elementary school age girls).
>
> 5. Development of group services for teen-age mothers.

This same agency lists additional functions of other group work positions on its staff:

Work with groups of mentally retarded adults.

Services to the aging (groups; visiting).

Services to mother's groups.

Teen-age leadership training.

Consultant to neighborhood youth services committees, several neighborhood planning councils, and citizen action groups.

The informal component of social group work allows for creation of new and necessary services if the administrative structure supports such creativity and does not stifle it by traditional bureaucracy. An account of such new approaches was presented by group work practitioner Antonia Pantoja when she described the group worker's role in intergroup relations:

"I have chosen three examples from activities typical of the work of the New York City Commission on Intergroup Relations. They will help to prove my point that group work is the profession which can bring to such situations the best skills and knowledge and the commitment that is necessary to function successfully and adequately in these and in similar situations.

"1. *Community tension in relation to school integration.* We are all familiar with the *de facto* segregation of a large number of the public schools in New York City. As part of one of the methods used to desegregate the school system during the early summer of 1959, the Board of Education decided to transfer about 365 Negro and Puerto Rican children from schools in the Bedford-Stuyvesant neighborhood into Queens. The Queens communities have an all-white population of homeowners of long residence in the area. Although the Board of Education did not announce this move as an integration measure, the parents in Glendale and Ridgewood realized that integration was the real reason for the shift, rather than an effort to utilize better school facilities.

"This situation brought about a series of disturbances carried on by Queens parents who tried to oppose the transfer of the Brooklyn children into their schools. The group which took the matter into their hands was the Glendale Taxpayers Association, composed of many local Parent-Teacher Association members and officers. Disorderly elements from the organized bigoted groups came to the area to aggravate the tension. During the summer months a job had to be done to check the negative activities, to mobilize the forces of good will, and to insure that when the children entered the schools in September, no violence would occur.

"The group workers who were involved in this crisis functioned in several different roles:

"*a*. As professionals representing an official city agency, they attended meetings of the opposing group to help tone down actions so that the group would act only within the law.

"*b*. As technicians and educators, they assembled the facts, reached groups within and outside the community, and helped them to disseminate these facts to check the rumors being spread by others.

"*c*. As enablers, liaisons, and mediators, they called a series of meetings with the clergy in the area, with heads of organizations, with the main intergroup relations agencies of the city, with the community leaders in Bedford-Stuyvesant and in Glendale-Ridgewood. At these meetings the different groups and agencies were helped to devise programs of action.

"*d*. As liaison between the community and the Board of Education, they planned and conducted meetings between the parents and the principals, teachers, and officials of the Board of Education.

"*e*. As program experts and planners, they prepared a network of services covering the first few weeks of school, in order to prevent any violence to the children, to allay the fears of the parents who were sending their children to the Queens schools, and to help foresee any problems that would be created in the schools by this situation. These programs were all performed by volunteers, community groups, and churches.

"2. ASPIRA: *the creation of a new agency.* One of the most important tasks in bringing about sound intergroup relations is that of helping the minority to develop its own resources, its own leadership. The measure of the success attained by minority groups in achieving their due place in society is directly related to the quality of their leadership. The Commission on Intergroup Relations has various programs directed to this need.

"ASPIRA, a project designed to develop new leadership in the Puerto Rican community of New York through the creation of a new agency, provides my second example of the efficacy of the group worker in inter-group relations.

"A group worker originated the idea of ASPIRA. The worker offered a new concept: the training of leadership in disadvantaged or minority groups must include the motivation and guidance of those members of the groups who possess the ability and talents to enter professional, technical, and artistic fields. This is necessary in order to create a pool of persons who can function on a par with the rest of the population, give leadership to their group, and place it on an equal basis with the organizations and leadership of the majority groups.

"As an organizer, the worker has brought together a board of directors to administer the project. The worker has also played the role of technical advisor to the chairman of the board and other officers to secure from foundations the funds necessary to sustain and fully develop the project. (ASPIRA has received two grants from two foundations.)

"When it opens its doors for service ASPIRA will be a private agency, staffed primarily by Puerto Rican professionals, with a Puerto Rican board of directors. It will represent a self-help effort. It will be in itself a symbol of its own purposes.

"3. *The neighborhood clinic.* My last example is that of a service offered by the Community Relations Division of the Commission on Intergroup Relations.

"The neighborhood clinic offers consultative services and guidance to groups from neighborhoods that are having intergroup problems. In cases where the group does not have the appropriate structure to work with the problems faced, the worker can help them to organize an intergroup relations committee. The worker will enable the group to identify and diagnose the problems that beset their area and will help them to secure the necessary facts and materials, including a survey of existing resources that they could use.

"The worker helps the group to devise a practicable plan of action to solve or alleviate their problems. As an expert, he brings in program aids and makes referrals to other agencies. Using the prestige of his agency, the worker helps the citizens' group take their problems to the proper city agencies and officials.

"These are not the only programs which the Commission

offers, but they indicate the kinds of problems with which people need help if they are to find answers and solutions.

"When the relationship among groups breaks down, the Commission staff find themselves propelled into dealing with tension and violence in local neighborhoods. We also engage, at the top levels of governmental and private agencies, in negotiations that will change, create, or modify policies and administrative decisions that affect minorities. We train minority leadership in the fields that govern their fate and progress, and we train 'majority' leadership in techniques and programs that will help their own groups learn how to live with people who are different. We work with neighborhood organizations to help integrate newcomers into homogeneous neighborhoods, to prevent changing neighborhoods from becoming ghettos, to involve the minority leadership in the decision-making structures, and to handle local incidents of prejudice and bigotry."[6]

B. Youth Services

This field is difficult to discuss as a unit because it involves a wide variety of clientele and is under different auspices—public and private, sectarian and non-sectarian. Some of the services are mostly building-centered: the Jewish Centers, the different Y's, and the various church- or synagogue-sponsored youth organizations. Others provide a wide net of group services in different meeting places: the Scouts, Campfire Girls, 4-H Clubs, etc. Most youth services are movements which subscribe to a common purpose or philosophy. Members frequently carry several roles: they are part of the policy-making body; they give direct service as volunteers or paid staff; and they are members receiving a service. Group participation is usually voluntary. The designation of "youth services" is not quite accurate, since membership consists also of adults who participate actively in these agencies or organizations.

In a democratic society the youth services are one of the major ways the society helps its youth perpetuate a democratic *way of life—*

---

6 Antonia Pantoja, "The Social Worker in Intergroup Relations," *Community Organization 1961*, New York: Columbia University Press, copyright by National Conference on Social Welfare, 1961, pp. 126-131.

not just a political form—and are also a means by which adults carry out their responsibilities toward the younger generation outside the one given to them as individual parents or as teachers and professional youth workers. The goals of youth organizations are to increase the mental health of their membership, youth and adults alike; to help them assume responsibility for the welfare of others; to enable them to participate intelligently in the life of their community, and to improve creatively the total culture of a given society. Services are predominantly group services. These agencies were the first ones, together with the settlements, to develop social group work. Group work as the core of their work appeared in numerous statements, of which the following is a representative sample:

> Members take part in developing the life of the Association through the democratic process of shared responsibility and cooperative effort. Through group experience, opportunities are provided for individuals to grow and become responsible leaders and citizens.[7]

In spite of the traditional close association between youth serving agencies and social group work in the past, this association has become problematic in the present. There are two major reasons for this:

1. Certain youth-serving agencies have taken on exclusively a recreational function, and therefore see little need for the services of social group workers.

2. Social group work, by virtue of its increasing identification with the profession of social work, has limited its own sphere of action in some instances to the restorative services and has neglected those other services represented by the youth-serving agencies.

There are signs, however, that these two impediments to integration of social group work in youth services are being removed to the benefit of adults and youngsters who participate in them.

Youth agencies widen their work to include qualitative services for *all* people so as to include those who are capable leaders as well as those who have special problems and those who deviate for one reason

---

[7] "Deep Roots and World Reach," *Work Book 21st National Convention YWCA of the U.S.A.*, St. Louis, 1958, New York: YWCA National Board, p. 126.

or another from the average youngster who can make his way into the community without special help. In 1961, Luada Boswell presented a paper at the National Conference reporting on two Girl Scout projects which had as their purpose:

> To broaden the reach of Girl Scouting to include a better cross-section of the community. Specifically, we proposed to carry it out by organizing troops for the daughters of migrant workers and the urban hard-to-reach, at places convenient for them to meet, with leadership indigenous to their neighborhoods.[8]

Y's work with groups of hard-to-reach youngsters, provide group work services for released mental patients, etc.

The social work profession is slow in accepting youth organizations as one of its fields of practice. The increase of youth population may hasten this acceptance.

Group workers in youth serving agencies rarely work directly with youth groups, since one of the purposes of the agencies is the involvement of adult volunteers. They do work with groups, but they usually are not *youth* workers. They work with *adult* groups for the purpose of helping them to lead youth groups intelligently and with regard to group work principles. They also help adults to learn about community problems, to accept differences in the population, to help with the integration of various groups, and to meet intelligently pressures of public opinion which may have direct bearing on youth as, for example, the wave of accusations against teen-agers.

The social group worker's functions in these agencies usually include:

1. Group work with adult committees.
2. Supervision of individual group leaders.
3. Teaching in-service training courses.
4. Occasional group work with specialized youth or children's groups.
5. Consultant for or participant in community committees concerned with youth services.

---

8 Luada Boswell, "A report on two girl scout pilot projects: migrant agricultural workers and urban hard-to-reach groups," *New Perspectives on Services to Groups: Theory, Organization, Practice; Social Work With Groups, 1961,* New York: National Association of Social Workers, 1961, p. 81.

6. Ongoing research into the needs and concerns of young people in a given community.

C. Child Welfare Services

The field of child welfare is a widespread one with many branches. "It encompasses services provided directly to children and is also concerned with the preservation and strengthening of family life and the bringing about of the kind of community life which makes for wholesome child development."[9]

The role of the group worker must be described separately in the different branches of this field:

1. *Aid to Dependent Children*. It is only recently that group workers have begun to function in this service. Originally it provided exclusively for financial aid to families without a father to allow mothers to stay at home and take care of their children. It is increasingly recognized that these mothers need additional help. They have many problems in regard to child-rearing and their own social needs. Attitudes of society (including those of social workers) have changed from a rigid objection to working mothers to a more individualized view of them.

In 1960, Louise Shoemaker described the use of the group worker with short-term groups of mothers on ADC grants.[10] She saw the aim of these groups as being that of helping the mothers gain strength to begin some long-term planning in casework, following the group experience, and of helping them understand the services and requirements of the public agency. The material which she presented showed how vital these meetings were for the clients: they could speak freely and they found companionship which many of them had sorely missed. In talking about this group experience one of the mothers remarked:

"I have attended every night and have never been to any group meetings where you could talk about your problems and feel like everyone cared."[11]

9   Maurice O. Hunt, "Child Welfare," *Social Work Year Book*, 1960, edited by Russell H. Kurtz, New York: N.A.S.W., 1960, p. 141.
10   Louise Shoemaker, "Use of Group Work Skills with Short-Term Groups," *Social Work With Groups 1960*, New York: N.A.S.W., 1960, pp. 37-51.
11   *Ibid.*, p. 44.

Louise Shoemaker continues:

> She acknowledged that she had little formal education and knew that she often used the wrong word, but no one in the group had laughed at her. She said her children have tried to help her with the selection of words and she had rehearsed at home, but when she got to the group meeting, words just came to her and she said them. She went on to say how much happier life was for her and her family now.[12]

Agency requirements are hard to understand. They frequently are resented when presented *only* by the person in authority. Group discussion, which allows expression of anger and doubt, helps with better understanding. Shoemaker records from another meeting:

> In answer to the question "What is ADC and why are you applying for it?" we had a discussion about the purpose of the program, the client's responsibility and agency responsibility. Two women in the group had received assistance before and gave helpful comments on what they feel ADC is. Mrs. Harris was able to say that she felt she did not need to change her life a great deal because she was receiving assistance—what she felt was important for her children were the same things that the agency said were important for them. This included keeping them well fed and well clothed and housed. Mrs. Evans, the other person who had received ADC aid, said the agency made them suffer. We looked at what they meant by suffering, what it is that makes them anxious and afraid, and what the agency can do to help them with this. In the discussion, it came out that they are very fearful and even angry, but some said that talking together like this was a help.
>
> We discussed what is meant by good physical care of children, and I said that we would trust them as adults to continue to give their children this care. We found that, in many cases, mothers responded well to having the worker come in to look at their home, and that in most homes the children were well cared for. Mrs. Harris said she found this to be true—she wanted her worker to feel proud of her children and of her. The others responded, saying that they could see how this might be and that they wanted the best things possible for their children.
>
> We discussed their need for assistance, the eligibility requirements, and what is expected of them in getting work or in staying at home with their children. Around establishing need [i.e. the establishment of eligibility for public assistance], there were many bitter comments about husbands. I said that they, the mothers, were taking responsibility in caring for their children and we, on our part, wanted to help them in giving financial

[12]   *Ibid.*, p. 44.

assistance and other help as it is needed. Even though their husbands may have acted irresponsibly, they, the mothers, are showing themselves to be responsible, and we want to deal with them on this basis. This is one of the reasons they are given a cash payment, leaving to them how the money is spent. There was a lot of head-nodding at this and Mrs. Harris spoke of her experience in a positive way.[13]

We see how one person's freedom of expression opens the way for the next one to speak up; how the group worker helps to understand agency procedures as being designed to *help* the mothers—not to deprive them or to pry into their affairs—and how the worker strengthens their self-confidence.

Groups were purposely conducted on a short-term basis so as not to discourage clients from attendance. It is easier for the client to know that one meets three times instead of having to plan for a long, undefined period.

This particular group work service is only in the beginning stage, but it shows a general trend in certain areas of public welfare. At present, the tasks of the group worker in the ADC program are:

a. Conducting short-term groups for mothers on ADC.
b. Providing consultation to and training of caseworkers in the method of social group work.
c. Participating in community interpretations of the ADC program and the needs it serves.

2. *Care of Children Away from Home.* This care is given in two forms: foster care in families and care in children's institutions. A new form, group boarding homes, is emerging.

The major contribution of the group worker lies in the institutional area or in the group boarding home. Institutional care is the oldest service given to children.

Social workers made a great contribution to child welfare in stressing the need for foster care for any child who is capable of living in a family. Unfortunately they neglected institutions completely for a long period, and did not help to improve their services. This has changed, though not yet sufficiently. Institutions are often still used only as a "last resort." They are looked upon as poor replicas of family living, with sometimes a few clinical services attached to them.

Children in institutions need a group life which allows for balance

13   *Ibid.*, pp. 47-48.

between activities and, as Fritz Redl once called it, "constructive loafing" between group living and privacy. They need all the services given to children in their own homes and some additional ones related to their anxieties, loneliness, and planning for life outside the institutional services. The quality of group living is therefore as vital as the clinical, educational, and other specialized services attached to the institution.

The persons who have most contact with the children, who take care of them during most of the twenty-four hours of the day, are the child care workers (sometimes called houseparents); they are no longer considered custodial personnel. They are group workers with a strong additional function of "parenting." They work with children who have been hurt, who are anxious and defiant; they must be understanding in order to be helpful to them.

The institutional team outside of the child care workers consists usually of the caseworker who carries the continuity between the child's home, the institution, and the return to the community and who helps the child individually with specific problems; the teachers who are responsible for individual or group schooling, depending upon the child's capacity; other clinical workers—such as psychologists or psychiatrists—as necessary, and the social group worker. Some larger institutions employ special service personnel such as recreation workers, art teachers, and so forth.

The functions of the social group worker on the institutional team are twofold: to help with the group living situation and to conduct clinical groups. His tasks include:

a. Direct group work with formed groups of children inside the institution—through both house councils and therapeutic groups.

b. Work with parent groups, where possible.

c. Supervision of child-care workers.

d. Supervision of volunteers who work with groups of children placed in the institution.

e. Responsibility for referral to resources for group association in the community, when the child is in the institution as well as when planning for his release.

f. Responsible participation in diagnosis of individuals and in decisions regarding placement in the institution, grouping of children, treatment plans, and plans for after-care.

g. Responsibility for better public understanding of the new concept of institutional care, of needed improvement of the totality of its services.

A new trend has appeared in the use of group workers in relation to foster care of children in families. A few private agencies have begun to use the social group worker as the person who conducts discussion or activity groups with a therapeutic intent with children placed in foster care who have strong negative or highly ambivalent feelings about this placement and difficulties in relating to adults. Sometimes their role also includes working with foster parents to enable them to use the group process in helping them fulfil their chosen task.

3. *Services to Unmarried Mothers.* These services are usually given as part of the services offered through the ADC program, through private family services, or in institutions for unmarried mothers. The group worker's responsibility in the ADC program was discussed earlier; his contribution to family services will be discussed under a separate heading. In homes for unmarried mothers he may, as in all institutional programs, take on major responsibility for the group living situation. His tasks will be the same as in children's institutions, with the exception of work with parents.

Work with house councils and therapeutic groups is especially important in such homes because the majority of these young women consists of teen-agers who need to find outlets for some significant activity and associations during a time when they are forced to *wait* under the added pressure of anxiety and body changes. Their stay in the institution is only for a short term period, but it is most significant for them. Every single girl is filled with anxiety and hostility. The atmosphere in such a home is an intensely emotional one. Group work services therefore are essential, because they offer relief from tension through activities and opportunity to gain insight and to learn to trust others through their relationships with each other and with the group worker who helps them in the reality of living together.

D. Family Services

In the North American culture, the family is *the* basic institution. It is therefore justified that the article discussing family social work, in the *Social Work Yearbook for 1960,* starts with the following sentence:

Family social work in its broadest sense covers all social services designed to improve and strengthen family life and to help individuals and families with problems of family interrelationship or social adjustment.[14]

The family agency, in this respect, is similar to the settlement or neighborhood house, which also offers such an inclusive service.

The purpose of family services is to help with specific problems the family group encounters. These lie mostly in the economic and socio-emotional areas. Both public and private agencies offer services to families. For a long period, private agencies took responsibility for social service help with marital relations problems, the rearing of children, or other crisis situations—such as sickness, death, desertion—which threatened the family, while public agencies provided for economic assistance. This separation between the functions of public and private agencies is disappearing. Public agencies accept more and more service functions in addition to those of financial help.

Basic family problems in a given society do not change greatly, but certain aspects of them are stronger at a given time than at another. At present, there is increased need to help *young couples* with marital adjustment. The marriage age has moved more closely to the period of adolescence, to a time in the human life cycle when the individual is still in his formative years. Its advantage lies in the fact that marriage partners have usually great flexibility and therefore may adjust happily to each other, but it also includes the hazard of personality change which one or the other, or both partners, had not anticipated at the time of marriage.

Adjustments to having to take over economic responsibility are frequently especially difficult because the wage-earner may not have completed his education.

A longer life span in our times is of special significance to family life. Again, as in all changes in human society, it brings with it advantages and problems. It frequently allows the younger generation to rely more heavily and for a comparatively longer time span on the protection or support by parents who can afford this; but it may also place a burden on grown children to support parents who may live for many years with diminished physical or mental capacities.

The *changing form of the family*, with less emphasis on the ruling power of the father, may make for happiness and security through a

---

[14] Rae C. Weil, "Family Social Work," in Russell H. Kurtz, Editor, *op. cit.*, p. 251.

feeling of mutual appreciation and working together, but it may also bring about serious problems of confusion and conflict.

Freer interaction and more unsupervised contact *between the sexes* than in earlier times in this culture may allow for better choice of marriage partners, but it also requires more self-discipline on the part of the young and provokes anxiety in the parents who must present values in social conduct and learn how to *motivate* voluntary compliance with them instead of enforcing submission.

Poverty has always produced many problems for a family. It means additional hardship in an abundant society, because the contrast between "have" and "have-not" is so great and one lives in such close proximity to goods and opportunities which are unreachable. The answer the individual may choose can be constructive group action to improve his lot and that of others, but it can also be delinquency or withdrawal expressed in many different forms.

Such are some of the problems with which family agencies must concern themselves. In general, family services are rendered through the use of social casework. Yet, a new trend is clearly discernible which makes social group work an important part of these services. It has come about through:

1. *The concept of the family as a group.* This includes a new diagnostic understanding of family problems as problems partially caused by the group process in the family and also a realization that treatment of interpersonal problems is sometimes done better by working with the family as a group and not only individually with each member;

2. *The general recognition that some people gain more through interaction in a group,* and

3. *The recognition that certain social work activities with an educational emphasis are more economically carried on through groups.*

Family agencies work today with the following kinds of groups:

1. The total family group;

2. Groups consisting of couples, whose focus is on general family life education;

3. Groups consisting mostly of mothers who work on problems of child-rearing;

4. Groups of present or prospective foster or adoptive parents,

who discuss agency requirements and procedures as well as the problems encountered in being a foster or adoptive parent;

5. Groups of children and adolescents who work through a variety of problems that these youngsters face at home, or school or with their peers.

Such groups are often conducted by caseworkers, many of whom have had some additional training in group work. With the increasing use of groups in family services, social group workers are employed in such agencies. Their functions are:

1. Direct group work with the variety of groups named above;

2. Training of other staff members in the use of the group work method (because of the shortage of social group workers);

3. Consultation to the agency in relation to community resources offering socialization services for children or adults;

4. Some casework with a number of clients to become acquainted with the major method used in this field;

5. Work on community action as it relates to the problems encountered by this agency. This may include leadership or participation in committees established by the family service agency or by other community organizations.

Group work method needs some adaptation when it is used in the family interview. The role of the group worker in this particular group usually must be a less active one than in almost any other group he conducts. He must avoid appearing as an "arbiter" in family conflicts. Each family member may tend to call upon the social worker as a judge and an ally. Conflicts in the family group are especially fraught with emotion. It takes a special skill to give each member present the feeling that the group worker is a warm listener concerned with every one of them and yet also with the total unit.

None of the other groups conducted in the family service field require special adaptation of the group work method.

E. Services to the Aging

Social work's interest in this field is comparatively new. Services given to the aged consisted for centuries mostly of provision of food and shelter and nursing care. The *Social Work Year Book for 1960*

states that in 1900 3.1 million persons or 4.1 per cent of the population of this age resided in the United States.[15] By 1958, their number
rose to 15 million or 8.6 per cent of the population. With this increase
in population, attention was drawn toward the aged and there is a
beginning of more understanding of their needs.

In our society, youth has been stressed as the most desirable period
of human life. Youth has been equated with being attractive, being
productive, being able to learn and therefore being an asset in a society that must constantly live for the future. Old age, then, was considered the reverse of all these desirable qualities. This general attitude
of society toward the aged was—and possibly still is—frequently intensified by the shrinking personal income of the aged and by their possible loss of physical or mental capacity. As parents, they usually have
fulfilled their task of child-rearing and feel a loss of importance as
heads of families. They have lost friends through death. The older
person often feels alone, unwanted and an outcast of his community.
This realization has changed social services.

Services to the aged are given by public and private agencies in the
health and welfare fields and by the churches and synagogues. They
are either agencies exclusively designed for this work or multi-purpose
agencies which include service to the aged as part of their activities. It
is easily understood by the particular nature of this age group that
these services must be given by a variety of professions.

Social group workers serve in the social programs, frequently called
Golden Age Clubs, and in the institutions for the aged. The activities
of these clubs have moved from being purely recreational to adding
aspects of education and serving particular psycho-social needs of their
participants. Jean Maxwell lists the special dimension of need for
group participation in older people:

> "1. Changed physical and psychological capacities require un-
> derstanding and acceptance of these changes, necessitating sub-
> stitutions and reorganizations of behavior. Peers who have lived
> or are living through such changes give a support and under-
> standing most helpful to individuals.
> "2. Groups offer the opportunity to renew old friendships and
> develop new ones to replace the losses from death of old friends.
> "3. Community groups and organization memberships increase

15   Geneva Mathiasen, "The Aging," in Russell H. Kurtz, Editor, *op. cit.*, p. 95.

in importance as a means of providing identity for older people. A person's identity is closely tied to his group affiliations. The question 'Who is he?' is directed to family, occupation or profession, company or organization worked for, organization represented. With the growth of larger urban and suburban areas and more moving from place to place, family names are less easily recognized and carry less identity value for the individual than in earlier days. With retirement, identity through the employing agent, occupation, or profession decreases or is lost. There are few doors open to 'Joe Smith, retired.' Group identification promotes a sense of self-worth and worth in the eyes of others.

"4. Groups are the means by which an older person belongs to something larger than himself or his family. They serve as a channel through which the individual can act in unison with others to express a point of view, accomplish tasks, enjoy experiences possible only through groups, and make his voice heard in the community and the world—feel useful, alive.

"5. Status and recognition are elements achieved by the individual within a group, or through a group in the broader community. In our society self-esteem is so closely related to the job one does and the money one earns from it that retirement can easily mean a loss in self-esteem. To be valued by a group for what one contributes to its success, to be rewarded by members' respect for what one is like as a person, to be praised for what one can make, all rebuild self-esteem.

"6. Every group requires its members to meet a set of specific expectations. These may concern ways of behaving, dress and grooming, manners, beliefs, type and quality of activity and so forth. We have seen that older people are often left completely on their own as to what they shall make of their retired or older years. Group membership helps to undergird and broaden, focus and define, these expectations.

"Thus we see that group participation represents far more than filling in time or having fun. . . ."[16]

The functions of the social group worker in community agencies giving service to the aged are:

[16] Jean M. Maxwell, "Group Services—Well-being for Older People," in Russell H. Kurtz, Editor, op. cit., pp. 83-84.

1. Working out a program of different kinds of groups related to the highly varied needs which this age group presents, from relatively self-directing persons to those who need much support. The common designation of being "aged" does not really present common characteristics. Groups must be, therefore, specifically formed and consideration must be given to their different constellations as well as to diversified programs. This function is partially an administrative one.

2. Direct work with certain groups of the aged, especially those who present problems in relationships.

3. As in all group work, some contact with individuals outside of the group, but more intensively in this particular age group. Home visits are indicated.

4. Supervision of volunteers or part-time workers in programs for the aged.

5. Consultant to committees of older citizens in relation to social action in their own behalf, if requested to do so.

Many of the problems of the aged are intensified when they enter an institution. As all institutionalized people, they feel that they are removed from the normal community life which centers around the family. They frequently are also those who have some impairment of their capacities. Self-respect is especially threatened.

> It is important that they feel that they are truly "senior citizens" in a community which accepts them as capable human beings. The social group worker's contribution to the institutionalized aged is to enhance this possibility by offering opportunities for making such contributions and to relate the older person more satisfactorily to the group which has taken on the vital replacement of the family.[17]

In the institution for the aged, the functions of the social group worker are:

1. Direct work with formed groups for the purpose of specific help to those who cannot easily enter the group life of the institution;

2. Responsibility for the stimulation of a rich and varied pro-

[17]   Gisela Konopka, *Group Work in the Institution*, New York: Association Press, 1954, p. 285.

gram in the institution designed to allow for satisfaction of individual needs, as described by Jean Maxwell, and to counteract the feeling of segregation from the community which may appear in an institution. This may be done by either being a consultant to the staff of one particular institution or by serving several smaller institutions at the same time.

In the community service for the aged, as well as in the institutional service, an additional function is to help with the change of community climate toward old age. From direct knowledge of aged people in social interaction grows a wealth of information in regard to their needs which must be transmitted to the community. In informal contacts, people speak freely about their concerns even if they otherwise may be too proud to ask for help. While playing cards, the members of a group may talk freely about the terrible cost of medical care, the impossibility of getting decent housing for which they can pay on social security, their yearning for contact with younger people and the wish to do something for them, or difficulties in finding a decent nursing home for a member of a discriminated-against minority. All this calls for action in relation to medical care for the aged, housing developments, foster grandparent plans[18] and action to fight discrimination.

The social group work method needs no particular adaptation to this field. It must be pointed out, though, that the group worker must work consciously through his own emotional response to the aged. He has been reared in an environment where the prevailing culture places little value on the older person, and he is part of this culture. This may influence him. He also works with people in a period in human life that he himself has not yet experienced. This is different from work with children or with other adult age groups, even if the group worker is somewhat younger than those with whom he works. When he works with senior citizens he must learn to project himself into an age group which is still before him but to which he usually does not look forward with happy anticipation. Self-knowledge and insight are necessary to overcome this.

18   There are many children who have never known grandparents and who would enjoy and profit by the kind of relationship grandparents offer to a child. On the other hand, there are those older people who yearn for contact with children but who have no grandchildren of their own. A foster grandparent plan should bring the two together.

F. Medical and Psychiatric Services

The fields discussed up to this point are indigenous to social work, although all of them also require the services of other professions. There are a number of fields, however, where social work has taken a prominent part in the given service but whose major function lies within the scope of other professions. Such fields are called in the literature "host settings" for social work. The four fields presented in the following pages—Medical Social Work, Psychiatric Social Work, Corrections, and School Social Work—will fall into this category. One of the oldest ones in which social work has been practiced is the health field; it has led to two specializations: medical social work and psychiatric social work. Both represent general social work practice adapted to those particular settings. The *Social Work Year Book for 1960* defines them in the following ways:

> *Medical social work* is social work practiced in a responsible relationship to medicine and public health within the structure of programs of health and medical care. Initially, this field of social work practice was concerned almost exclusively with the social needs and problems of ill persons under care in hospitals and clinics. Over the years, medical social work has progressively related itself to the goals and functions of such other social and health institutions as official health agencies (local, state, federal), voluntary health agencies (for example, the National Foundation), rehabilitation centers, and medical care divisions of public welfare agencies.[19]
>
> *Psychiatric Social Work* is social work undertaken in psychiatric agencies and mental health programs. Its purpose is to contribute to those services which promote mental health in the community and to serve people with mental or emotional disturbances. It is generally practiced in hospitals, clinics, or other psychiatric settings as a part of the activities of a clinical team including psychiatrists, psychologists, and frequently other professional personnel concerned with the treatment of patients and the extension of psychiatric services.[20]

Sick people need more than direct medical services. The physically ill patient in a hospital may be concerned with mounting bills, with

[19]   Eleanor E. Cockerill, "Medical Social Work," in Russell H. Kurtz, Editor, *op. cit.*, p. 375.
[20]   Daniel E. O'Keefe, "Psychiatric Social Work," in Russell H. Kurtz, Editor, *op. cit.*, p. 451.

holding his job, or with the way his family manages without the bread-winner or father. Youngsters worry about school and the classes and social contacts they miss. They wonder whether they have done "something bad" for which they have been removed from the family. The epileptic in the community suffers still under an old stigma and frequently does not dare to make social contacts even though his seizures may be controlled by medication. The handicapped child in a camp may "take" her physical therapy, but may feel so hopelessly inadequate and "ugly" that the effort to improve is made only half-heartedly or she may try to control everybody by tantrums because of the nagging fear of being so unattractive. Relatives of a long-term sick person need practical help with arrangements for care of the patient. They also need help with their feelings about his illness. A physician may recommend and insist upon institutionalization of a wife because of increasing physical deterioration caused by a serious sickness; some-one is needed to help the husband with his anguish: is he institu-tionalizing her too soon? Or maybe not soon enough? The parents of a child with a cardiac disease may be told about this in every detail, but what meaning does it have to them? Do they blame themselves? So much of what they will do depends on how they relate to the sick-ness and to the child.

Mental and emotional illnesses present even more problems of this kind. Aside from the stigma still attached to them, they involve so much more of the total personality than most forms of physical ill-ness. Much of their etiology—as far as we know today—is understood as a problem of previous or present relationships in a person's life. This theory underlies, for example, the policy of child guidance clinics which treat a child only when the parents are also willing to involve themselves in treatment.

Both medical and psychiatric social work were originally conceived of as casework services, mostly with relatives of the patients. Social group work was introduced later (See Chapter I). Group workers usually work directly with patients. This has at times retarded its identification with social services. A milestone in the development of clinical group work was the Waveland Conference of 1955, a confer-ence conducted by what was then known as the American Association of Group Workers and made possible by a grant of the National In-stitute of Mental Health. It was directed toward Group Work in the Psychiatric Setting, but had implications for the total health field.

One of the observers at this conference, Joseph W. Eaton[21] summarized the general contributions of the social group worker to psychiatric treatment:

". . . recovery is a social process and . . . group workers have demonstrated this in the following way:

"A. By preparing patients to accept help through social channels, relationships, and group encouragement.

"B. By gathering data for diagnosis from the social behavioral dimension.

"C. By helping patients to be more comfortable.

"D. By demonstrating treatment through milieu-group treatment.

"E. By helping patients to help themselves."[22]

The conference report states:

"Dr. Eaton made reference to our problem of professional identification. He pointed up concern with our development as a branch of social work, a branch of the helping professions in general, or as a new entity. He voiced the feeling of the group that it was important to maintain our identification with social work, but he also indicated the need for us to contribute much of our learning to the fields of education and administration.

"Dr. Eaton went on to point up the potential of meeting a vast amount of presently unmet needs for treatment through the use of the group work method."[23]

Another observer at the same meeting, Dr. Raymond Feldman,[24] stated:

". . . that social group work in treatment settings can be of tremendous value to the psychiatrists because there is so little emphasis on the group in their training. Particularly in our state

---

21 Russell Sage Foundation; Visiting Professor of Sociology, Western Reserve University, School of Applied Social Sciences, at the time the conference was held.

22 Joseph W. Eaton, Dr. Raymond Feldman, and Eileen Blackey, "Evaluation and Plans for the Future," in Harleigh B. Trecker, Editor, Group Work in the Psychiatric Setting, New York: Whiteside and Morrow, 1956, pp. 171-172.

23 Ibid., p. 172.

24 Veterans Administration Central Office, Department of Medicine and Surgery, Psychiatry and Neurology Division; Representative, American Psychiatric Association at the time of the institute.

hospitals, there is a lack of knowledge as to how to make the most effective use of group experience. He stated in this regard that extension and expansion of group work is certainly in order."[25]

Both comments point to the major responsibilities of the group worker in this field, namely, direct service to patients, consultation, and in-service teaching.

In both psychiatric and medical settings there is great variation from agency to agency and from one patient population to another. Work with adult mental patients in a state hospital is different from work with children in an out-patient child guidance clinic; residential treatment for emotionally disturbed children demands a different approach than do services to people who come to a community rehabilitation agency in search of help with vocational planning.

Job descriptions, therefore, will be only samples of possible combinations of services the group worker is asked to perform. We will begin with in-patient work. The rationale of the group worker's contribution to in-patient work was so well presented by Fritz Redl at the Waveland conference that his remarks are reproduced here:

> "The contribution of group work as a method in residential therapy is important. We should get over our 'professional neurosis' which arises from our being a minority group. This produces the tendency to swallow everything wholesale or the tendency to overidentify with the so-called higher status groups and leave our skills behind.
>
> "We don't yell loud enough about what we know regarding design. There is a readiness to hear more than group work assumes. Group workers do not talk enough. . . .
>
> ". . . What does a group work program in a residential setting mean? . . .
>
> "Group work must be a part of the total design of the institution.
>
> "*The Therapeutic Ingredients:*
>
> "1. The group worker can provide the diagnostic assessment of group relevant data and secondary individual characteristics of high treatment relevance. . . .

[25]   *Ibid.*, p. 172.

"2. The group worker is highly important in figuring group composition—the clinician and the group worker as a team make the decisions. This is the framework within which group and individual treatment can function. . . .

"3. *Treatment* is a multidefined term. Whenever you talk of a residential treatment center you speak not of an educational polishing process but of an 'unpacking' process. This process must be related to particular phases of individual therapy. The group worker must design group life to support the individual therapy process and must also indicate to the individual therapist where the individual therapist's limits must be placed at any one time. Because of the interrelatedness of the two on the life process of the child, there must be constant cooperation between group life development and individual therapy development at any one time.

"4. The group worker must take responsibility for the total hygiene of the program. He has a responsibility to protest when program is not hygienic. Every part of life in the institution must be coordinated. . . .

"5. Rules, regulations, routines and policies have great importance. They are just as relevant as individual therapy. Group work must contribute to the plan. . . .

"6. There is a tendency to forget that *what* you do with people is important, not only how you feel about them. It is frequently up to the group worker to see that handling remains hygienic—not only the affects on what we do on one child, but the group psychological hygiene is important as well.

"7. We need to develop the use of the 'life space interview' and learn to interview a child when something has stirred him, in close proximity to the event. This must be done by someone who 'smells like' the others in the child's environment. The group worker needs to decide, 'What will I pick up; what will I leave?' He needs to help make decisions about timing.

"8. The group worker can contribute his knowledge about climate, group atmosphere, contagion pile-up, build up of we-feeling and the like.

"9. The group worker has to raise his voice about the functioning of the staff group. . . .

"10. The group worker must assist in the role distribution and the function of the team. Not only is what you do important, but in what role you do it. . . .

"11. The group worker must understand group pathology as well as individual pathology. Group pathology may or may not be related to individual pathology.

"12. It is the group worker's job to evaluate the group's help to a child. Sometimes the child does not need a group. The group worker must make a professional judgment as to when to withdraw the child or lower the level of group life intensity. In free life children may drop out of groups. In the residential center, they are psychologically forced into groups—it is our responsibility to determine exposure to or relief from group activity."

The responsibility of a social group worker in a children's treatment center may therefore be:

1. Supervision of the child care workers (sometimes called group counselors, houseparents, and so forth). The child care worker is the person with whom the child has contact during most hours of the day. Since the living situation is a group situation and must provide for the needs of a growing child as well as help these particular children to overcome their problems, the child care worker must be capable of translating understanding of the individual and the group into everyday practice. It is the group worker's responsibility to help with this through individual or group supervision and to provide for continued in-service involving other members on the team.

2. Direct work with children in formed groups.

    A. Newcomer or diagnostic groups in larger treatment centers. Such groups must offer the children the opportunity to freely discuss their anxieties and expectations and give information about the treatment center. The group worker offers in this group a relationship with an adult whom the children have to share but who gives each of them a high degree of individual attention. He can observe the children in their interaction with others for the purpose of helping to work out proper placement of the child and a purposeful treatment program.

[26] Fritz Redl, "The Therapeutic Ingredients in the Group Work Program in a Residential Treatment Center for Children," in Harleigh B. Trecker, Editor, *Group Work in the Psychiatric Setting, op. cit.,* pp. 43-46.

B. Discharge groups. In these groups the group worker helps
the children face the problems of moving out of the protective institutional environment and work through re-
activated anxieties. This may be done through discussions,
through role-playing, or through planned activities—such
as trips, etc.—which allow the child to experience his new
environment.

C. Treatment groups. The group worker helps select the
children to work through their problems in interaction
with contemporaries in a structured group. Such groups
may be discussion groups or activity groups.

D. Group living councils. These are groups which help the
child to gain the feeling of participating responsibly in the
life of the institution and to have a place where he can
express his feelings about institutional living and suggest
changes.

3. "Life space interviews," as Fritz Redl called them. The group
worker does not take over the role of the caseworker or the psychiatrist, but is available for short individual contacts "on the
spot" to handle serious problems in the reality of the living
situation.

4. Responsible participation on the team in relation to intake of
children. The group worker's responsibility is (1) to help with
assessment of the social capacity of the individual child and to
determine his degree of readiness for group life and (2) to help
with the assessment of each cottage group or other sub-unit in
the treatment center, and to determine its capacity to accept
newcomers and the kind of newcomers it can absorb.

5. Responsible participation in the consideration for discharge.
The group worker's responsibility here is to consider particularly
the child's social ability and to know what informal group life the
particular child will need when he leaves the treatment center.
He must be aware of community resources which are appropriate
for those needs and must help to prepare the child and the family
to use them.

6. Work with the family. Occasionally parents' groups are considered necessary and possible. Selection of parents for such
groups usually will be made by the caseworker, but the group
worker is responsible for the composition of such groups and for

direct work with them. The purpose of such groups is to help parents share their concerns in regard to their children or foster children, to help them understand the work of the treatment center, and to prepare them for the return or entrance of the child into their homes.

7. Consultation to special service staffs. Most of the need for play in a child's life should be fulfilled in the cottage and through the creative efforts of the child care worker. Larger treatment centers do employ special service staffs concerned with this area of the child's life. Swimming instructors, art teachers, recreation workers, and so forth, are professionals in their own right, but they may want consultation from the group worker as to the group process occurring in those activities and how to make it most helpful to individual children.

8. Supervision of volunteer group leaders. Whenever possible, treatment centers must keep open the channels to the community. Volunteers help with this. They also bring specific skills which are not always available on the staff. If they work with groups, the group worker must take responsibility for helping them with their task.

9. Continuous re-evaluation of the total group living situation. The social group worker is the person on the team who must be particularly sensitive to the total "atmosphere" of the treatment center. This includes staff relations as well as relations among the children.

As in every other institution where teamwork is indicated, the social group worker must responsibly share information with other members of the team and, in turn, make responsible use of the information they share with him. He also may be asked to teach other team members his specific knowledge and skill and he may be taught by others.

In recent years mental hospitals have made an effort to penetrate their total program with therapeutic intent. (There are still many such hospitals which serve only to provide for shelter and food. Increasingly this is changing with emphasis on *hope* for the mental patient and therefore purposeful work with the aim of discharge.) There has been increasing recognition of the vital importance of hospital environment and the relationship of patients with each other. Most state mental hospitals are vastly understaffed. It is impossible to give psychiatric services to all patients. Individual treatment can reach only a small minority of them. The greatest effort at this time must be directed toward the making of a "therapeutic community." One of the functions of the social group worker therefore—as always when he becomes part of institutional work—must be participation in hospital programs for in-service training of those members of the staff who are directly responsible for the daily living situation of the patient. In addition to this, the group worker carries responsibility for working with formed groups. Marion B. Sloan presented these functions in the following outline:

"A. *Direct work with patients in small formed groups:*

"Patients are referred for group experiences by their doctors, social caseworkers and other professional personnel. Referrals and selections of these patients for group experiences are based on specific problem areas and/or common treatment experiences. Frequent conferences with other professional personnel help the group experiences to become an integral part of the total treatment plan for each patient.

"The program for each group includes both discussion and informal activities, determined in each case according to the needs, interests and readiness of the individual group members and the treatment objectives for the particular group. . . .

"Groups which have demonstrated their usefulness in meeting the needs of patients . . . have been developed around the following:

"1. *Patients with common treatment experiences:*

"a. *Admissions:*

"A short-term group experience for new patients which is focused on helping the patient with his initial adjustment to the hospital milieu, acceptance of mental illness and the need for treatment.

"b. *Insulin and Electrocoma:*

"Fear is a common element among patients on physical treatment. Sometimes this is realistic, but often fears, apprehensions and anxieties arise from misconceptions about treatment. Emphasis in these groups is on developing collective support, clarification and understanding through common social experiences and discussions. The observations of these group interactions are shared by the staff and used in effectively structuring the treatment experience with other members of the treatment team.

"c. *Pre-discharge:*

"Through support and identification the group offers help in handling difficulties which arise in the process of discharge from the hospital and return to family and community. The group serves as a medium of helping one another face realistically their common concerns and problems related to having been mental patients, seeking employment, meeting friends and re-entering family life.

"2. *Patients with common psychosocial problems:*

"These are planned, directed group experiences for patients whose mental illnesses are complicated by psychosocial problems associated with age, sex, and marital status. These groups include:

"a. Adolescents
"b. Older Adults
"c. Young Mothers
"d. Young Single Men

"3. *Patients with common activity interests:*

"These are groups where common interests serve as a basis for the formation of positive social relationships. Purposes for such groups include need satisfaction through success and recognition, channeling of physical and emotional energies, encouragement of self-expression through creative activities and the development of social skills.

"4. *Suggested groups to be developed in the future are:*

"a. Post-discharge
"b. Pre-transfer
"c. Relatives of patients.[27]

It may be added that a group worker must also know when groups are not appropriate—when they are either harmful or not helpful. Patients selected for special groups must be grouped with this in

[27] Marion B. Sloan, "The Role of the Group Worker in the Adult Psychiatric Hospital," in Harleigh B. Trecker, Editor, *Group Work in the Psychiatric Setting, op. cit.,* pp. 58-60.

mind. It must be realized that hospital life in itself means constant exposure to other people who were not chosen by the individual patient. This means that the one part of working on constructive social environments in the hospital lies in the provision for privacy and for opportunities to patients to be alone if they so desire and if this does not contradict treatment aims.

Group workers frequently are not used in general hospitals serving patients with short-term physical illnesses. The living situation has neither the same purpose nor the same impact on a patient who is hospitalized only for a limited time. Group workers have worked, though, in children's wards for the purpose of relieving the child's feeling of isolation. Children's general hospitals have accepted more and more the fact that they must provide for special needs of children in addition to the necessary medical care. These special needs, however, are more likely to be met through recreational specialists, occupational therapists, and so forth, than through group workers.

Group work services are needed more in hospitals or camps for patients with long-term illnesses or with serious physical handicaps, such as summer camps for handicapped children and adults. The functions they carry in such camps parallel those in children's institutions and treatment centers.

Outpatient services which employ social group workers include child guidance clinics, societies for the deaf, societies for the blind, general rehabilitation centers, organizations for released mental patients, and, occasionally, general or psychiatric hospitals which give outpatient service. The most established group-work positions are found at present in child guidance clinics. To diagnose children's behavior correctly, experts are agreed that one needs to observe the child in interaction with his contemporaries as well as in interaction with the adult. Also, most children show difficulties in their relations with contemporaries and need to work them through in a protected environment. Younger children especially are incapable of working out problems in interviews, and need activities to work through them. The responsibilities of the group worker in child guidance clinics are usually:

1. Work with diagnostic groups: Every child coming into a clinic is automatically referred to such a group in the same way that he is referred for psychological and psychiatric interviews. Such

groups meet for a limited period—about once a week for three or four consecutive meetings. This equals the period during which the child is seen by other members of the team. On the basis of such observation, the group worker then participates responsibly in diagnosing the child and in working out an adequate treatment plan for him.

2. Work with formed treatment groups: Children are referred to these groups after decision of the total treatment team. They are either activity or discussion treatment groups or a combination of both. They usually meet once a week over a longer period of time. These groups may have a changing membership, since some children recover earlier than others. The group worker is responsible for assessing the individual's needs for referral to or discharge from the group as well as the total group situation and its capacity to let go of an individual member or accept a new one.

During school vacations, such groups may meet more frequently or for a full day instead of the usual two-hour sessions.

3. Intimate knowledge of and referral to appropriate community agencies which can give the child or adolescent helpful and healthy group experiences when he is ready to leave the protected and therapeutic atmosphere of the clinic.

4. Work with parent groups: Not all parents should be involved in group services. These groups serve parents who cannot be reached in individual interviews and where it is hoped that group interaction will make involvement easier for them. Sometimes these groups are also established as short-term help when the agency has a long waiting list and cannot accept the child and his parents for immediate treatment. Such groups then serve to provide the parents with pertinent information and to afford them some relief from anxiety; they also alert the agency to any emergency problem which requires immediate attention. Occasionally they provide sufficient help so that further help is unnecessary.

Permanent physical handicaps require of the person who is afflicted with them an inner adjustment to them. The feeling about such handicaps is highly related to the social environment. This is based partially on the nature of the handicap and partially on the attitude of society toward it. Blindness, for instance, is socially handicapping because of the restrictions it imposes on the blind person as long as he has not learned how to handle himself and how to move without constant assistance from another. Yet blindness is a socially accepted handicap and there are few prejudices toward the blind.

The deaf or hard-of-hearing, on the other hand, frequently faces individual hostility in addition to the restrictions imposed on him because of his handicap. His handicap is not visible and therefore the person who meets him may consider him unfriendly or conceited. Communication with the deaf or hard-of-hearing is difficult and after some effort, others often withdraw from him. The deaf person needs special help to overcome his isolation.

Epileptics and former mental patients may be handicapped little by their present or former illness, but the social stigma of it alone may drive them into isolation. Outpatient group work services, therefore, are directed toward resocialization of people with such handicaps by helping them to increase their skill in meeting others and by helping non-handicapped persons to understand them better and to integrate them into community groups. This means that the social group worker works directly with outpatient groups and is responsible for community interpretation of those handicaps. He must help to change community climate.

In the total health field, the trend is toward increasing use of the group as a medium of treatment and community education. About two decades ago, it was thought that the group work method needed particular adaptation to this field. This does not seem to be so today.

G. Corrections

"The field of correction involves the operation of prisons, reformatories, training schools for boys and girls, and the administration of probation and parole systems. These correctional agencies are charged with a twofold objective: that of maintaining the secure custody of offenders committed to their care, and that of providing such treatment as will direct their behavior into more law-abiding channels. The achievement of these two objectives requires the skills of trained custodial administrators in combination with the services of many professional groups including psychiatrists, social workers, psychologists, educators, and chaplains. In meeting the many needs of any correctional institution, one of the major administrative problems is to mobilize and integrate the specialized skills required for the custody and treatment of the inmate population."[28]

The field of correction not only includes a variety of services, but also a variety of philosophies which determine those services. In addition, the clients of this field present every kind of human being and every category of human problem. They have in common only the fact that they have violated the law. One of the major tasks in this field is the development of a classification system to make it possible to fit services to specific needs.

A clear understanding of crime and delinquency is still in its beginning stage. The older theories of explaining them by heredity or environmental influences alone are no longer accepted. It is understood that a large complex of factors is involved to trigger a delinquent act. Whatever the person or the problem, crime and delinquency always include a component of a *social* disorder. They are violations of human interaction. In treatment of the offender, not enough attention has yet been paid to this. Group situations in which the offender finds himself are not used purposely to change his mode of relating to others. Group associations in prisons are too frequently left to the hazard of daily encounter of inmates with each other.

In 1946, the National Conference on Prevention and Control of Juvenile Delinquency recognized the need for group treatment. Several of its deliberations, which were later published, stressed this. It was stated:

> Group work services should be provided for those apprehended for delinquent behavior, for those in institutions for detention, and for long-term treatment of juvenile delinquency.[29]

The standards for detention care of delinquents place group work in the core of its service. Group work functions are presented on two levels:

1. Group Work Staff:

"The most important staff members are those who have direct contact with children. These persons are variously known as

---

28 James V. Bennett, "Corrections," in Russell H. Kurtz, Editor, *op. cit.*, pp. 205-206.
29 "Case Work-Group Work," A Report of the National Conference on Prevention and Control of Juvenile Delinquents, Washington, D.C., Nov. 1946, p. 38.

group supervisors, group counselors, child care workers, group leaders, etc. The term 'group worker' is used throughout this book because of the professional standing which ought to be given this type of work. Group work functions are not confined to supervision, counseling, care or leadership. The distinguishing mark of a good group worker is his ability to meet individual and group needs with knowledge and skill. The trend in detention homes is toward the employment of college-trained personnel for this work. Few have had graduate training in social group work; they should be supervised by one who has. Group workers should be encouraged to secure graduate training in social group work just as many caseworkers in the field of probation have acquired graduate training in social casework. . . ."[30]

2. Group Work Supervisor:

"Institutions with nonresident personnel should have a trained and experienced group worker to supervise and assist the group workers on each shift. In *single-unit* institutions for fifteen or twenty children, the superintendent, assistant superintendent, and caseworker may perform this function. However, constant coverage must be given during the hours of the two day shifts with at least an 'on call' resident available to those on duty at night. *Institutions of two or more units* should have, for each 'group worker shift,' a group work supervisor free of other responsibilities or attachments to a particular group. Where possible, the group work supervisor (head of shift) should have graduate training in social group work. In institutions of four or more units, the head of each shift should have experienced assistants so that there is at least one 'roving group worker' for every two units."[31]

"Group discussions, planned and unplanned, should be encouraged, but should be conducted only under the guidance of a social worker trained in group discussion techniques."[32]

There are other signs also, in the institutional field for delinquents, that the need for social group work is beginning to be recognized.

[30] National Council on Crime and Delinquency, *Standards and Guides for the Detention of Children and Youth*, Second Edition, New York: N.C.C.D., 1961, p. 48.
[31] *Ibid.*, p. 49.
[32] *Ibid.*, p. 88.

Functions of the social group worker in these parallel closely those of the treatment centers and institutions in child welfare. Resistance to adults and refusal to accept personal responsibility are especially strong among the youngsters in delinquency institutions. August Aichorn understood this when he wrote in 1935:

> To the dissocial child we are a menace because we represent society which he is in conflict with. . . . They do not tell the truth.[33]

The group worker in the institution works only rarely with voluntary groups; more often he works with living groups or with groups formed for treatment purposes. Groups with relatives have also been comparatively rare in corrections, although there have been some experiments with group work with wives of long-term inmates who are scheduled for parole or discharge. These sessions prepare the wives for the problems and discouragements they will have to face. Simultaneously the inmates themselves have group sessions.

In probation and parole services some attempts have been made to use the group work approach. The group worker's functions in this service include:

1. Direct work with groups of probationers or parolees for the purpose of discussing their present adjustment or for the purpose of offering constructive group activities to those who are not yet ready to enter into community group services.

2. Summer programs for youth probationers or parolees who are still in school, but who cannot find employment during the summer and who are not yet ready to participate in other youth camps.

3. Week-end programs for the same kind of youngsters.

4. Discussion groups with parents of children and adolescents adjudicated delinquent to help them understand court services, to allow them to express concern, anxieties and hostilities, and to enable them to become more helpful to their children.

5. Helping children or adults under his supervision to become aware of and to use different community resources.

6. Casework services.

[33] August Aichorn, *Wayward Youth*, New York: The Viking Press, 1935, p. 125.

In the correctional field especially, the same person must often be able to use both case work and group work methods and to use them judiciously.

There has been much discussion as to whether group work needs much change in an authoritarian setting such as the court. Group work method includes the constructive use of limitations. This makes the method more easily adaptable to this setting than a more permissive approach. Yet the informal approach, usually characteristic of group work, needs to be modified. Furthermore, group attendance may frequently be required. Special skill is needed to motivate participation in spite of this.

H. School Social Work

"School Social Services represent some of the efforts being made in education to meet the needs of certain individual children who have social and emotional problems which interfere with their school functioning and achievement. These services have increased and expanded as new knowledge has enhanced the understanding of behavior and of the needs of children when learning difficulties are encountered.

"Social services, an integral part of the total school program, may include psychological service, psychiatric service, attendance service, vocational counseling, and school social work service. The teacher uses these resources to supplement her own work with children in the classroom in order that her teaching efforts may be more effective. Social services help by working directly with children who have school adjustment problems and with their parents. Opportunity is provided also, through consultation, for the teacher to gain a deeper understanding of the children in her classroom—understanding of their feelings, attitudes, and behavior that may be thwarting or enhancing the opportunity for learning which the school provides."[34]

The school setting is definitely a group setting, and teachers work with groups. When group work was more closely related to informal education, it was not part of school social work programs as it is understood today, but those informal groups were widely used by the schools to help youngsters. School social work, as developed in this country, was more traditional casework combined with the task of the "truant officer." This was symbolized by the designation of the

---

[34] Opal Boston, "School Social Services," in Russell H. Kurtz, *op. cit.*, p. 517.

school social workers as "visiting teachers." The function of the school social worker has changed, and with the change has come an appreciation of possible contributions to be made in this field by the group worker. Representatives of this field of social work are especially open to experiments with group work services as part of their specialization. Some departments have employed social group workers. Their function has included:

1. Direct work with groups of children who have showed school difficulties.

2. Consultation with teachers to help them with the handling of children who are difficult in the classroom situation.

School social work using the group work method is more frequently done at present outside the formal school system. Outstanding examples of this are Big Sisters organizations and neighborhood houses which serve school referral groups. They meet usually over a comparatively long period of time.

Summary

In looking over the fields in which the group work method is used, certain trends can be ascertained:

1. A trend toward the use of the group as a conscious helping tool in *all* social services, including those which formerly used the casework method alone.

2. A widening of the traditional social work function toward inclusion of the educationally-oriented ones as exemplified in the youth services.

3. A concern with social action, not only *on behalf* of clients, as has been traditional in social welfare, but with involvement of group members as allies of the professional social worker.

4. A concern with the individual, the group, and necessary culture change.

Activities of the social group worker in different fields are not always the same. They include a wide variety consisting of:

1. Work with client or membership groups;

2. Work with committees, boards, or other community groups;

3. Work with individuals related to group services;

4. Supervision of volunteers or part-time staff;

5. Consultation to other professionals working with groups;

6. Participation or leadership in social action;

7. Continuous research into the psycho-social phenomena which confront the group worker;

8. Evaluation of group worker practice.

The wide range of agencies in which group work is practiced opens questions of agency structure and education, which are not yet wholly answered. For instance, the separation of casework and group work originally indicated different agency functions; now they are methods often used in the same agencies. Should social work keep the separation in professional training?

At the time this book is being written, the social work profession has not yet answered this question.

BIBLIOGRAPHY

SETTLEMENTS AND NEIGHBORHOOD CENTERS

Addams, Jane, *Forty Years at Hull House*, New York: The Macmillan Co., 1935.

Berry, Margaret, "Settlements and Neighborhood Centers," in Russell H. Kurtz, Editor, *Social Work Year Book, 1960*, New York: N.A.S.W., 1960, pp. 523-528.

Carpenter, H. Daniel, "The Neighborhood-Grass Roots of American Democracy," *Ethical Frontiers*, New York: New York Society for Ethical Culture, 1948.

Dillick, Sidney, *Community Organization for Neighborhood Development—*

Past and Present, New York: Woman's Press and William Morrow & Co., 1953.

Hillman, Arthur, "Experimental Approaches in Deprived Areas," *Community Organization 1961*, New York: Columbia University Press, 1961, pp. 109-123.

International Federation of Settlements, *The Building of Human Relationships in Our Times*, Conference Report of the 6th International Conference of the International Federation of Settlements, Amsterdam, Holland, June 1952; Utrecht, Holland, 1953.

National Federation of Settlements, *Neighborhood Goals in a Rapidly Changing World*, A Report of the Action-Research Workshop held at Arden House, Harriman, New York, 1958.

Pacey, Lorene M., *Readings in the Development of Settlement Work*, New York: Association Press, 1950.

Taylor, Graham, *Pioneering on Social Frontiers*, Chicago: University of Chicago Press, 1930.

Woods, Robert A., *The Neighborhood in Nation Building*, Boston: Houghton Mifflin Co., 1923.

YOUTH SERVING AGENCIES

Boswell, Luada, "A report on two girl scout pilot projects: migrant agricultural workers and urban hard-to-reach groups," *New Perspectives on Services to Groups: Theory, Organization, Practice*, New York: N.A.S.W., 1961.

Coyle, Grace L., *Group Work and American Youth*, New York: Harper & Row, Publishers, 1948.

———, "Social Group Work in Recreation," *Proceedings of the National Conference of Social Work, 1946*, New York: Columbia University Press, 1946, pp. 202-208.

Fisher, Galen M., *Citadel of Democracy*, Berkeley, Calif.: Howell-North Press, 1955.

Height, Dorothy I., *Step by Step with Interracial Groups*, New York: Publications Services, Y.W.C.A. National Board, 1955.

New York City Youth Board, *Reaching Teen-Agers through Group and Recreation Programs*, New York: N.Y.C. Youth Board, 1954.

Serotkin, Harry, "Youth Services," in Russell H. Kurtz, Editor, *op. cit.*, pp. 607-617.

Solender, Sanford, "The Place of the Jewish Community Center in Jewish Life," *Journal of Jewish Communal Service*, Fall 1957.

Basic Standards for the Triennium, 1958-1961, "Deep Roots and World Reach," Work Book 21st National Convention YWCA of the U.S.A., St. Louis, 1958, New York: YWCA National Board.

CHILD WELFARE SERVICES

Bettelheim, Bruno, *Love is Not Enough*, Glencoe, Ill.: The Free Press, 1950.

Cole, Minerva G. and Lawrence Podell, "Serving Handicapped Children in Group Programs," *Social Work*, Vol. 6, No. 1, Jan. 1961, pp. 97-104.

Jones, Howard, *Reluctant Rebels*, New York: Association Press (copyright 1959 by Tavistock Publications, Ltd.).

Hunt, Maurice O., "Child Welfare," in Russell H. Kurtz, Editor, *op. cit.*, pp. 141-157.

Keane, Sister M. Charles, R.S.M., *The House Mother*, Washington, D.C.: National Conference of Catholic Charities, 1954.

Konopka, Gisela, "Part 4. The Role of the Group in Residential Treatment," Symposium 1954, The Role of Residential Treatment for Children, *American Journal of Orthopsychiatry*, Vol. XXV, No. 4, Oct. 1955, pp. 679-684.

Maier, Henry W., "The Meaning of Repeated Adult Requests," *Child Welfare*, Dec. 1958, p. 7.

Reid, Joseph H. and Helen R. Hagan, *Residential Treatment of Emotionally Disturbed Children*, New York: Child Welfare League of America, 1952.

Schulze, Susanne, *Creative Group Living in a Children's Institution*, New York: Association Press, 1951.

Schwartz, William, "Characteristics of the Group Experience in Resident Camping," *Social Work*, Vol. 5, No. 2, Apr. 1960, pp. 91-96.

Seabloom, William, "Group Therapy with Emotionally Disturbed Adolescent Boys," *Lutheran Social Welfare Quarterly*, Vol. 1, No. 1, 1961, pp. 22-28.

FAMILY SERVICES

Konopka, Gisela, "Group Work Techniques in Joint Interviewing," *Social Welfare Forum*, 1957, New York: Columbia University Press, 1957.

Parsons, Talcott and Robert F. Bales, *Family, Socialization and Interaction Process*, Glencoe, Ill.: The Free Press, 1955.

Seabloom, William, "Group Therapy with Emotionally Disturbed Adolescent Boys," *Lutheran Social Welfare Quarterly*, Vol. 1, No. 1, 1961, pp. 22-28.

Shoemaker, Louise, "Use of Group Work Skills with Short-Term Groups," *Social Work With Groups*, 1960, New York: N.A.S.W., 1960, pp. 37-51.

Thomas, Carolyn, "The Use of Group Methods with Foster Parents," *Children*, Vol. 8, No. 6, Nov.-Dec. 1961, pp. 218-222.

Weil, Rae C., "Family Social Work," in Russell H. Kurtz, Editor, *op. cit.*, pp. 251-257.

SERVICES TO THE AGING

Farrar, Marcella and Nelida Ferrari, "Casework and Group Work in a Home for the Aged," *Social Work*, Vol. 5, No. 2, Apr. 1960, pp. 58-62.

Hoge, Evelyn B., "Developing Clubs for Older People," Pamphlet No. 3, *How Public Welfare Serves Aging People*, Chicago: American Public Welfare Association, 1954.

Kaplan, Jerome, "Mobilizing Community Resources," Pamphlet No. 5, *How Public Welfare Serves Aging People*, Chicago: American Public Welfare Association, 1955.

————, *A Social Program for Older People*, Minneapolis: University of Minnesota Press, 1953.

Kubie, Susan H. and Gertrude Landau, *Group Work with Aged*, New York: International Universities Press, 1953.

Margolin, Lillian, "Residential Camping Services for Older Adults," *New Perspectives on Services to Groups: Theory, Organization, Practice*, New York: N.A.S.W., 1961, pp. 133-142.

Mathiasen, Geneva, "The Aging," in Russell H. Kurtz, Editor, *op. cit.*, pp. 95-102.

Maxwell, Jean M., "Group Services—Well-being for Older People," *Social Work with Groups*, 1960, New York: N.A.S.W., 1960, pp. 74-85.

McCarthy, Henry L., "Day Centers for Older People," Pamphlet No. 4, *How Public Welfare Serves Aging People*, Chicago: American Public Welfare Association, 1954.

McGowen, Virginia A., "Helping Older People Find Good Nursing Home Care," Pamphlet No. 8, *How Public Welfare Serves Aging People*, Chicago, American Public Welfare Association, 1955.

Shapiro, Sidney, "The Old Cronies," in Harleigh B. Trecker, Editor, *Group Work—Foundations and Frontiers*, New York: Whiteside, Inc., 1955, p. 172.

Tibbitts, Clark and Wilma Donahue, Compilers, "Guidebook for Leaders," Vol. III, *Aging in the Modern World*, Ann Arbor: University of Michigan, Division of Gerontology, 1957.

————, "A Handbook for Group Members," Vol. 1, *Aging in the Modern World*, cited above.

Tine, Sebastian, Katherine Hastings, and Paul Deutschberger, "Generic and Specific in Social Group Work Practice with the Aging," *Social Work with Groups 1960*, New York: N.A.S.W., 1960, pp. 86-99.

MEDICAL AND PSYCHIATRIC SERVICES

Blackey, Eileen, "Social Work in the Hospital: A Sociological Approach," *Social Work*, Vol. 1, No. 2, Apr. 1956, pp. 43-49.

Cockerill, Eleanor E., "Medical Social Work," in Russell H. Kurtz, Editor, *op. cit.*, pp. 375-382.

Coyle, Grace L., "Group Work in Psychiatric Settings: Its Roots and Branches," *Social Work*, Vol. 4, No. 1, Jan. 1959, pp. 74-81.

Coyle, Grace L. and Raymond Fisher, "Helping Hospitalized Children through Social Group Work," *The Child*, Vol. 16, No. 8, Apr. 1952.

Felix, Robert H., *et al.*, *Mental Health and Social Welfare*, New York: Columbia University Press, 1961.

Frey, Louise A., "Social Group Work in Hospitals," *New Perspectives on Services to Groups: Theory, Organization, Practice*, New York: N.A.-S.W., 1961, pp. 92-103.

Guzie, Frances P., "Psychiatrically Oriented Groups," *Use of Groups in the Psychiatric Setting*, New York: N.A.S.W., pp. 123-129.

Harlow, Minnie Maude, "Group Work in a Psychiatric Hospital," in Felix, Robert H., *et al.*, *op. cit.*, pp. 152-174.

Harm, Carl S. and Joseph Golden, "Group Worker's Role in Guiding Social Process in a Medical Institution," *Social Work*, Vol. 6, No. 2, Apr. 1961, pp. 44-51.

Herman, Melvin, "Reintegration of Handicapped Persons in the Community," *New Perspectives on Services to Groups: Theory, Organization, Practice*, *op. cit.*, pp. 70-78.

Impallaria, Constance, "Some Contributions of Therapeutic Group Work in a Medical Setting," *Selected Papers in Group Work and Community Organization*, National Conference of Social Work, 1952.

Jones, Maxwell, *The Therapeutic Community*, London: Tavistock Publications, 1952.

Kaplan, Irving H., "Some Aspects of Group Work in a Psychiatric Setting," *Social Work*, Vol. 5, No. 3, July 1960, pp. 84-90.

Konopka, Gisela, "The Generic and the Specific in Group Work Practice in the Psychiatric Setting," *Social Work*, Vol. 1, No. 1, Jan. 1956, pp. 72-80.

———, "Group Work and Group Therapy in a Psychiatric Setting," *Education for Psychiatric Social Work*, Proceedings of the Dartmouth Conference, New York: A.A.P.S.W., June 1950, pp. 89-103.

———, "Implications of a Changing Residential Treatment Program," *American Journal of Orthopsychiatry*, Vol. XXXI, No. 1, Jan. 1961, pp. 17-39.

———, "The Role of the Group Worker in the Psychiatric Setting," *Ameri-*

can Journal of Orthopsychiatry, Vol. XXII, No. 1, Jan. 1952, pp. 176-185.

——, "Team Relationships and Operations in Social Group Work," in Marjorie Murphy, *The Social Group Work Method in Social Work Education*, Vol. XI, *A Project Report of the Curriculum Study*, Werner W. Boehm, Director and Coordinator, New York: Council on Social Work Education, 1959, pp. 106-114.

——, *Therapeutic Group Work with Children*, Minneapolis: University of Minnesota Press, 1949.

Lane, Dorothea M., "Psychiatric Patients Learn a New Way of Life," *New Perspectives on Services to Groups: Theory, Organization, Practice, op. cit.*, pp. 114-123.

Lindsay, Doreen, "Group Placement of Long-Term Mental Hospital Patients," *New Perspectives on Services to Groups: Theory, Organization, Practice, op. cit.*, pp. 104-113.

Maier, Henry W., "Group Living: A Unique Feature in Residential Treatment," *New Perspectives on Services to Groups: Theory, Organization, Practice, op. cit.*, pp. 124-132.

National Association of Social Workers, *Use of Groups in the Psychiatric Setting*, New York: N.A.S.W., 1960.

O'Keefe, Daniel E., "Psychiatric Social Work," in Russell F. Kurtz, Editor, *op. cit.*, pp. 451-460.

Pennock, Mary and Grace Weyker, "Some Developments in the Integration of Casework and Group Work in a Child Guidance Clinic," in Harleigh B. Trecker, Editor, *Group Work—Foundations and Frontiers*, New York: Whiteside, Inc., 1955, p. 76.

Perlman, Bernice, "Group Work with Psychotic Veterans," *American Journal of Orthopsychiatry*, Vol. XIX, No. 1, Jan. 1949, pp. 69-78.

Sloan, Marion B., "Factors in Forming Treatment Groups," *Use of Groups in the Psychiatric Setting*, New York: N.A.S.W., 1960, pp. 74-86.

——, "The Special Contribution of Therapeutic Group Work in a Psychiatric Setting," in Harleigh B. Trecker, Editor, *Group Work—Foundation and Frontiers, op. cit.*, p. 208.

Trecker, Harleigh B., Editor, *Group Work in the Psychiatric Setting*, New York: Whiteside, Inc., and Wm. Morrow and Co., 1956.

Weiner, Hyman J., "Group Work in a Medical Setting," *The Group*, Vol. XVII, No. 4, Apr. 1955.

——, "The Hospital, the Ward, and the Patient as Clients: Use of the Group Work Method," *Social Work*, Vol. 4, No. 4, Oct. 1959, pp. 57-64.

White, Grace, "The Distinguishing Characteristics of Medical Social Work," *Medical Social Work*, Vol. I, No. 1, Sept. 1951, pp. 31-39.

Wilson, Gertrude, "Hospital Group Work," Pittsburgh: University of Pittsburgh, mimeographed, No. 677, undated.

Wilson, Gertrude and Gisela Konopka, "Social Group Work in a Psychiatric Setting," *The News-Letter of the American Association of Psychiatric Social Workers*, Vol. XIV, No. 2, Autumn 1944, pp. 35-43.

Woodruff, Robert R., "Group Work in a Children's Hospital," *Social Work*, Vol. 2, No. 3, July 1957, pp. 56-61.

CORRECTIONS

Austin, David M., "Goals for Gang Workers," *Social Work*, Vol. 2, No. 4, Oct. 1957, pp. 42-50.

Bennett, James V., "Corrections," in Russell H. Kurtz, Editor, *op. cit.*, pp. 205-211.

Blake, Mary, *Youth Groups in Conflict*, Washington, D.C., U.S. Department of Health, Education and Welfare, 1958.

Cloward, Richard A. and Lloyd E. Ohlin, *Delinquency and Opportunity*, Glencoe, Ill.: The Free Press, 1960.

Donohue, John K., *Baffling Eyes of Youth*, New York: Association Press, 1957.

Fenton, Norman, "The Prison as a Therapeutic Community," *Federal Probation*, Vol. XX, No. 2, June 1956, pp. 26-29.

Jereczek, Gordon, "Gangs Need not be Delinquent," *Federal Probation*, Vol. XXIV, No. 2, June 1960.

Konopka, Gisela, "The Group Worker's Role in an Institution for Juvenile Delinquents," *Federal Probation*, Vol. XV, No. 2, June 1951, pp. 15-23.

————, *Group Work in the Institution*, New York: Whiteside, Inc., 1954.

————, "Institutional Treatment of Emotionally Disturbed Children," *Crime and Delinquency*, Vol. 8, No. 1, Jan. 1962, pp. 52-57.

————, "The Social Group Work Method: Its Use in the Correctional Field," *Federal Probation*, Vol. XIV, No. 1, Mar. 1950.

————, *Therapeutic Group Work with Children*, Minneapolis: University of Minnesota Press, 1949.

Lerman, Paul, "Group Work with Youth in Conflict," *Social Work*, Vol. 3, No. 4, Oct. 1958, pp. 71-77.

McCleary, R. D., "Group Work with Delinquents," *The Group*, Vol. VIII, No. 4, June 1946, pp. 1-4.

National Council on Crime and Delinquency, *Standards and Guides for the Detention of Children and Youth*, Second edition, New York: N.C.C.D., 1961.

National Conference on Prevention and Control of Juvenile Delinquents, Reports of the National Conference on Prevention and Control of Juvenile Delinquents, Washington, D.C., Nov. 1946.

New York City Youth Board, "Pattern for Prevention," New York: N.Y.C. Youth Board, Jan. 1953.

Nolte, Robert E. and John J. Fallon, "Delinquency Treatment by a Public-Private Agency Team," *Social Work with Groups, 1960*, New York: N.A.S.W., 1960, pp. 100-107.

Rahm, Harold J. and Robert J. Webert, "Office in the Alley," report on a project with gang youngsters, The Hogg Foundation for Mental Health, 1958.

Redl, Fritz and David Wineman, *Children Who Hate—Controls from Within*, Glencoe, Ill.: The Free Press, 1951.

Smith, Alexander R. and Alexander Bassin, "Group Therapy with Adult Probationers," *Federal Probation*, Vol. XXIV, No. 3, Sep. 1960, pp. 15-21.

Studt, Elliot, "The Nature of Hard-to-Reach Groups," *Children*, Nov.-Dec. 1957, pp. 219-224.

Tolman, Norman G., "Approaching the Institutionalized Female Delinquent through Group Therapy," *Federal Probation*, Vol. XXV, No. 2, June 1961, pp. 34-40.

Witmer, Helen L., and Ruth Kotinsky, *Personality in the Making*, New York: Harper & Row, Publishers, 1952.

SCHOOL SOCIAL WORK

Bennett, Margaret Elaine, *Guidance in Groups: A Resource Book for Teachers, Counselors and Administrators*, New York: McGraw-Hill Book Co., Inc., 1955.

Poole, Florence, "An Analysis of the Characteristics of School Social Work," *Social Service Review*, Vol. XXIII, No. 4, Dec. 1949, pp. 454-459.

Quattlebaum, Virginia, *School Social Work Practice: Proceedings of the Lake Forest Workshop*, New York: N.A.S.W., 1958.

Wright, Barbara H., *Practical Handbook for Group Guidance*, Chicago: Science Research Associates, 1948.

Epilogue

*I believe that we should make room in
our outlook for tested knowledge about
human nature and social behavior. But
if we are wise we shall also provide for
the revision of this knowledge—for what
we know, or think we know, is not the
last word. And I am equally convinced
that we should find out how to make
more constructive use of the knowledge
we have.*[1]

We have described the particulars of one of the helping
methods in social work, its change in the course of history, its underlying values, its view of individual, group and society, its principles
and techniques and the fields in which it is practiced.

A thirteen-year-old girl exclaimed after a group meeting in which
the youngsters had worked through many conflicts, "I feel *so* much
better—and we begin to like each other! You surely have done this,
Miss Summer. Alone, we would just have bickered around; you did
it!—Oh no, you didn't! *We* did it, We!"

She put in a nutshell the basic helping intent of social group work.

---

[1] Merle Curti, Probing Our Past, New York: Harper & Row, Publishers, p. 170.

Out of the group worker's understanding and skill had emerged the essential totality of helping people to help themselves.

Work with human beings seems simple on the surface—something anyone can do. Yet the history of thousands of years of human life has shown how difficult it is. The aim, the demand for living together harmoniously, has been pronounced by all the great philosophers, religious leaders, and statesmen. Practice has not yet been able to follow them. Help with human relationships is not easy. The human being is one of the most complicated entities in the world. Relationships among them produce conflicts, problems, satisfactions. Knowledge and theory about man is in constant development. A helping profession is dependent on this knowledge, since it is actively engaged in change—change of the individual, the group, the community. This is a difficult and responsible task, and must therefore be harnessed by disciplined use of available knowledge. *Discipline* here means an honest understanding of oneself, so that one does not misuse the helping position for one's own purposes; it also means an open and searching mind to participate in better and deeper understanding of people. While the group worker must place his major effort on practice, he must also take on responsibility for raising questions growing out of this so that new insights can be obtained. Progress in understanding human beings cannot come from the laboratory alone. It is incumbent upon the practitioner to raise questions, to observe, to analyze and thus contribute to knowledge and better practice. As in the science concerned with "matter"—physics—an effort has to be made to analyze for the purpose of finding new ways of working effectively. And just as in the natural sciences, this must be the work of many, not only of one genius.

There is sometimes reluctance on the part of the person who works with people and who has an intuitive gift to help, to analyze. He is afraid he may destroy the essential totality of the phenomena with which he works. Yet he will discover that his work becomes enhanced by theory, that he can help better.

The botanist dissects the flower to discover its secrets of color, of reproduction, of life cycle. He sees parts, but in the end he knows that he has studied *a flower*, not just petals, stamens, and pollen. In understanding human beings, the same applies. Beyond the parts necessary for analysis, the total human being in his environment must be seen and experienced. The final work of the group worker must not show the parts, the technique, the effort. It uses all of them, but it becomes valuable only because of the fusion of the parts in the fire of creativity.

Social group work is a helping process which becomes increasingly significant in the social welfare field. The skill of individualization in a group is desperately needed in a world with a growing population and with much awareness of its interdependence. Eduard C. Lindeman's words, written into one of his notebooks, summarize its essence:

> Group Work is a mental hygiene experience—a venture in sanity. Small groups, conscious discipline in human relations, nuclear democracy, leadership laboratory. . . .

To practice in accordance with this goal, much knowledge and learning are needed. To the student of social group work who works through this to arrive at an integrated capacity to help, the old Zen saying may apply:

> To a man who knows nothing, mountains are mountains, waters are waters and trees are trees. But when he has studied and knows a little, mountains are no longer mountains, waters no longer waters and trees no longer trees. But when he has thoroughly understood, mountains are once again mountains, waters are waters and trees are trees.[2]

[2] Bryan Holme and Thomas Forman, *Poet's Camera*, New York: Studio Publications, Inc., 1946, p. x.

Index